"Careful research, lots of Scripture, and a demonst
'you are washed clean' to those who feel like outc
abuse."

    Ed Welch, Counselor and Faculty, The Christian Counseling and
    Educational Foundation

"I can't express how grateful I am that someone is tackling this subject with both a
pastoral heart and an understanding of how the devastating effects of sexual assault
can wreak havoc for decades after the abuse. It is an epidemic issue where resources
are scarce. There isn't a weekend that goes by when we aren't told a gut-wrenching tale
of innocence stolen, then left trying to help a man or woman make sense of the pain. I
praise God for the gospel that can heal and restore and for the Holcombs that had the
courage and wisdom to write this book for us."

    Matt Chandler, Pastor, The Village Church, Dallas, TX

"God sees, knows, heals, restores, and redeems. This is the message of hope this book
offers to all who have suffered from abuse. How desperately needed this message is in
our culture today! In my interaction with teens and young adults, I have heard many
stories of sexual abuse. I am so thrilled that there is a resource like this book that offers
relevant, practical, biblical hope and healing words of life."

    Rebecca St. James, singer; author; actress

"Having experienced much sexual brokenness in my own life and now having pastored
a church that ministers to thousands of broken people, I can say with confidence that
this book is desperately needed. Justin and Lindsey write to help the abused and to help
those who help the abused. It is a must read for all those who live and minister in this
sexually broken world."

    Darrin Patrick, Lead Pastor, The Journey, St. Louis, MO; Vice President,
    Acts 29 Church Planting Network

"Jesus says, 'Blessed are those who mourn.' *Rid of My Disgrace* gives sexual assault victims, and those who love and serve them, the freedom to grieve the violence against
them and the tools to experience healing and hope in Jesus. I am so thankful for this
major contribution to my life and the people I love."

    Grace Driscoll, pastor's wife; mother of five; conference speaker; author

"Justin and Lindsey demonstrate a unique level of compassion and concern for victims
of sexual assault and the hope for them for healing. The gentle and empathetic tone,
along with a sincere belief that victims can experience healing, make this book indis-
pensable for both victims and those who care for them."

    Craig Groeschel, Founding and Senior Pastor, LifeChurch.tv

"The world—and too often the church—encourages victims of sexual assault to do more. Self-help advice just adds more layers of guilt and a sense of powerlessness. The authors of this excellent book have good news: literally, a gospel that answers our disgrace with the grace of God in Christ. For anyone who suffers from abuse—as well as those who minister to them—*Rid of My Disgrace* is powerful, healing medicine."

> **Michael Horton**, J. G. Machen Professor of Systematic Theology and
> Apologetics, Westminster Seminary California; author, *The Gospel-Driven Life*

"This is a sad and disturbing book. The 'dark' of it will keep you awake at night. But the 'light' will cause you to sing with joy and hope. What a gift to the church and to those who have felt the shame of sexual assault or who love those who have! Read it and give it to your friends. They will rise up and call you blessed! It is the best book I've ever read on the subject of abuse . . . and I've read a lot of them."

> **Steve Brown**, Professor of Preaching Emeritus, Reformed Theological
> Seminary; author, *When Being Good Isn't Good Enough* and *When Your Rope Breaks*

"Where will you find a 'theology of the victim' from a Reformed theologian? You just found it. If you've been the victim of abuse, you won't find yourself blamed in this book. You'll find yourself embraced by the love of a God who meets you in your pain. This will be required reading for all of my students."

> **Chuck DeGroat**, Academic Dean, Newbigin House of Studies; Director,
> City Church Counseling Center

"*Rid of My Disgrace* reminds victims of sexual assault that they are not alone and it is not the end of the story. From King David's daughter Tamar to the courageous survivors telling their stories today, the Holcombs take sexual assault out of the shadows of shame and isolation and into the light of the gospel. With a solid grasp on both the effects of sexual assault and of redemptive history, the Holcombs thoroughly identify sexual assault and its aftermath. This book calls readers to let even such a painful, hideous act be a part of their stories of redemption through Christ's sufficient work on the cross."

> **Monica Taffinder**, cofounder and counselor, Grace Clinic Christian
> Counseling

"Written passionately from the agony that haunts victims, this book also offers a message of hope and healing. It is an invaluable resource for those who have been victimized and a must read for family, friends, pastors, or counselors of victims to be equipped to serve and love them well."

> **Jud Wilhite**, Senior Pastor, Central Christian Church, Las Vegas, NV;
> author, *Eyes Wide Open*

"Some books are easy to read, but this isn't one of them. Its difficulty, however, is not a matter of style or prose but of substance. We don't like thinking about sexual assault and abuse. We'd rather pretend they don't exist. But the church can no longer afford to turn a blind eye to the extent of this problem or to ignore the devastation it brings to both body and soul. What makes this book so worthy of your attention, notwithstanding the discomfort it may cause you to feel, is the wealth of wisdom, gospel grace, and pastoral sensitivity that the Holcombs bring to bear on those affected by this experience. No matter how deep the pain or sense of loss endured by the victims of sexual assault, God's healing grace and power are greater still. Highly recommended!"

Sam Storms, Senior Pastor, Bridgeway Church, Oklahoma City, OK

"This important book places the powder keg of gospel truth where it is most needed: on the frontline of pastoral ministry. A mixture of clear writing, real-life stories, and faithful Bible exposition makes this a powerful resource in the fight for redemption in the lives of those we are called to serve."

Joel Virgo, Church of Christ the King, Brighton, UK

"This book helped us understand the painful emotions that go along with the particular suffering of sexual assault. But more than that, it showed us how to respond to our twelve-year-old son who was assaulted."

Parents of a child victim

"I thought I had gotten over the abuses in my past—I had forgiven my abusers, stopped feeling like a victim, and felt like I was a stronger person. After reading *Rid of My Disgrace*, I realized there were still underlying issues I hadn't dealt with that were preventing me from getting close to other people and, worst of all, preventing me from having a deeper relationship with God. Each chapter not only discussed each emotion that had been secretly weighing on me, but also showed me that those emotions don't have to rule me. Jesus' death and resurrection apply not only to my sins, but also to the burden of someone else's sin against me. My identity is no longer as 'damaged goods.' It is as a 'child of God' and with that comes God's unending love. I highly recommend this book for anyone who has experienced not only some form of sexual abuse, but also other abuses as well."

Adult female victim

Re:Lit Books

~~Rid of My Dis~~grace

Hope and Healing for Victims of Sexual Assault
Justin S. Holcomb & Lindsey A. Holcomb
Foreword by Mark Driscoll

:: CROSSWAY

WHEATON, ILLINOIS

Library of Congress Cataloging-in-Publication Data
Holcomb, Lindsey A., 1981–
  Rid of my disgrace : hope and healing for victims of sexual assault /
Lindsey A. Holcomb, Justin S. Holcomb ; foreword by Mark Driscoll.
    p. cm. — (Re:Lit)
  Includes bibliographical references and index.
  ISBN 978-1-4335-1598-9 (tpb)
   1. Sexual abuse victims—Religious life. 2. Abused women—
Religious life. 3. Abused men—Religious life. 4. Sex crimes—
Biblical teaching. 5. Sex—Biblical teaching. I. Holcomb, Justin S.
II. Title.
BV4596.A2H65   2011
248.8'6—dc22   2010028915

Contents

Foreword

This book matters.

There is an epidemic of sexual assault, and victims need the kind of hope and help that only the gospel of Jesus Christ can provide. Tragically, most churches and Christians are woefully unprepared to help the one in four women and one in six men who have been abused sexually. Worse still, many Christian leaders (including parents) are ignorant of this epidemic because ashamed victims are reticent to simply declare what has been done to them, and untrained leaders do not recognize the signs of sexual assault or know how to inquire lovingly of victims.

What qualifies as sexual assault? What does the Bible say to victims? What does a victim of abuse experience? What effect does sexual assault have on a person's entire life if he or she is not given appropriate help? How does sexual abuse damage intimacy, freedom, and joy in marriage? What assistance can family, friends, coworkers, and loved ones provide to victims who have suffered? How is the gospel of Jesus Christ—the God who became a human being to endure horrific abuse—a healing hope for fellow victims?

This book gives answers.

What makes this book unique is that it is written by a married couple with both the academic credentials and pastoral experience to qualify them to give professional, pastoral, and practical counsel. Justin and Lindsey are personal friends and fellow leaders at Mars Hill Church, where the victims of sexual assault alone number enough to constitute their own megachurch. I am deeply thankful they have taken the time to write this book to serve our ministry and yours. I would urge fellow ministry leaders, as well as anyone who wants to help hurting people, to read this book, ask the Holy Spirit for wisdom, search the Scriptures, and invest the time and emotional energy it takes to ask hard questions of wounded people about the cause of their suffering in order to get started on their redemption.

This book is risky.

If you are considering reading this book, you are brave. You are likely a victim of sexual assault yourself, although you may be resisting that truth because of your shame. But by taking the risk of shedding some light on the darkness of your past, you are courageously taking the first steps toward a new life. God bless you. We pray this would also be the first step toward a new ministry, with you—in time—bravely telling your story and inviting others to do the same. In God's grace, we pray this book would be used by God to see horrendous evil used for honorable ministry to God's glory, your joy, and others' good, because what Jesus has done for you is the answer for what has been done to you.

Pastor Mark Driscoll

Acknowledgments

First of all, in terms of friends who have helped in so many ways, we would like to thank Mike Wilkerson, Amanda Hightower, and Dave Johnson.

A special thanks to Mark Driscoll for his support of this book and for his friendship. Additionally, we admire and respect the pastors at Mars Hill Church for how they care for so many victims.

Much gratitude for our research crew from the Docent Research Group: Nick Roark, Matt Johnson, B. J. Stockman, and James Gordon.

Lindsey would like to thank her coworkers at the Sexual Assault Resource Agency and the Shelter for Help in Emergency. Justin would like to thank his colleagues, students, and friends at the University of Virginia and Reformed Theological Seminary.

At Crossway, we would like to thank our editor, Mattie Wolf, who supported the book marvelously.

Finally, our sincere thanks go to all our brave friends who in this book tell their stories of the disgrace they experienced and the grace upon grace they received from Jesus.

Introduction

If you are reading this, it's likely someone did something to disgrace or shame you. That "someone" may have been a stranger or an acquaintance and that "something" could have been any form of non-consensual sexual behavior. It may have occurred yesterday or decades ago.

The number of occurrences of sexual assaults is staggering. At least one in four women and one in six men are or will be victims of sexual assault in their lifetime.

We wrote this book for the many victims of sexual assault, both female and male, to offer accessible, gospel-based help, hope, and healing.

Also, we wrote this book to help equip pastors and ministry staff as well as family members and friends of victims. As they read what we are saying to victims, we hope they learn to respond and care for victims in ways that are compassionate, practical, and informed.

For many years we have ministered to victims who want and need a clear explanation of how the gospel applies to their experience of sexual assault and its effects in their lives. We have talked to many parents, spouses, ministers, and friends who are looking for solid, gospel-based information that would be helpful in serving victims.

Our experience in the area of abuse, both personally and professionally, led us to write this book. While avoiding platitudes, suspicious questions, and shallow theology, we combine practical victim advocacy, biblical and theological depth, and up-to-date academic research.

Lindsey currently counsels victims of sexual assault. Previously, she worked at a sexual assault crisis center where she provided crisis intervention to victims of assault and conducted a variety of training seminars to service providers. Lindsey also worked at a domestic violence shelter. Many of the women she served were also victims of sexual assault. Her graduate research was on sexual violence and public health responses.

Justin is a pastor and has counseled numerous victims of sexual assault. Since 2001, he has taught theology at Reformed Theological Seminary. Justin also taught courses on sexual violence in the Sociology and Religious Studies departments as well as in the Studies of Women and Gender program at the University of Virginia.

In *Rid of My Disgrace*, we address the effects of sexual assault with the biblical message of grace and redemption. Jesus responds to your pain and past. Your story does not end with the assault. Your life was intended for more than shame, guilt, despair, pain, and denial. The assault does not define you or have the last word on your identity. Yes, it is part of your story, but not the end of your story.

The message of the gospel redeems what has been destroyed and applies grace to disgrace.

✝This book contains both footnotes and endnotes. Letters are used to indicate footnotes, which were included so that Scripture references would be readily available to the reader.

1

Disgrace and Grace

If you have suffered as the result of a sexual assault, this book is written to you and for you—not about you. What happened to you was not your fault. You are not to blame. You did not deserve it. You did not ask for this. You should not be silenced. You are not worthless. You do not have to pretend like nothing happened. Nobody had the right to violate you. You are not responsible for what happened to you. You are not damaged goods. You were supposed to be treated with dignity and respect. You were the victim of assault and it was wrong. You were sinned against. Despite all the pain, healing *can* happen and there *is* hope.

While you may cognitively agree that hope is out there, you may still feel a major effect of the sexual assault—disgrace, a deep sense of filthy defilement encumbered with shame.

Disgrace is the opposite of grace. Grace is love that seeks you out even if you have nothing to give in return. Grace is being loved when you are or feel unlovable. Grace has the power to turn despair into hope. Grace listens, lifts up, cures, transforms, and heals.

Disgrace destroys, causes pain, deforms, and wounds. It alienates and isolates. Disgrace makes you feel worthless, rejected, unwanted, and repulsive, like a *persona non grata* (a "person without grace"). Disgrace silences and shuns. Your suffering of disgrace is only increased when others force your silence. The refusals of others to speak about sexual assault and listen to victims tell the truth is a refusal to offer grace and healing.

To your sense of disgrace, God restores, heals, and re-creates through grace. A good short definition of grace is "one-way love."[1] This is the opposite of your experience of assault, which was "one-way violence." To your experience of one-way violence, God brings one-way love. The contrast between the two is staggering.

One-way love does not avoid you, but comes near, not because of personal merit but because of your need. It is the lasting transformation that takes place in human experience. One-way love is the change agent you need for the pain you are experiencing.

Unfortunately, the message you hear most often is self-heal, self-love, and self-help. Sexual assault victims are frequently told some version of the following: "One can will one's well-being"[2] or "If you are willing to work hard and find good support, you can not only heal but thrive."[3] This sentiment is reflected in the famous quote, "No one can disgrace us but ourselves."[4]

This is all horrible news.[5] The reason this is bad news is that abuse victims are rightfully, and understandably, broken over how they've been violated. But those in pain simply may not have the wherewithal to "pull themselves up by their bootstraps." On a superficial level, self-esteem techniques and a tough "refusal to allow others to hurt me" tactic may work for the short term. But what happens for the abused person on a bad day, a bad month, or a bad year? Sin and the effects of sin are similar to the laws of inertia: a person (or object) in motion will continue on that trajectory until acted upon by an outside force. If one is devastated by sin, a personal failure to rise above the effects of sin will simply create a snowball effect of shame. Hurting people need something from the outside to stop the downward spiral. Fortunately, grace floods in from the outside at the point when hope to change oneself is lost.[6] Grace declares and promises that you will be healed. One-way love does not command "Heal thyself!" but declares "You will be healed!" Jeremiah 17:14 promises:

> Heal me, O LORD, and I shall be healed;
> save me, and I shall be saved,
> for you are my praise.

God's one-way love replaces self-love and is the true path to healing. This is amazingly good news and it highlights the contrast between disgrace and grace or one-way violence and one-way love. God heals our wounds. Can you receive grace and be rid of your disgrace? With the gospel of Jesus Christ, the answer is yes. Between the Bible's bookends of creation and restored creation is the unfolding story of redemption. Biblical creation begins in harmony, unity, and peace (*shalom*),[7] but redemption was needed because tragically, humanity rebelled, and the result was disgrace and destruction—the vandalism of *shalom*. But because God is faithful and compassionate, he restores his fallen creation and responds with grace and redemption. This good news is fully expressed in the life, death, and resurrection of Jesus, and its scope is as "far as the curse is found."[8] Jesus is the redemptive work of God in our own history, in our own human flesh.

Martin Luther describes this good news: "God receives none but those who are forsaken, restores health to none but those who are sick, gives sight to none but the blind, and life to none but the dead. . . . He has mercy on none but the wretched and gives grace to none but those who are in disgrace."[9] This message of the gospel is for all but is particularly relevant to victims of sexual assault. The purpose of this book is to proclaim this message of healing and hope to you, because you know too well the depths of suffering and the overwhelming sense of disgrace.

Rid of My Disgrace

To illustrate the trauma of sexual assault and hope for redemption, we will investigate 2 Samuel 13. This passage is the biblical account of Tamar's assault by her half-brother Amnon. Tamar's assault reflects the contrast between disgrace and grace. Disgrace versus grace is similar to the contrasts between destruction and redemption, sin and salvation, brokenness and healing, despair and hope, shame and compassion, guilt and forgiveness, violence and peace.

> [1]In the course of time, Amnon son of David fell in love with Tamar, the beautiful sister of Absalom son of David. [2]Amnon became so obsessed with his sister Tamar that he made himself ill. For she was a virgin, and it seemed impossible for him to do anything to her. [3]Now Amnon had an adviser named Jonadab son of Shimeah, David's brother. Jonadab was a very shrewd man. [4]He asked Amnon, "Why do you, the king's son, look so haggard morning after morning? Won't you tell me?" Amnon said to him, "I'm in love with Tamar, my brother Absalom's sister." [5]"Go to bed and pretend to be ill," Jonadab said. "When your father comes to see you, say to him, 'I would like my sister Tamar to come and give me something to eat. Let her prepare the food in my sight so I may watch her and then eat it from her hand.'" [6]So Amnon lay down and pretended to be ill. When

the king came to see him, Amnon said to him, "I would like my sister Tamar to come and make some special bread in my sight, so I may eat from her hand." [7]David sent word to Tamar at the palace: "Go to the house of your brother Amnon and prepare some food for him." [8]So Tamar went to the house of her brother Amnon, who was lying down. She took some dough, kneaded it, made the bread in his sight and baked it. [9]Then she took the pan and served him the bread, but he refused to eat. "Send everyone out of here," Amnon said. So everyone left him. [10]Then Amnon said to Tamar, "Bring the food here into my bedroom so I may eat from your hand." And Tamar took the bread she had prepared and brought it to her brother Amnon in his bedroom. [11]But when she took it to him to eat, he grabbed her and said, "Come to bed with me, my sister." [12]"No, my brother!" she said to him. "Don't force me! Such a thing should not be done in Israel! Don't do this wicked thing. [13]What about me? Where could I get rid of my disgrace? And what about you? You would be like one of the wicked fools in Israel. Please speak to the king; he will not keep me from being married to you." [14]But he refused to listen to her, and since he was stronger than she, he raped her.

[15]Then Amnon hated her with intense hatred. In fact, he hated her more than he had loved her. Amnon said to her, "Get up and get out!" [16]"No!" she said to him. "Sending me away would be a greater wrong than what you have already done to me." But he refused to listen to her. [17]He called his personal servant and said, "Get this woman out of my sight and bolt the door after her." [18]So his servant put her out and bolted the door after her. She was wearing an ornate robe, for this was the kind of garment the virgin daughters of the king wore. [19]Tamar put ashes on her head and tore the ornate robe she was wearing. She put her hands on her head and went away, weeping aloud as she went.

[20]Her brother Absalom said to her, "Has that Amnon, your brother, been with you? Be quiet now, my sister; he is your brother. Don't take this thing to heart." And Tamar lived in her brother Absalom's house, a desolate woman. [21]When King David heard all this, he was furious. [22]And Absalom never said a word to Amnon, either good or bad; he hated Amnon because he had disgraced his sister Tamar.[a]

Second Samuel 13 provides an insightful analysis of sexual assault because it is portrayed through Tamar's eyes. Tragically, her experience

---

[a]2 Sam. 13:1–22 NIV.

includes manipulation, force, violence, negation of her will, emotional trauma, debilitating loss of sense of self, display of grief and mourning, crushing shame, degradation, forced silence, and prolonged social isolation with desolation. Tamar's social and personal boundaries are clearly violated.[10]

It's clear in verses 12, 14, and 22 that Amnon's actions of assault are violating, shaming, forceful, and humiliating. Violence permeates his words and actions. The words used to describe Amnon's feelings and physical state express sick emotions rather than life-giving ones. According to Phyllis Trible, Amnon reduces Tamar to the state of a "disposable object."[11] After he assaults Tamar, Amnon commands her to leave by telling his servant, "Get this woman out of my sight."[b] Other translations say "Throw this woman out."[c] Amnon barely speaks of her as a person. She is a thing Amnon wants thrown out. To him, Tamar is trash.[12]

Regarding biblical accounts of sexual assault, Mieke Bal writes, "Rape is an expression of hatred, motivated by hate, and is often accompanied by offensive verbal language."[13] Amnon failed to consider Tamar as a complete person, created with dignity in the image of God. The intensity of Amnon's desire for Tamar was matched only by the intensity with which he hated her.

Verses 13, 19, and 22 repeatedly describe the effects of Tamar's assault: disgrace, shame, and reproach. After the assault, Tamar is privately and publicly traumatized by shame. The description of her outward appearance intends to show her inward feelings. Verse 19 is one sentence made up of four clauses that describe Tamar's state: "Tamar put ashes on her head and tore the ornate robe she was wearing. She put her hands on her head and went away, weeping aloud as she went."

Dressing the head with a headdress symbolizes dignity, but to the contrary, applying ashes is a symbol of lowliness.[d] Figuratively, ashes signify that which is without value or what is loathsome. Ashes on the head are a sign of humiliation and disgrace.[14] The "shame" that Tamar spoke of before the assault in verse 13—"Where could I get rid of my disgrace?"—is now a reality.

Tamar's robe is a special symbol of her elevated social status; however, she tears her robe. The rending of clothes—often articulated bibli-

---

[b]2 Sam. 13:17 NIV.
[c]New American Standard Bible and New Living Translation.
[d]Isa. 61:3.

cally as "sackcloth and ashes"—is an act of grievous affliction, revealing the sorrow of the heart, and is an expression of loss and lament. Tamar had her dignity torn from her, and the invasion is now expressed with physical gestures. The narrator describes Tamar as a person.[e] But after this violation, her beauty is exchanged for feelings of shame and loss expressed through symbols of emotional distress. Tamar has become a person who has experienced loss of control over her body, over her life, and over her dignity.

To put her hands on her head is a gesture of grief.[15] The book of Jeremiah describes the image of hands on the head to express shame.[f] Covering the head with one's hands and with ashes is a double image intensifying the expression of the abused person's state of deep shame and anguish.

The basic meaning of "cry" is to plead, from a disturbed heart, for help in time of distress. Tamar's cry is not to summon another, but to express her deeply felt distress. Tamar's "crying aloud" is an audible expression of pain, emphasizing the distress already conveyed through her visual appearance and gestures.

While we read that she leaves crying, we are not specifically told where she goes. The image produced is one of Tamar wandering aimlessly, with her torn dress, wailing like one in mourning, publicly announcing her grief and her disgrace. The assault has reduced her to a state of aimless despair.[16]

Tamar's body language portrays deep pain. Her actions resemble a rite of shame and link her with all other victims of assault. The post-assault scene is dominated by physical symbols that express Tamar's inner trauma. She has been grievously wronged by Amnon and left alone by everyone else. Her brother Absalom said, "Be quiet now, my sister. . . . Don't take this thing to heart" (v. 20). He would rather have kept her assault and suffering hidden. Even though the text says her father, the king, was furious, he did nothing. It was appropriate for David to be angry. However, he should have reached out to Tamar and protected her, even if it was only in a gesture of articulating that anger to her that she had been wronged. When victims are abused and shamed, often the

---

[e]2 Sam. 13:1.
[f]Jer. 2:36–37. "How much you go about, changing your way! You shall be put to shame by Egypt as you were put to shame by Assyria. From it too you will come away with your hands on your head, for the LORD has rejected those in whom you trust, and you will not prosper by them."

response (or lack thereof) of family and friends continues to pile on the shame. Those who should have been supportive and taken her side did not. They minimized what had happened, showing that they did not understand the depth of Tamar's pain.

Second Samuel 13 describes well the destruction wrought by sexual assault, which includes the violation and its effects, the sin against Tamar, and its consequences. An important question asked by assault victims is echoed in verse 13 when Tamar asks, "Where could I get rid of my disgrace?" Her question was left unanswered in the text. Absalom, her brother, responded to Tamar's pain by plotting to kill Amnon and by silencing her. David, Tamar's father, ignored her disgrace.

However, there was one who later came and entered her pain and shame. Jesus Christ was killed, not for revenge but to bear her shame on the cross[g] and to offer her a new robe of righteousness to replace her torn robes of disgrace.[h] How Tamar felt after the assault, described in verse 19, is shockingly similar to what Jesus experienced leading up to and during his crucifixion.[i] Jesus entered her pain and shame as Tamar's substitute to remove the stain of sins committed against her, and he rose from the dead to bring her healing and hope.

Disgrace, Grace Applied, and Grace Accomplished

The message of this book is that the gospel applies grace to disgrace and redeems what is destroyed. This good news for victims is explained in the three parts of the book.[17]

Part One—Disgrace

In order to deal with the issue honestly and directly, the first part (chapters 2 and 3) presents a clear definition of sexual assault and a description of its effects. Numerous misconceptions surround the issue of sexual assault as victims are often unsure if their experiences classify as assault. Sexual assault is not just rape by a stranger with physical force or a weapon. Most victims (approximately 80 percent) are assaulted by an acquaintance (relative, spouse, dating partner, friend, pastor,

---

[g]Heb. 12:2.
[h]Isa. 61:10.
[i]He was betrayed by a close friend, abandoned by his other friends, mocked, beaten, publicly shamed and humiliated, and he felt abandoned by God (Psalm 22 and Matt. 27:45–46).

teacher, boss, coach, therapist, doctor, etc.). Sexual assault also includes attempted rape or any form of nonconsensual sexual contact.

Many victims feel the effects of sexual assault but are isolated or confused because they believe a popular misconception of what sexual assault entails. The purpose of chapter 2 is to let victims know the prevalence of their experiences and the truth about assault. Chapter 3 on the effects of sexual assault is central for this book as it mostly describes the emotional damage done to victims, which is the focal point for applying the gospel of redemption.

Part Two—Grace Applied

Chapters 4 through 9 focus on ways that grace is applied to the disgraceful experiences and effects of sexual assault. Denial, shame, distorted images of self and God, guilt, anger, and the despair that comes with it all can only be dealt with one way: through God's compassion, faithfulness, and grace.

We believe that the only thing that gets to the depth of the devastation of sexual assault is God's one-way, unconditional love expressed through, and founded on, the person and redemptive work of Jesus Christ. And in response to sin and its effects, God's radical grace and redemption are at the center of responding to the pain and needs brought on by a victim's experiences.

Part Three—Grace Accomplished

The third part (chapters 10 through 12) is for further study for anyone who wants to read about the biblical understanding of sin, violence, and sexual assault, and God's response of redemption. Chapter 10 investigates the original peace (*shalom*) inherent to God's creation, the cosmic treason of human sin, and the violence that follows. We will trace a biblical theology of violence in general and explore what the Bible says about sexual assault in particular. The fall and sin invert mutual love and harmony into domination of and violence against each other. Sex, the very expression of human union and peace, becomes a tool for violence after the fall.

Chapters 11 and 12 trace the drama of redemption starting in the garden of Eden leading to the cross and resurrection and finally to completion in the new creation. God's steadfast unfailing love (*hesed*)[18] and grace are the threads throughout the Old and New Testaments.

Chapter 11 surveys significant, redemptive events in the Old Testament while chapter 12 shows how God's desire to restore peace and bring redemption is fulfilled in the life, death, and resurrection of Jesus Christ. When victims can identify with the horrendous victimization of the cross, they are more meaningfully able to celebrate the victorious resurrection of Christ. Jesus suffered violence that mirrors much of what victims experience today (shame, humiliation, silence, betrayal, pain, mockery, injustice, loneliness, etc.). While Jesus' suffering and death were real and brutal, there was resurrection after Good Friday. The cross is both the consequence of evil and God's method of accomplishing redemption. Jesus proves, by the resurrection, that God redeems, heals, and makes all things new.

As we explore how one-way love heals and replaces the destruction caused by one-way violence, it is helpful to look at the prayer of Psalm 6. Imagine this psalm as Tamar's cry and yours—a mourning of disgrace and longing for grace from God:

> O LORD, rebuke me not in your anger,
>> nor discipline me in your wrath.
> Be gracious to me, O LORD, for I am languishing;
>> heal me, O LORD, for my bones are troubled.
> My soul also is greatly troubled.
>> But you, O LORD—how long?
> Turn, O LORD, deliver my life;
>> save me for the sake of your steadfast love.
> For in death there is no remembrance of you;
>> in Sheol who will give you praise?
> I am weary with my moaning;
>> every night I flood my bed with tears;
>> I drench my couch with my weeping.
> My eye wastes away because of grief;
>> it grows weak because of all my foes.
> Depart from me, all you workers of evil,
>> for the LORD has heard the sound of my weeping.
> The LORD has heard my plea;
>> the LORD accepts my prayer.
> All my enemies shall be ashamed and greatly troubled;
>> they shall turn back and be put to shame in a moment.

PART ONE

Disgrace

2

What Is Sexual Assault?

Many victims are not sure if what happened to them was assault because numerous misconceptions surround the issue. Our goal in this chapter is to present the facts about sexual assault by looking at its definition and prevalence. Sexual assault is not just rape by a stranger with a weapon. Approximately 80 percent of victims are assaulted by an acquaintance (relative, spouse, dating partner, friend, pastor, teacher, boss, coach, therapist, doctor, etc.). Sexual assault also includes attempted rape or any form of nonconsensual sexual contact.

Many victims experience the effects of sexual assault, but feel isolated or confused because they believe misconceptions of what sexual assault entails. This may result in you feeling self-blame, denial, shame, guilt, anger, distorted self-image, and despair. We want you to know the prevalence of your experience and offer a definition of sexual assault. To accomplish this we endeavor to be as precise and comprehensive as possible.

Definition

Sexual assault is used as an overarching term, encompassing a large number of sexual behaviors—physical, verbal, and psychological—that violate the agency and well-being of an individual. Sexual assault is the current legal term that replaced the narrow definition of rape. Some states use this term interchangeably with rape. The exact definition of "rape," "sexual assault," "sexual abuse," and similar terms varies from state to state.[1]

With some definitions of sexual assault, it is difficult to truly discern between those who are victims of sexual assault and those who are not. When this happens, many victims feel as if they do not fit into the rigid qualifications of sexual assault, hence ignoring the ongoing or past situations in which they are or were victimized.

There are varying definitions of sexual assault.[2] For some researchers, a very narrow interpretation of sexual assault is preferable, as it avoids over reporting, a phenomenon that would provide inflated statistics. Conversely, those who favor a more broad explanation of sexual assault support its expanded definition, because it includes behaviors that often go unreported.[3]

The fluid definitions used to define this issue can, at times, exclude victims as well as add to the misconceptions held by many victims surrounding their experiences, society in general, and those in support roles. Slight changes in the definition and perception of sexual assault can change whether a person is considered a victim or not. This is why defining sexual assault is very important.

A definition that is too narrow can cause some victims of assault and those who should be supporting them to downplay the experience. Our definition of sexual assault is *any type of sexual behavior or contact where consent is not freely given or obtained and is accomplished through force, intimidation, violence, coercion, manipulation, threat, deception, or abuse of authority.* This definition gets beyond our society's narrow understanding of the issue and expands the spectrum of actions to be considered sexual assault.

The reasoning behind our cohesive and comprehensive definition of sexual assault is manifold. First, clarity helps victims know that they are not alone in their experience. Second, victims would be more motivated to report if they knew that what happened to them was a crime. Third, a clear definition would reduce myths and victim blaming. Fourth, it would also enable more services to be established to cater to the needs of victims of an extremely violating crime, in addition to educating authorities on how to properly handle such a sensitive topic. Fifth, surveys and studies indicate that most people know almost nothing about the dynamics of sexual violence and have little or no experience in dealing with it.

There are three parts to our definition of sexual assault: 1) any type of sexual behavior or contact 2) where consent is not freely given or obtained and 3) is accomplished through force, intimidation, violence, coercion, manipulation, threat, deception, or abuse of authority. We will look at each of these separately.

Sexual Behavior or Contact

Sexual assault is a display of power and control by the perpetrator against the victim. It is not a product of an "uncontrollable" sexual urge. Sexual assault is mainly about violence, not sex. Even though perpetrators use sexual actions and behaviors as a weapon, the primary motivation is to dominate, control, and belittle another. This can be done with physical sexual contact and nonphysical sexual behavior. Sexual assault is about power, and a victim may be physically or emotionally unable to resist even when there is no actual physical violence involved.

When defining sexual assault as any sexual act that is nonconsensual—forced against someone's will—it is important to understand that the "acts" can be physical, verbal, or psychological. There are four types of sexual violence. Each type involves victims who do not consent, are unable to consent, or refuse to allow the act:[4]

1) A completed sex act that is defined as contact between the penis and the vulva or the penis and the anus involving penetration, however slight; contact between the mouth and penis, vulva, or anus; or penetration of the anal or genital opening of another person by a hand, finger, or other object

2) An attempted (but not completed) sex act

3) Abusive sexual contact that is defined as intentional touching, either directly or through the clothing, of the genitalia, anus, groin, breast, inner thigh, or buttocks of any person

4) Noncontact sexual assault that is defined as assault that does not involve physical contact. Examples of noncontact sexual assault include voyeurism (peeping Tom); intentional exposure of an individual to exhibitionism (flashing); exposure to pornography; verbal or behavioral sexual harassment; threats of sexual violence; and taking nude photographs of a sexual nature of another person without their consent.

Sexual assault occurs along a continuum of power and control ranging from noncontact sexual assault to forced sexual intercourse. Sexual assault includes acts such as nonconsensual sexual intercourse (rape),[5] nonconsensual sodomy (oral or anal sexual acts), child molestation, incest, fondling, exposure, voyeurism, or attempts to commit these acts.

Using these categories of sexual acts and behaviors, some examples of sexual assault include:

- Unwanted vaginal, anal, or oral penetration with any object
- Forcing an individual to perform or receive oral sex
- Forcing an individual to masturbate, or to masturbate someone else
- Forcing an individual to look at sexually explicit material or forcing an individual to pose for sexually explicit pictures
- Touching, fondling, kissing, and any other unwanted sexual contact with an individual's body
- Unwanted contact between the mouth and genitals
- Voyeurism: spying on someone engaged in intimate behavior, sexual activity, or other activity usually considered to be of a private nature; also includes the abuser watching while the victim is made to perform sexual acts
- Exhibitionism: also known as flashing, a behavior by a person that involves exposure of private parts of their body to another person in a situation in which they would not normally be exposed; also includes making the victim watch while the abuser performs sexual acts
- Putting a finger, tongue, mouth, penis, or any object in or on an individual's vagina, penis, or anus when they do not want them to
- Touching an individual's intimate parts (defined as genitalia, groin, breast, or buttocks, or clothing covering them), or compelling them to touch his or her own or another person's intimate parts without consent
- Forcing an individual to look at sexually explicit material or forcing them to pose for sexually explicit pictures or video recordings
- A doctor, nurse, or other health care professional giving the victim an unnecessary internal examination or touching their sexual organs in an unprofessional, unwarranted, and inappropriate manner

Consent

In addition to the wide scope of sexual behaviors and contact that are included in the definition of sexual assault, another key issue is consent. Consent is when an individual is freely able to make a choice based upon respect and equal power, and with the understanding that there is the freedom to change her or his mind at any point.

There are three main considerations in judging whether a sexual act is consensual or an assault. First, are both people old enough to consent? Second, do both people have the capacity to consent? Third, did both agree to the sexual contact? If any of these are answered "no," it is likely that sexual assault has occurred.

Consent requires communicating "yes" to engaging in a particular act. Consent is not given when one person says "no," says nothing, is coerced, is physically forced, is mentally or physically helpless, is intoxicated, is under the influence of drugs, or is unconscious. Nor does it occur any time that consent is not explicitly given. Having given consent on a previous occasion does not mean that a person has consented for any future sexual encounter. The law generally assumes that a person does not consent to sexual conduct if he or she is forced, threatened, or is unconscious, drugged, a minor, developmentally disabled, chronically mentally ill, or believes they are undergoing a medical procedure.

Methods

There are varying methods perpetrators use to violate victims. In some cases, sexual assault may involve the use of force, which may include but is not limited to physical violence, use or display of a weapon, or immobilization of the victim. Sexual assault may also involve psychological coercion and taking advantage of an individual who is incapacitated or under duress and, therefore, is incapable of making a decision on her or his own.

Sexual assault occurs when a nonconsensual sexual act or behavior is committed either by 1) physical force, violence, threat, manipulation, or intimidation; 2) ignoring the objections of another person; 3) causing another's intoxication or impairment through the use of drugs or alcohol; or 4) taking advantage of another person's incapacitation, state of intimidation, helplessness, or other inability to consent.

Prevalence

Victims

Sexual assault affects millions of women, men, and children worldwide. The prevalence of sexual assault in the United States is difficult to determine because the crime is vastly underreported, yet the statistics are still overwhelmingly high: One in four women[6] and one in six men[7] will be sexually assaulted at some point in their lifetimes. These statistics are probably underestimates.

Some victims are sexually assaulted from when they are a few days old, and some are in their nineties. People can be assaulted regardless of their color, race, religion, nationality, lifestyle, sexual preference, education, class, occupation, ability, or disability. It is clear that sexual assault is a frequent phenomenon and is well within the range of being labeled a "common experience" for women, men, and children. According to most recent statistics, every two minutes someone in the United States is sexually assaulted.[8]

Most victims of sexual assault are female. According to numerous studies, between 88–92 percent of sexual assault victims are female and 8–12 percent are male.[9] One out of six women in the United States has been raped at some time in her life.[10] African-American women are assaulted at a higher rate than white women[11] and are much less likely to report it and get help.[12]

According to the Bureau of Justice, women sixteen to nineteen years old have the highest rate of sexual victimization of any age group.[13] The National Center for Juvenile Justice reports that 14 percent of victims (girls and boys) are under age six and that 67 percent of females and 70 percent of male child sexual assault victims know their offender.[14]

Sexual assault can occur in marriage and between dates and friends. Researchers have estimated that sexual assault occurs in 10–14 percent of all marriages.[15] Studies estimate that incest is experienced by 10 to 20 percent of children in the general population.[16] Studies indicate different prevalence rates of incest for females and males. One study reported that as many as one-third of all girls and one-fifth of boys have experienced incest.[17] Researchers agree that girls are much more often the victims of incest. Others report that the incidence for males is less than half of that for females because a higher proportion of males are sexually abused by adults outside the home.[18] Male incest victims may also report less frequently because they are socialized to not express feelings of helplessness and vulnerability.

Research shows that there are differences between females and males with respect to the characteristics of sexual assault and the events surrounding it. When victimized, women are more likely than men to be injured, to use medical services, and to report the violence to the police.[19] Men are more likely than women to have had multiple assailants during their attack.[20]

Regarding the age breakdown of sexual assault, 15 percent of sexual assault victims are under age twelve, 29 percent are ages twelve to seventeen, and 80 percent are under age thirty.[21] The highest risk years are ages twelve to thirty-four, and girls ages sixteen to nineteen are four times more likely than the general population to be victims of sexual assault.

Most victims of child sexual assault know their attacker; 34.2 percent of assailants were family members, 58.7 percent were acquaintances, and only 7 percent of the perpetrators were strangers to the victim.[22] Of child sexual abuse victims, approximately 10 percent of victims are age three and under, 28 percent are between ages four and seven, 26 percent are between ages eight and eleven, and 36 percent are twelve and older.[23]

Those who experienced childhood assault are at a higher risk of adult revictimization.[24] Childhood sexual assault is especially common among sexually assaulted women and men (59 percent and 61 percent respectively).[25] Women who had been sexually assaulted in childhood are at least twice as likely to be assaulted in adulthood.[26] It was found that the respondents with more physically and emotionally severe adolescent sexual assault experiences were at a significantly greater risk of revictimization. They are 4.4 times more likely to be revictimized than the respondents who had not experienced adolescent sexual assault.[27]

The findings regarding male victims are even more dramatic. One study reports that 61 percent of men who report a sexual victimization during adulthood also report having been sexually assaulted as a child.[28] Men who experienced sexual assault as adults are five times more likely to have a history of childhood sexual assault than men with no adult sexual assault experience. Two major studies have shown a strong correlation between childhood sexual victimization and subsequent adult sexual victimization.[29]

Perpetrators

Predominately, perpetrators responsible for sexual assaults are male[30] and are usually someone the victim knows.[31] Although strangers are stereotyped as perpetrators of sexual assault, the evidence indicates that a high percentage of offenders are acquaintances of the victim.[32] Most sexual assault perpetrators are white, educated, middle-class men.[33]

With only 7 percent of the perpetrators armed, sexual assault is the least likely to involve a weapon of any other violent crime.[34]

If individuals who commit sexual assault offenses are not apprehended and prosecuted, they will likely continue to commit sexual offenses. One widely recognized study found that 126 admitted perpetrators had committed 907 sexual assaults involving 882 different victims. The more sex offenders that are apprehended and prosecuted, the fewer victims there will be of sexual assault.[35]

Reporting

With regard to the reporting of sexual assault, there are two major issues to consider—false reporting and under reporting. While under reporting is a major concern, false reporting is not. Actually, false reports are quite rare. The figure often used by sexual violence experts for estimating falsified reports is 2 percent, which is a slightly lower rate than other crimes.[36]

Given the horrific nature of sexual assault and the shame it brings to victims, it is not shocking that it is one of the most underreported crimes. The fear of intrusive and revictimizing court procedures prevents many sexual assault survivors from reporting their assaults. Most sexual assault victims choose not to report their assaults. Factors that keep a victim from reporting the crime include shame and embarrassment, self-blame, fear of media exposure, fear of further injury or retaliation, fear of one's own family and community response, and fear of a legal system that often puts the victim's behavior and history on trial.

According to the FBI, sexual assault is "one of the most underreported crimes due primarily to fear and/or embarrassment on the part of the victim."[37] One research report claims that only between 5 percent and 20 percent of sexual assaults may actually be reported.[38] At the most, less than 40 percent of all sexual assaults were reported to law enforcement.[39] Under reporting skews all recordable statistics. Therefore, statistics on the incidence of sexual assault vary greatly and are believed to underrepresent the prevalence of the crime. Despite the inability to paint a complete picture of the occurrence of sexual assault, statistics can provide victims with a greater understanding of the scope of the issue.

It is important to acknowledge that most researchers believe that male sexual assault is severely underreported, perhaps even more so than sexual assaults of women. Male sexual assault victims are much less likely to disclose information regarding their experiences than are females.[40] Therefore, they constitute an extremely underidentified, underserved, and frequently misunderstood population.

Though sexual assault is underreported by both females and males, males are in a unique position. They are far less likely to disclose being sexually assaulted to anyone. Two trends are evident in the existing statistics on male victims of sexual abuse: 1) the more recent the research, the higher the incidence of assault, and 2) with growing awareness, more men seem willing to disclose their experiences of sexual assault.[41]

Acknowledgment

Naming and describing the evil done to you does not ensure automatic personal healing. However, it does provide clarity regarding sexual assault, and it allows for acknowledgment. If sexual assault is not defined, named, or described, then it remains hidden. Telling the truth about sexual assault by acknowledging the traumatic experience is one important aspect of healing, but it is not the whole picture. Further healing comes as you are able to interpret the effect of what happened to you within a larger pattern of meaning. The first step toward doing this is to look closely at the effects of sexual assault and the accompanying emotions.

3

What Are the Effects of Sexual Assault?

This chapter on the effects of sexual assault is central to this book. Internal trauma is not only *done to*, but also *experienced by*, victims. These internal—and deeply personal—places of a victim's heart, will, and emotions need a clear application of the gospel of redemption.

The number of occurrences of sexual assaults is staggering. At least one in four women and one in six men currently are or will be victims of sexual assault in their lifetimes. The only thing more staggering than the prevalence of abuse is the acute damage done to the victims. This damage can stem from, but is not limited to, the denial of their wills and the violation of their bodies. The effects are physical, social, emotional, psychological, and spiritual.

We will focus on the distress experienced by victims that is caused by sexual assault. We do this for redemptive purposes, not just to be descriptive. Typically, people who have been sexually assaulted have a hard time finding the words to describe how they feel or what they are thinking in response to the trauma. Because of this, it is often helpful that the language of pain be offered by those who are not currently in traumatic pain themselves, but are able to empathize and speak on behalf of those who are. Describing the pain is a way to normalize how the victims are feeling rather than to alienate them by not talking about it at all.[1]

Sexual assault is not simply an event that happened to you, ended, and now is over. It can have an impact on every aspect of your life—your faith, your daily attitudes and emotions, your self-image, your relationships, and your sexuality. These are not just past issues but remain very real and current. Regardless of how long ago the assault took place, the traces of an assault can reach into the present life of a victim and trigger ongoing problems.

Effects

The effects of sexual assault discussed in what follows are potential but not inevitable. Research shows that victims of human-induced trauma tend to experience a greater degree of harm,[2] and that sexual assault causes more harmful psychological effects that are more severe than effects of other crimes.[3] During an assault, most victims feel terrified, fearful, helpless, humiliated, and confused. Afterward, any of these feelings can persist and intensify, especially terror and fear.

From the earliest studies, the most common psychological symptoms associated with sexual assault were anxiety and fear. Research consistently reports high levels of anxiety and fear immediately after the assault, and for some, even years later.[4] A number of studies have clearly indicated the prominence of depression in the symptomatology of sexual assault victims, particularly in the first three months[5] after the incident, and some considerably longer.[6]

After a person has been sexually assaulted, it is normal to experience a range of feelings and reactions. Everyone copes in his or her own way. Some people have very strong reactions; others are calm or numb. It is not uncommon for victims to alternate between moments of terror, anger, or rage and moments of numbness.[7] Some feelings and reactions might be experienced directly after the assault while others can occur days or sometimes weeks later. Understanding that these feelings are normal and experienced by others who have been sexually assaulted may make the emotions and reactions less frightening.

Some victims will find they heal relatively quickly, while others will feel the lasting effects of their victimization throughout their lifetimes. Since every person and situation is different, victims will respond to an assault in various ways. Many factors can influence individuals' responses to, and healing from, what happened to them.[8]

Sexual assault is a massive violation of the physical, psychological, and personal boundaries of another person. The acute damage of an assault stems not only from the denial of the victim's will but also from the violation of the body's physical boundaries. The trauma of sexual assault involves losing control of your own body and possibly fearing death or injury.

Immediate physical effects may be pain and bodily injuries, especially if the perpetrator used force. Specific physical effects may include:

bruises, broken bones, STIs, nausea, vomiting, headaches, and pregnancy. Longer-term physical effects may be disturbed sleep patterns, nightmares, insomnia, loss of appetite, and stomach pains.

Sexual assault causes harmful emotional, psychological, and/or physiological effects that are more severe than the effects of other crimes.[9] These effects include: shame, self-blame, guilt, embarrassment, anxiety, stress, fear, anger, confusion, sexualized behaviors, loss of sex drive, interpersonal problems, denial, irritability, depression, despair, social withdrawal, numbing/apathy (detachment, loss of caring), chronic and acute somatizing (experiencing of physical symptoms in response to emotional distress), feelings of isolation and alienation, restricted affect (reduced ability to express emotions), nightmares, flashbacks, headaches, difficulty concentrating, diminished interest in regular activities, negative self-image, loss of self-esteem, emotional shock or numbness, erratic mood swings, feeling powerless, disorientation, OCD, panic attacks, body memories, loss of security, confusion of sex with love, extreme dependency, impaired ability to judge the trustworthiness of others, various phobias, hostility, aggression, change in appetite, suicidal ideation (thoughts of suicide and death), hypervigilance (always being "on your guard"), insomnia or other sleep disturbance, decreased energy and motivation, exaggerated startle response (jumpiness), eating problems/disorders, self-mutilation (cutting, burning, or otherwise hurting oneself), sexual dysfunction (not being able to perform sexual acts), sexual effects (ranging from avoidance to compulsive promiscuity), hyperarousal (exaggerated feelings or responses to stimuli),[10] inability to concentrate or focus, feeling uncomfortable being alone, gastrointestinal disturbance, substance use and abuse (alcohol and other drugs) and other compulsive behaviors, shock, impaired memory, and post-traumatic stress disorder (PTSD).

In a study investigating trauma symptoms, victims of sexual assault were much more symptomatic than their peers.[11] They reported significantly more distress than did their nonassaulted peers.[12] This attests to the incredible long-term effects sexual assault has on both women and men. Post-traumatic symptoms of startle response and emotional volatility can make victims ashamed of their behavior, and attempts to control these responses lead to a life of suppression and avoidance.[13]

Trauma

It is appropriate to call sexual assault a traumatic event. "Trauma" is understood as a state of being negatively overwhelmed. It is the experience of terror, loss of control, of helplessness during a stressful event that threatens one's physical and/or psychological integrity. Jennifer Beste writes: "The especially sinister side of trauma is that, even when the event has ended, it has only begun to shatter one's key assumptions about one's self and one's relation to others in the world.... The disintegration of one's perception of self and world disrupts one's normal pattern of functioning."[14] After a traumatic event such as a sexual assault, many victims experience intense emotional distress and frequent flashbacks of the assault(s) as they struggle emotionally and cognitively to adjust their sense of reality.

While some victims eventually experience a gradual decrease in the intensity of emotions and memories surrounding the assault, others reexperience the traumatic memories as though the original assault were presently occurring. Subsequently, they develop a host of responses now identified as post-traumatic stress disorder (PTSD) symptoms,[15] which is usually associated with combat war veterans. Bessel van der Kolk, a trauma theorist, explains that the inability to integrate the traumatic event into one's understanding of reality results in a "repetitive replaying of the trauma in images, behaviors, feeling, physiological states, and interpersonal relationships."[16]

Because sexual assault is always traumatizing, victims are three times more likely than nonvictims to suffer from depression, six times more likely to suffer from post-traumatic stress disorder, thirteen times more likely to abuse alcohol, twenty-six times more likely to abuse drugs, and four times more likely to contemplate suicide.[17]

Negative Stereotypes

Social psychology research on attitudes toward sexual assault has demonstrated that individuals in our society hold many prejudices about and negative views of sexual assault victims.[18] Thus, victims often suffer not only from the trauma of the assault itself but also from the effects of these negative stereotypes. The result is that victims feel socially derogated and blamed following their sexual assault, which can prolong, continue, and intensify the substantial psychological and emotional distress the victim experiences. It is clear that negative reactions from family, friends, loved ones, and society have a harmful effect on victims. Because sexual assault is a form of victimization that is particularly stigmatized in American society, many victims suffer in silence, which only intensifies their distress and disgrace. There appears to be a societal impulse to blame traumatized individuals for their suffering. One rationale is that this provides nonvictims with a false sense of security if they can place blame on victims rather than on perpetrators. Research findings suggest that blaming victims for post-traumatic symptoms is not only erroneous but also contributes to the vicious cycle of traumatization. Victims experiencing negative social reactions have poorer adjustment.[19] Research has proven that "the only social reactions related to better adjustment by victims were being believed and being listened to by others."[20]

Self-Blaming

Self-blaming is a common behavior among victims. As a coping technique and to make sense of the assault, victims make attributions for why the assault occurred. There are two types of self-blame: behavioral and characterological self-blame. Behavioral self-blame reflects the victim's belief that his or her own behavior led to the assault. Characterological self-blame focuses not on the behavior but on the victim's personality or character as the cause of assault. Regarding this type of self-blame, victims feel there is something inherently wrong with them, causing them to deserve to be assaulted. Many studies have shown that self-blame is associated with more distress and poorer adjustment.[21]

Difference between Female and Male Victims

While the effects are the same between female and male victims, there are variations of intensity and length of the distress between the two. Women have been shown to internalize psychological effects like depression and anxiety more than men. Up to 60 percent of women reported having some feeling of "mental pollution" after the assault.[22] While most female victims experience some symptom reduction by three months postassault, many effects, including fear, anxiety, depression, post-traumatic stress, decreased self-esteem, social difficulties, and sexual dysfunction may continue at significant levels for a number of years.[23]

Studies that include both women and men indicate that immediately following the sexual assault, men present with more denial and emotional control[24] and higher levels of depression and hostility.[25]

Although men reported being less symptomatic than women, men were actually found to be more symptomatic. Most research on the differences between men and women in symptom expression suggests that women are generally more willing to acknowledge distress than men.[26] However, male victims of sexual assault report significantly higher levels of distress than female victims on eight of the ten scales and equivalent levels on the remaining two scales (depression and intrusive experiences). This suggests that sexual assault may be especially trauma-producing for men. This could be because of the sex-role violation associated with sexual assault within a society where men are expected to be strong, aggressive, and avoidant of any (even forced) sexual contact with other men. Sexual assault can be particularly destabilizing to the man's sense of self and sexual identity.[27] Perhaps this is why male victims appear to respond to assault-related distress by engaging in externalizing activities, tension reduction behavior, and dysfunctional sexual behavior.[28]

Men with a history of adult sexual assault reported higher levels of distress than females on the Trauma Symptom Inventory tests, despite females' tendencies to acknowledge psychological distress more so than men.[29] This reveals an additional layer of stress and experience that sexual assault may have on male victims. Because of the socially constructed notion of the male gender role, emphasizing their strength and aggressiveness, an experience of sexual assault may lead them to question their sexuality more than women. This claim is supported by the same study which reports men having greater difficulty in the "self and sexual domains" than women.[30] Men are often a forgotten group in the realm of sexual assault, but as a population, they may be at risk of experiencing higher levels of trauma as a result of the experience.

Emotions and Grace

There are similar ways that both women and men react to trauma. Sexual assault can bring physical, psychological, emotional, and spiritual pain that often leads to shame, embarrassment, degradation, denial, a profound sense of emptiness, guilt, a sense of powerlessness, anger, a sense of helplessness, vulnerability, fear, depression, isolation, and/or anxiety. These emotions are generally associated with the victim's response to sexual assault.[31] Counselors and therapists report that sexual assault victims experience these emotions more than those who have not been sexually assaulted. As a result, victims understandably want many things: relief, protection, hope, justice, and vindication.

A wide range of physical, emotional, psychological, and physiological effects has been discussed. Over the past two decades, sexual assault has increasingly been conceptualized as a traumatic experience. This has been done by the growth of studies reporting the prevalence of PTSD among victims.[32] Various factors are linked to traumatic distress or feelings of disgrace from sexual assault. These include denial, shame, guilt, anger, distorted self-image, and despair. For the purpose of this book, we are focusing on these most prevalent responses to sexual assault.

Emotions

Since we are dealing with the negative and destructive emotions that result from sexual assault, we must deal with what emotions are and are not. Emotions are based on cognitive assessment and belief; they are not simply experienced. An emotion is not an impression—a feeling or a unique sort of internal experience that just happens to a person and then is named and described.[33] Emotions are not merely physiological impulses that can be simply ignored, trivialized, or controlled.[34]

Rather, emotions are based on and require beliefs, standards, and judgments. Emotions result from an individual's evaluation of an event, situation, or object, and they reveal whether that individual sees some aspect of the world threatening or welcoming, pleasant or painful, regrettable or as a solace, and so on.[35]

In *Faithful Feelings*, Matthew Elliot offers a clear summary about emotions:

> Emotion is always about something; it has an object. Emotion tells us about our values and beliefs. It can also tell us about the beliefs and values of others. Emotions are not necessarily rational, not

because they are intrinsically irrational impulses, but because we can be irrational people. Emotions are often a powerful motivation. . . . Emotions are highly complex phenomena that rely upon both our conscious and unconscious mind, memories, cultural forces, family upbringing, and our personalities. These factors interact and respond to one another in an incredibly complex web of interdependent beliefs and values to produce particular emotions in particular circumstances.[36]

What this means for victims of sexual assault is that your emotions are important and valid. They are not just chemicals in your brain and physiological responses to stimuli. Your emotions are to be taken seriously and listened to. They reveal what you believe about God, yourself, your experience of sexual assault, others, and the world. What you believe has a huge connection to how you respond to disgrace, violence, denial, shame, guilt, fear, anxiety, bitterness, despair, and so on.

New Emotions

The beliefs that accompany the development, maintenance, and increase of disgrace and distress are directly responsible for generating dysfunctional emotions and their effects for victims. This means that emotions can be fed or fought by the one experiencing them. Our hope is that the grace of God would fight against the emotions accompanying your disgrace and nurture in you new emotions. Paul Holmer writes: "Part of the whole sense-making that Christianity provides is a whole panoply of new emotion. Hope, fear of the Lord, contrition about oneself, love—these and more are not just variations of the familiar or permutations of something we already have, they are new affects, new forms of pathos."[37]

We need to look at the gospel of Jesus, especially related to sexual violence, in order to investigate the new emotions available to victims and how they relate to the current emotions victims experience.

Too many people want to separate emotion and suffering from faith and theology, but we will do the opposite. We wish to integrate suffering, faith, emotions, and theology. Don Saliers writes: "Whatever else it may include, the Christian faith is a pattern of deep emotions."[38]

Healing

What grace offers to the victim experiencing disgrace is the gift of refuting distortions and faulty thinking and replacing their condemning, counterfactual beliefs with more accurate ones that reflect the truths about God, yourself, and God's grace-filled response to your disgrace. This is an important point to highlight. We are all powerless to heal ourselves. Research shows that self-help statements have been found to be ineffective and even harmful by making some people with low self-esteem feel even worse about themselves in the long term.[39] As a matter of fact, positive self-statements frequently end up reinforcing and strengthening one's original negative self-perception they were trying to change.[40]

Tragically, positive self-statements "have more impact on people with low self-esteem than on people with high self-esteem, and the impact on people with low self-esteem is negative."[41] The consequences are that positive self-statements are likely to backfire and cause harm for the very people they are meant to benefit—people with low self-esteem.[42]

What victims need are not self-produced positive statements but God's statements about his response to their pain. How can you be rid of these dysfunctional emotions and their effects? How can you be rid of your disgrace? God's grace to you dismantles the beliefs that give disgrace life. Grace re-creates what violence destroyed. Martin Luther writes that "the love of God does not find, but creates, that which is pleasing to it."[43] One-way love is the change agent you need. Grace transforms and heals; and healing comes by hearing God's statements to you, not speaking your own statements to yourself. The rest of the book focuses on God's redemptive response to your experience of sexual assault (Part Two) and to violence and sin in general (Part Three).

As we explore the effects caused by sexual assault and how grace can heal them, it is helpful to look at the prayer of Psalm 13. It is a request for God to deal with our sorrow, distress, and disgrace with his steadfast love, in the hope that we may rejoice in salvation:

> How long, O Lord? Will you forget me forever?
> How long will you hide your face from me?

How long must I take counsel in my soul
>and have sorrow in my heart all the day?
How long shall my enemy be exalted over me?
Consider and answer me, O LORD my God;
>light up my eyes, lest I sleep the sleep of death,
>lest my enemy say, "I have prevailed over him,"
>lest my foes rejoice because I am shaken.
But I have trusted in your steadfast love;
>my heart shall rejoice in your salvation.
I will sing to the LORD,
>because he has dealt bountifully with me.

PART TWO

Grace Applied

Allen's Story

My name is Allen. It wasn't until my midthirties that I finally discovered something that had happened to me, something I had suspected but kept denying. I'd been molested as a little boy.

When I was eight years old I had what I thought was a recurring nightmare—a large dark figure coming into my room in the middle of the night. I remember it happening several times—screaming for help and crying in fear, with no one ever coming to help. The rest I had blanked out. These "nightmares" stopped when I moved into a different bedroom a year or so later.

Over the next twenty years life went on; I experienced the typical joys and challenges of adolescence and young adulthood. I got married at twenty-one, and my wife and I started a family of our own. Four daughters came along within six years—I felt so blessed, so fortunate.

During all those years there had been recurring signs that I had been molested as a child. I was hypervigilant, had bouts of insomnia, depression, and an obsession with appearing strong and tough (lifting weights like crazy) and, something rather embarrassing, the absolute inability to have a rectal exam.

When I was eighteen I underwent a physical as part of applying for an ROTC scholarship, and when it came time for the rectal exam I started shaking and crying uncontrollably. I was humiliated and embarrassed, and the doctor ended up not doing it. The exact same thing happened about ten years later when I underwent a routine physical exam. Another similar incident occurred when I was on a cruise with my wife after we had been married for years. I got food poisoning, and after a horrendous night I went to the infirmary on board for a shot to stop the nausea. When I pulled my pants down to receive the shot, I started shaking and crying again, just as I had years earlier at my ROTC physical. My wife and I eventually had our fifth child, a son who joined his four sisters. Once he started getting older, I began having massive anxiety attacks and bouts of depression, which felt like they had come out of left field. At times I found myself literally shaking in my office at work for no reason. I had no idea what was happening or why.

Finally in my midthirties I started seeing a Christian counselor, and he helped me put the pieces together to something I had been denying for over twenty years, being molested as a little boy. The perpetrator was my grandfather. He had come to visit us at the exact time of my recurring "nightmares." I later learned he had also molested my two sisters. When it all came together, I just shook and sobbed in the counselor's office. But at least now it all made sense, and the truth of what I had been denying all those years finally came out. After all those years of suspecting that something had happened to me but denying it, it all became clear. It hurt so badly. It still does sometimes. After all, how could a grown man do that to a trusting, helpless little boy, especially his own grandson?

All the years of denial solved nothing. Time did not heal those wounds. Facing the reality of what actually happened was the beginning of the healing process, a process that continues and will not be complete until we are in heaven. What has given me comfort is the fact that the truth is now clear, and while the truth hurts, it also sets us free (John 8:32). I know God wept when I was molested, and I know that he cared for me as an eight-year-old kid, and he still cares for me. I know that through the death and resurrection of Jesus Christ there is forgiveness available for all of us, including me, and including my grandfather. My grandfather died years before everything became clear, but I have forgiven him; Scripture is clear that we need to forgive others as God forgives us (Matt. 6:14–15; Eph. 4:32; Col. 3:13). There are still traces of lingering hurt and anger in my heart—I won't deny that—but the anxiety attacks and the bouts of depression have stopped. I still have insomnia sometimes, with the accompanying hypervigilance, but markedly less than before. I still lift weights regularly, but as a way to relieve stress and stay in shape, not out of a compulsion to appear strong and tough.

One benefit of all this is that it has made me extra careful and protective of my own kids—in a healthy and not controlling way—so that hopefully they will not experience what I did. As an ordained minister, it has also given me a deeper sense of compassion for those in our church who have been traumatized by sexual assault or in other ways. And while I am gradually experiencing the healing power of the grace of God as related to this, I look forward with hope to the day when the healing will be complete. In the meantime, I am grateful that the denial has stopped and that God cares for me.

4

Denial

Sexual assault often communicates to victims that they are alone, unimportant, beyond hope, and not worthy of sympathy. It tempts victims to deny and minimize. Denial and minimization are key methods victims use for lessening or coping with the pain and trauma from an assault. When we experience pain, our impulse is to escape the bombardment of betrayal and loss. In our desperation, we deny our suffering in an attempt to dull the pain.

Following the initial shock of the assault—and even months later—victims may deny to others or to themselves that anything has happened by suppressing memories in an attempt to gain control of their lives again. If and when there is an acceptance of the assault, victims often minimize it by saying "it doesn't bother me anymore." Denial of the assault and its effects can lead victims to minimize the anxiety and distress they are feeling, which can lead to isolation and loneliness. Sadly, some would rather deny or minimize their own emotions than grieve the irretrievable loss of their innocence and trust in others.

Many victims do not fully acknowledge what has happened to them, or they minimize the intensity of the experience. This is especially true for survivors of childhood sexual assault. Initially, denial can slow the process down to create a buffer or safety zone so survivors can begin to cope with difficult emotions.

We all have experiences of disgrace that allow us to learn to cope with the occasional failures, defeat, or rejection inherent in life. In the case of severe trauma such as sexual assault, the interpersonal experience of disgrace is internalized. Once internalized, its distorting effects may function apart from the original experience with progressively destructive consequences. Disgrace becomes a core dimension of their identity. The experience of disgrace can be so painful that victims set in motion the processes of denial, repression, and minimizing. However, instead of lessening suffering, too much denial and minimization may increase the pain. Denial does not allow the victims to deal with the severe mental and emotional tolls, the psychological destruction, and the traumatic effects of the assault.

One of the most debilitating consequences of sexual assault is victims' suppression of their feelings. Understandably, victims cope by suppressing their terror, pain, and rage, but rather than fostering avoidance tactics, victims need encouragement to grieve. Victims' experiences threaten their semblance of internal and external safety, so it's unrealistic to expect them to simply abandon their reliable survival strategies even amid objective safety. Family and friends should give grace as some level of denial may help as victims learn to cope with how they feel.

You may have learned to cope over the weeks, months, or years by consciously or unconsciously driving the abuse and pain from your memory and conversations. You may find yourself saying to others "Everything is fine," or "It could have been worse." It may be more comfortable to refuse any discussion as if nothing happened. While self-preservation schemes may help to manage your pain and protect against the nightmare of powerlessness, betrayal, confusion, and rejection, no amount of denial will erase your pain; it only postpones healing.

Denial fuels the myth that time heals all wounds. But memory knows no time. Over time the pain may diminish in severity or be masked in other ways, but time alone will not heal the wounds from what has been done to you. Perhaps you try to manage your pain through drugs, alcohol, food, anger, fear, getting tough, running from God, being sexually promiscuous, or isolating yourself. But in order to heal, you need God's compassion and redemptive work applied to your suffering. The more realistic and honest you can be regarding your emotions in response to what has happened to you, the more you will understand that you are not responsible. You have permission to grieve and mourn what has happened, and know that God has compassion for you amid your suffering.

Impulses toward denial are most common among victims assaulted by someone they know. It can be extremely difficult to face the fact that someone you should have been able to lovingly trust betrayed you. In addition, perpetrators often use their own form of denial and when confronted may defend or rationalize their actions. A perpetrator's denial can be incredibly confusing to victims as they wrongly ponder their own culpability or blame. Sadly, perpetrators often give astonishing rationalizations by saying that what they've done (or are doing) is a form of misunderstood love. Tragically, some victims believe the lies and consequently have difficulty identifying that they've been assaulted at all.

Additionally, societal and familial norms silence victims by preventing them from speaking out about their experience of sexual assault. This is particularly the case for victims assaulted by their relatives, partners, or acquaintances. Families and friends often encourage denial and minimization because the facts are uncomfortable to hear, they don't know how to respond, or they are worried about embarrassing the family.[1] You may have been told not to talk about your assault in a number of different ways: "Don't air the family's dirty laundry," "This did not happen to you," or "Forget the past and move on." In response to the confusion brought about by family and friends, excuses for perpetrators or nonoffending parents are often made. "It wasn't his fault, he was drinking," "I'm sure I did something to lead him on," or "I know my mother would have protected me if she only knew."

In addition, victims from culturally and linguistically diverse backgrounds may be denied access to mainstream support systems. Victims with a disability may also be unable to voice their experiences to others due to the nature of their disability. If you are unable to share your emotions and needs with others, you may understandably feel confused, alienated, isolated, in despair, or angry.

In light of all this, adopting a "forget the past and move on" mentality may sound attractive when you are besieged with painful memories of an abusive past or experience. But this strategy is ineffective and is a barrier to healing.

Some level of resistance to restoration is normal for sexual assault victims. There is either a conscious refusal to admit that the assault has any impact, or there is an absence of memory of the past damage. Specific attention to the harm done is needed before the restoration is begun.

While denial is used for self-preservation, if it is never addressed it is actually a major barrier to healing. Denial can turn from a natural reaction, to a shocking and traumatic event, to a mode of self-protection and self-reliance that avoids honest engagement of one's emotions and God's response to what happened.

As you engage your emotions, feelings of helplessness and grief may grow stronger. While grief can be excruciating at first, the Bible says that you do not mourn alone. God grieves for and with you. God's response toward you is compassion. In light of that, you can cry out honestly to God about what happened and how it affects you. Scripture is filled with people crying out to God and God's gracious and redemptive responses.

The Psalms in particular provoke us out of denial. The book of Psalms is not filled with 150 hymns of joy. The psalms of complaint and accusation—the music of confusion, doubt, and heartache—significantly outnumber the hymns of joy.

While our natural impulse is to deny painful emotions, the psalms expose them to us, others, and God. In light of this exposure, Calvin writes that psalmists "lay open their inmost thoughts and emotions, call, or rather draw, each of us to the examination of himself in particular, in order that none of the many infirmities to which we are subject, and of the many vices with which we abound, may remain concealed."[2]

God Sees, Hears, and Knows

Instead of denying, minimizing, or ignoring what happened to you, God mourns what happened. Through Jesus he identifies with you and he has compassion. God calls sexual assault what it is: violence, evil, and sin. He doesn't minimize it; he doesn't ignore your hurt. Your dignity as an image-bearer of God has been assaulted, and it is an assault against him since you reflect his glory.[3]

God knows your suffering. He sees, responds, and invites you to participate in the sorrow and grief he has for your situation. You are not encouraged to be silent or deny, but to feel and express your emotions, to cry or weep, to grieve the destruction you experienced. God has compassion for the victims of injustice, and at the root of his compassion is the fact that he witnesses the suffering of the abused. His real (and constant) presence amid violence allows us to understand God's hatred for sin.

Exodus

The exodus story[4] begins with God's people being oppressed in Egypt. At their time of greatest need, God heard Israel's desperate cries for help: "And God heard their groaning, and God remembered his covenant with Abraham, with Isaac, and with Jacob. God saw the people of Israel—and God knew."[a] God sees, hears, and knows the suffering of his people: "I have surely *seen* the affliction of my people who are in Egypt and have *heard* their cry because of their taskmasters. I *know* their sufferings."[b] God sympathizes with the groans of his people and gets involved with their suffering. He already sees, hears, and knows your suffering and is facing it in its fullness even before you cried out. Now he is inviting you to face it with him, not alone.

Psalms

Many of the psalms reveal the compassionate disposition of God toward those who suffer: "The LORD is near to the brokenhearted and saves the crushed in spirit."[c] Suffering does not repel God. Instead it draws God near. God promises never to cut himself off from those who cry to him in distress.[d] This divine attention toward those who are suffering is incarnated in the suffering servant, who we now know is Jesus Christ: "He was despised and rejected by men; a man of sorrows, and acquainted with grief."[e]

Jesus Christ

God's compassion for and solidarity with the oppressed is embodied in Jesus Christ. Christ not only suffered for his people but also suffers with them.[f] "The descent of God to earth is the descent of God to the underside of the knife, plague, or rain of fire."[5] He understands our sufferings. His identity was attacked.[g] He was rejected and betrayed by others.[h] He was abandoned.[i] He was lied about, slandered, and person-

---

[a]Ex. 2:24–25.
[b]Ex. 3:7, emphasis added.
[c]Ps. 34:18.
[d]Ps. 9:9, 12.
[e]Isa. 53:3.
[f]Acts 9:4–5; 1 Cor. 12:26–27.
[g]Matt. 4:3; 27:40.
[h]Matt. 26:47–50, 69–75; Mark 3:21; 14:43–45, 66–72; Luke 22:47–52; John 7:5.
[i]Matt. 26:56; Mark 14:50.

ally attacked.[j] He was humiliated. He was in emotional agony.[k] He was in physical agony from being beaten and tortured. He was murdered. He experienced the worst agony imaginable, not only physically on the cross, but also emotionally and spiritually as well. At one point, he cried out: "My God, my God, why have you forsaken me?"[l]

Jesus endured the cross because of his compassion and love for you. The New Testament repeatedly turns to the cross of Christ as the supreme demonstration of the love of God. John provides the most famous example: "By this we know love, that he laid down his life for us.... God is love.... In this is love, not that we have loved God but that he loved us and sent his Son to be the propitiation for our sins."[m] We can begin to appreciate the contours of God's compassionate love by reflecting on the cost of the cross and the depth of our need.[6]

Jesus shared in absolute abandonment and the pain of sufferers. He carries the burden of pain with you. Jesus understands your pain, because he was a victim of violence and suffered injustice. He knows what it means to bear shame. He knows what it means to be alone, naked, bleeding, and crying out to God. You can more meaningfully celebrate the victorious resurrection of Christ when you can identify with the horrendous victimizing of the cross. Jesus mirrors much of what you experienced (shame, humiliation, silence, betrayal, pain, mockery, travesty of justice, loneliness, etc.). In your suffering, you can be armed with the confidence that Christ also suffered unjustly.

When considering God's solidarity in Christ with victims, it is important to highlight how Jesus is merciful and faithful. Hebrews 2:17 connects Jesus' suffering to his disposition toward us: "Therefore he had to be made like his brothers in every respect, so that he might become a merciful and faithful high priest in the service of God."

Commenting on this passage, Calvin explains Christ's desire to sympathize with us as we suffer:

> And it is the true teaching of faith when we in our case find the reason why the Son of God undertook our infirmities. For all knowledge without feeling the need of this benefit is cold and lifeless. But he teaches us that Christ was made subject to human affections, that He

[j]John 8:41, 48.
[k]Matt. 26:36–46; Luke 22:39–46.
[l]Matt. 27:46.
[m]1 John 3:16; 4:8, 10.

might be a merciful and faithful high priest. . . . For in a priest, whose office it is to appease God's wrath, to help the miserable, to raise up the fallen, to relieve the oppressed, mercy is especially required, and it is what experience produces in us. For it is a rare thing for those who are always happy to sympathize with the sorrows of others. . . . The Son of God had no need of experience that He might know the emotions of mercy. But we could not be persuaded that He is merciful and ready to help us had He not become acquainted by experience with our miseries. But this, as other things, has been as a favor given to us. Therefore whenever any evils pass over us, let it ever occur to us, that nothing happens to us but what the Son of God has Himself experienced in order that He might sympathize with us; nor let us doubt but that He is at present with us as though He suffered with us. . . . An acquaintance with our sorrows and miseries so inclines Christ to compassion, that He is constant in imploring God's aid for us.[7]

Jesus' solidarity with those who suffer is also a ministry of acknowledgment. The humiliation and death of Jesus acknowledges the ongoing reality and striking power of violence and injustice. It is a powerful acknowledgment on God's part of the persevering affliction of pain and suffering. This reflects the seriousness with which God takes the presence of innocent suffering.

God's Sorrow

God's solidarity with and compassion for those who suffer is the motivation for his response of grief. Grief is not negative. People may claim that grief is usually negative and not something God does, but the Bible teaches that sorrow and grief are profound human emotions that help us come to grips with reality. When something of great value is lost, we express sorrow.

In the Bible, people grieve and express sorrow because God is a God who hears and responds. The sorrow of God plays a major role in the Old Testament. Because of his loving-kindness (*hesed*), the Bible reveals that God actually suffers for his people. His love for his people and his desire to be loved by them drives God to suffer with and for us. This is seen most clearly in the cross but is taught throughout the entire Bible. The way toward our healing is painful for God, as Walter Brueggemann writes: "But the way of healing is not an easy one for Yahweh; Yahweh goes through loss, anguish, rage, and humiliation. The healing costs the healer a great deal."[8]

Jesus was a man of sorrows and grief.[n] His grief is both for others in their suffering and sin and for what lies ahead of him at the cross. This is not just because he is the God-man and now experiences human emotions since he has a body. In his grief for others, Jesus is expressing the emotions of Yahweh as revealed in the Old Testament. As one who grieves, Jesus has compassion for and knows how to give comfort to those who weep and mourn.[o]

Resurrection

Rather than minimize grief, Jesus experiences it and comforts others in it. But mourning is not the final word. Resurrection is. He gives a word of comfort to those in distress. The knowledge of his resurrection is our hope and a major way of dealing with sorrow: "Let not your hearts be troubled. Believe in God; believe also in me. In my Father's house are many rooms. If it were not so, would I have told you that I go to prepare a place for you? And if I go and prepare a place for you, I will come again and will take you to myself, that where I am you may be also."[p]

The Bible teaches that our suffering is a place to experience God's sustaining grace in our weakness.[q] It is clearly taught that grief is a natural response when one experiences loss, but it can be tempered by the knowledge of Christ and the resurrection.

The loss that causes grief is very real, but it is temporary. The knowledge that softens the blow of grief is not an abstract platitude but the real resurrection of Jesus.[r] Our grief now is in the context of a future hope.[s] The hope of the new creation frames, but does not erase our present mourning: "Behold, the dwelling place of God is with man. He will dwell with them, and they will be his people, and God himself will be with them as their God. He will wipe away every tear from their eyes, and death shall be no more, neither shall there be mourning, nor crying, nor pain anymore, for the former things have passed away."[t]

[n]Matt. 23:37; 26:38; Mark 7:34; 8:12; 14:34; John 11:35; 12:27.
[o]Luke 7:13.
[p]John 14:1–3.
[q]2 Cor. 1:8–9.
[r]1 Corinthians 15.
[s]1 Thess. 4:13–18.
[t]Rev. 21:3–4.

The type of grieving and mourning we see in light of God's redemption is not despair, but one of honesty and trust in the character of God with assurance that he knows, sees, hears, and cares. God uses this grief and mourning for your restoration. Geerhardus Vos describes this redemptive grief:

> What the Lord expects from us at such seasons is not to abandon ourselves to unreasoning sorrow, but trustingly to look sorrow in the face, to scan its features, to search for the help and hope, which, as surely as God is our Father, must be there. In such trials there can be no comfort for us so long as we stand outside weeping. If only we will take the courage to fix our gaze deliberately upon the stern countenance of grief, and enter unafraid into the darkest recesses of our trouble, we shall find the terror gone, because the Lord has been there before us, and, coming out again, has left the place transfigured, making of it by the grace of his resurrection a house of life, the very gate of heaven.[9]

Grief

Victims frequently ask: Is it okay to grieve what happened to me? Why do I feel guilty for mourning? Is it because I feel like I'm questioning God's goodness? The cross is God's solidarity with and compassion for the assaulted, and the resurrection is his promise that he can heal and redeem your suffering.

Grief is not a sinful emotion but is the result of sin. God and his people have legitimate grief because of sin and the pain it brings.[u] Because of God's redemptive work, he will wipe away all of your tears.[v] We look forward to the day when grief will be banished. Therefore, you can have hope, which invites you to grieve, but not to grieve as one who does not have hope.[w] We grieve with hope because Jesus' resurrection is proof to us that God is about healing, redeeming, and making all things new.

In Matthew 5:4 Jesus says, "Blessed are those who mourn, for they shall be comforted."[x] Grief and mourning are a pivotal part of restoration. It can involve an extensive and painful process of identi-

---

[u]Acts 8:2; 20:37–38; Phil. 2:27.
[v]Rev. 7:17; 21:4.
[w]1 Thess. 4:13; 5:10; 1 Cor. 15:55–57.
[x]Also see Isa. 61:2.

fying and experiencing many losses. There is much to grieve because much has been taken from you: the loss of control over your own body, sometimes a loss of an entire childhood, the loss of not having had a protective or nurturing family or appropriate role models, and/or the loss of trust.

Grief might be ongoing, not just a step that is done and completed quickly, as victims face multiple losses they have suffered and are involved in the process of engaging grief as it emerges. Grieving outside of God's redemptive work can be so overwhelming that it leaves no room for introspection and leads to despair. However, participating in God's grief can be redemptive because you don't have to deny or minimize what happened to you. Sorrow is embracing the sadness of losses that have grieved and angered the heart of God. Victims often fail to realize that God's own sorrow for what has happened is deep and profound. Mourn. Grieve. Cry. God is grieved by and angry at what happened to you. He is even more grieved and angry than you are, so you are invited to participate with God in his grief and anger.

That is why your cry does not need to be one of despair but can be a cry of hope and faith. While the cross shows us that God understands pain and does not judge you for your feelings of grief, the resurrection shows you that God is active in restoring peace (*shalom*), and that he conquered sin and is reversing its effects.

Your mourning and grief can be a protest at how things are. Things are not the way they're supposed to be. And these can be cries of hope that the way it will be—peace restored, no more pain—might be known more fully now.

Grief is not the main or only response to the pain you feel, but it is an appropriate and good response. Grief intensifies the sadness in facing the loss. Grief admits that there are scars that can be removed only in heaven. Grief opens the heart, replacing hardness and contempt with tenderness and vulnerability.

Facing the Truth

The first step in facing the truth about victimization begins when you say, "Yes, I was assaulted, and those who hurt me took something away I can never get back." The past, no matter how painful and overwhelming, may seem like an enemy. But in the process of healing, such memories are being used by God to transform us, not destroy us. What others did to you with evil intents to harm, God uses for good for you and others.[y] Romans 8:28 promises: "And we know that for those who love God all things work together for good, for those who are called according to his purpose."

Admitting the Damage

In addition to facing this truth, it is necessary to admit the damage that has occurred. Minimizing your loss may seem courageous and charitable, but it helps no one. You do not help yourself by living in the darkness of denial. It takes courage to admit the devastating effects of the assault to yourself and others. In the process of telling others, you might see that in your denial you tried to protect yourself from further betrayal or comfort yourself by relying on obsessive-compulsive behaviors, abusing drugs or alcohol, creating distance in relationships and isolating yourself, and/or promiscuity.

Naming Evil

The only way to move from denial, isolation, and self-protection is to look honestly at the assault that has been done to you. Healing begins when the secret is disclosed and the shackles of silence are broken. Healing involves naming evil for what it is and seeing how God rages against it to reestablish *shalom* and proclaim his steadfast love for you. About naming the wounds caused by wrongdoings, Miroslav Volf wites:

> We must name the troubling past truthfully—we must come to clarity about what happened, how we reacted, and how we are reacting to it now—to be freed from its destructive hold on our lives. Granted, truthful naming will not by itself heal memories of wrong suffered: but without truthful naming, all measures we might undertake to heal such memories will remain incomplete.[10]

God's Presence

As you grieve, no magic words or pious platitudes will make the pain go away. But in the middle of your suffering, you are not alone. This

---

[y]Gen. 50:20.

is not the entire message of redemption, but it is a significant part of it. Somehow, God is present in the darkness and pain. This does not remove the fear, the anxiety, and the struggle, but it does remind us that God is there when we reach out into the darkness.

Psalm 46:1 proclaims, "God is our refuge and strength, a very present help in trouble." David does not promise there will be no trouble or any heartache in this life. He only promises that God is with you in the trouble. The cross and resurrection show you that God mysteriously pulls you toward him even as you squirm and resist. And he is there in the dark places when you feel most alone.

In all of this anguish, God is present even when you feel alone. This is a paradox: How can you feel so alone and yet sense deeply that God is near? David describes much the same experience in Psalm 10. David cries out in verse 1: "Why, O LORD do you stand far away? Why do you hide yourself in times of trouble?" But then David declares unequivocally in verse 17: "O LORD, you hear the desire of the afflicted; you will strengthen their heart; you will incline your ear." The laments of this psalm encourage us to risk the danger of speaking boldly and personally to God. Walter Brueggemann reminds us that "the laments are refusals to settle for the way things are. They are acts of relentless hope that believes no situation falls outside Yahweh's capacity for transformation. No situation falls outside of Yahweh's responsibility."[11] Psalm 10 can serve as a prayer for you as you reflect on the temptation of denial and the need for grief and mourning while still hoping in God's healing and restoration.

Confidence

Because of Jesus, you have the privilege to confidently go to God and receive grace and mercy. Your need and your cries don't cause God to shun you or distance himself from you. Rather, he has compassion on you. Hebrews 4:14–16 says: "Since then we have a great high priest who has passed through the heavens, Jesus, the Son of God, let us hold fast our confession. For we do not have a high priest who is unable to sympathize with our weaknesses, but one who in every respect has been tempted as we are, yet without sin. Let us then with confidence draw near to the throne of grace, that we may receive mercy and find grace to help in time of need."

What happens if you remain in denial? You ignore your need and cling to things that offer false confidence and settle for something besides grace and mercy. However, you are invited to go confidently to God when you grieve and acknowledge your weakness and suffering. He joyfully responds with grace and mercy.

Crystal's Story

My name is Crystal. I grew up in a non-Christian home where life was never happy. I have awful memories of my father coming into my bedroom late at night when he would crawl into my bed, fondle me, and masturbate. I always pretended to be asleep because I was scared of what he would do if he knew I was awake. Because of this, I grew up believing that I somehow caused my father's evil behavior, which left me feeling dirty and dishonored. And because I led him to believe I was asleep, I wrongfully believed that I played a culpable role.

Sadly, as I developed from a girl into a woman, I continued to carry around the lie of this distorted sense of self. My parents divorced—which was a relief—but my father moved on to other victims. All the while I continued to experience a deep sense of dirtiness. I felt damaged. To avoid thinking about the pain from my childhood, I immersed myself in my school studies. I excelled academically and by the end of high school was elated to leave home after I had received a scholarship to a top university.

I believed that college would give me a fresh start on life and help me find a new identity. I never wanted anyone to know what my father had done to me as a little girl. I instantly found new friends in campus groups and activities and was able to hide amid all the fun. I was desperate to fit in and have a normal college experience. And because of what I'd suffered, I figured that life owed me.

The fun I believed I was entitled to came to an end. I'd spent an evening bar hopping with my girlfriends and at the end of the night I met a cute guy who bought me a few drinks, and I spent the evening chatting with him. For the first time, I felt confident around a guy and was enjoying his attention. When the bar closed, he offered to drive me home. And while I was hesitant to be alone with a guy, I didn't want to appear anything less than carefree to him or to my girlfriends. Instead of driving me home, he took me to a neighborhood park where he started kissing and fondling me.

Suddenly, the memories from childhood that I had tucked away came flooding back. I froze in shock. Despite my refusing his advances by pushing his hands away and saying "No!" he persisted by whining, begging, and more touching. But his determination scared me. He even threatened to leave me at the park to find my own way home, so I gave up. I figured that back at the bar I must have led him to believe that I wanted this, and I was afraid of what my girlfriends would think of me if I were to tell them I refused his advances. His touching and kissing continued. He grabbed my hand and had me masturbate and orally stimulate him. He held my head down until he was finished and then drove me home in silence as I cried. As I wept I kept asking myself: "Do I only exist for men's perverted and controlling pleasure?" First, my father masturbated while he touched me, and now I'm forced to masturbate this stranger.

I felt like damaged goods. How could I have let this happen again? I was scared; I felt sick, dirty, and disgusted with myself and the world. I had spent years as a nervous, anxious little girl feeling unloved and dirty and had worked so hard to transform myself into a seemingly fun, carefree, and confident woman. I realized that I wasn't what I had been pretending to be. Suddenly I was that anxiety-ridden little girl again who made men do bad things to her. I made a vow that no one would ever touch me again or hurt me in any way. No one could be trusted. I shut down emotionally and became depressed, withdrawn, and unconcerned about my future.

Eventually my roommate convinced me to speak with one of the college mental health counselors, where I was told that I needed to reclaim my life. I had to reassert my sense of self and believe again that I was worthwhile by reclaiming the power and control taken from me. I walked out of her office determined to regain my life. But what developed out of that was an eating disorder, isolation from all men, depression, and an obsession with academics and performance. This continued for many years.

Then I met Jesus. A girlfriend kept inviting me to church, and I decided I'd finally go, just once, so she would leave me alone. I always assumed that Christianity was about following a list of "dos and don'ts." I thought, especially I because I felt so dirty and damaged, that if I wanted to participate in church, I'd have to fix myself up first.

The message I heard that morning was the exact opposite. Instead, I heard that if I have faith in Jesus, God knows me, loves me, forgives me, vindicates my suffering, and calls me his own. It is all about Jesus and not what I have done, will do, need to do, or even what has been done to me. Because of what Jesus did on the cross, God does not see me as defiled, damaged, dirty, or unworthy. Never in all my life had I heard such good news before.

It took a while for me to trust in Jesus, but God was gentle and patient with me. And I knew I was in good company as I began to realize that Jesus suffered and felt like no one cared. I was deeply comforted to know that the Creator of the universe understood me and cared in the middle of my loneliness.

However, I didn't feel secure in his love for me. I feared that once God realized how messed up I really was he would eventually leave me. Initially, I fought him, determined to deal with life in my own way. I knew how life played out; outwardly I was friendly and nice with people around me, but I always made sure to keep a distance.

Then the light dawned on me—God created me and knows me. He knows everything that happened to me, everything I've done, and all the dirtiness, filth, and shame I'd felt. His grace is bigger than my life, bigger than my pain, bigger than my sin. He came down from his throne, took on flesh, and willingly went to the cross for me. There is no greater love than this. As people have lied, hurt, abused, mistreated, and abandoned me, I, too, had lied, hurt, abused, mistreated, and abandoned God; yet he still loves me. I am not "damaged goods." I am his daughter, more precious than gold. I am a child of God—the God who rules everything. With this new identity comes much. I have an inheritance that will never perish, a Savior in Jesus who knows my struggles and empathizes with me, and a God who will never leave me nor forsake me.

One of my favorite Bible verses is Joel 2:25, "I will restore to you the years that the swarming locust has eaten." He has restored so much, my purpose, my dignity, my trust in others, my relationships, and most of all, my identity. I'm a child of God made in the image of a good and loving Father. Life is not perfect and it won't be until Jesus comes again or God takes me to my eternal home, but life is different. He is still redeeming and restoring me for his glory and my joy.

5

Distorted Self-Image

Sexual assault maligns a victim's sense of self and communicates that victims are stupid, foolish, worthless, defiled, or dirty. A profoundly negative self-image or what some call low self-esteem is a pervasive consequence for sexual assault victims. Some victims had a distorted sense of self before the assault, and the violence against them simply reinforces the negative feelings about themselves. Others may have had a healthy sense of self, but after being victimized, a negative self-image develops. Either way, sexual assault commonly results in victims feeling a strong sense of disgust at the core of their self-understanding.

Given that sexual assault inflicts powerlessness, betrayal, confusion, and rejection, it is not surprising that victims often experience a distorted self-image. This can fuel self-blame, self-hate, and self-harm. Distorted self-image can also lead to isolation from others who might help restore a sense of safety, grace, and love. It may even convince the victim to pursue relationships and interactions with others that lead to further chronic suffering, thereby perpetuating and intensifying the negative self-perception.

The distortion of a victim's sense of self can range from feeling "not myself" to losing any sense of self at all.[1] The reasons for such self-concepts are various. The experience of sexual violation involves being objectified and used for the satisfaction of another. Experiencing one's own desires as being utterly disregarded is an intense loss of dignity.

The fact that the violence was sexual adds the stigma of feeling defiled, dirty, and damaged. It is not uncommon for some victims to be physically aroused at some point during the assault. If victims experience any emotional gratification or physical pleasure during the assault, they might feel a sense of guilt or shame that further reinforces the already distorted negative self-image. Feeling as if they "failed" to protect themselves from bodily violation, threat, and humiliation can cause victims to direct profound feelings of blame, anger, and shame at themselves.

In addition to victims having a negative self-image due to the experience of assault, perpetrators also reinforce all these negative self-beliefs. Many perpetrators can detect and exploit their victims' distorted sense of self and inflict verbal and psychological abuse on their victims by degrading, insulting, and blaming them for the assault. Victims may internalize all of this, which further perpetuates and strengthens their negative self-images.

Family and friends may also reinforce negative self-concepts. Sometimes they cause disgrace and judgment when they question a victim's role in the assault or imply that the victim cued the assault, brought it on themself, or asked for it in some way.

Additionally, myths about sexual assault are part of the general culture. The overwhelming cumulative impact of these myths is to further intensify the negative self-image of victims. Unchallenged sexual assault myths perpetuate feelings of guilt, shame, and self-blaming tendencies for victims. Existing myths contribute to the distorted meaning victims attach to their sexual victimization.

Calling what victims feel "low self-esteem" is not accurate because it fails miserably to convey adequately the extent of damage to one's self-concept. Many victims perceive themselves as being vile, defiled, filthy, and dirty as opposed to them having had a vile, defiled, and dirty act done to them. Disgrace done to victims can result in them feeling disgust toward themselves. The issue of identity is a significant part of a victim's distorted self-image. A sense of identity confusion about "who I am" can contribute to an identity of self-condemnation or a view of the self as nothing.

In response to the negative self-image many victims suffer under, some family members, friends, or counselors may suggest various forms of self-esteem enhancements that usually focus on positive self-statements and other self-healing exercises. These are used to reconstruct the victim's identity. However, these self-enhancements end up being only "home-made rituals."[2]

The truth is we are powerless to heal ourselves. Research shows that self-help actually results in self-harm. Self-help statements have been found to be ineffective and even harmful because "they may even backfire, making some people feel worse rather than better."[3] If the positive self-statement does not "stick," the result is to return to one's original negative self-perception and hold it more strongly.[4] For example, if people who believe that they are unlovable repeat, "I am a lovable person," they may dismiss this statement fairly quickly and perhaps even reinforce their convictions that they are unlovable.[5]

With regard to negative self-concepts, our powerlessness to heal ourselves is evident: "Positive self-statements have more impact on people with low self-esteem than on people with high self-esteem, and the impact on people with low self-esteem is negative."[6] The consequences are that positive self-statements are especially likely to backfire and cause harm for the very people they are meant to benefit: people with low self-esteem.[7]

This rejection of simplistic self-esteem enhancement methods is not because we want you to continue in self-loathing but because something better exists. To experience healing and freedom, your identity must be established on the work of Christ, not on the foundation of the shame and self-hate that frequently results from assault. Making a transition from a "victim" identity to an identity in Christ is offered in God's redemptive work through Jesus.

You need to know God's statements and images about who you are, not self-produced positive statements or the lies being told to you by your experience of disgrace. Confronting your distorted self-image and having your identity reconstructed is not a chore you do but is the fruit of having faith in the person and work of Jesus.

Renewed Identity

We cannot avoid questions like "Who am I really?" and we can only answer it by answering the prior question "Of what story do I find myself a part?" Story is powerful. The link between story and identity cannot be overstated.

Being a victim of sexual assault is part of your story that you should not deny or minimize. If it becomes *the* story about you, then your identity will be founded on disgrace. Confusion about who you are can contribute to an identity of self-condemnation and a view of self as "worthless" or "unlovable." Perhaps you've adopted false identities like these messages because of what you repeatedly tell yourself or because of what others have told you about who you are. Some false identities adopted by survivors of sexual assault are: worthless, damaged, gross, disgusting, defiled, screwed up, used, impure, and unwanted. Messages we are told about ourselves and messages we speak to ourselves throughout life shape our identity.

Whether you were assaulted as a child, teenager, and/or adult you may be tempted to define your life by the abuse, by your wounds, by your quests for comfort or revenge, or by the relationships that secure approval or self-control. Whether you realize it or not, you may be placing expectations on those around you to relate to you as a victim who must be protected yet who is slow to trust anyone's protection. You may be expecting them to play their part in the new story that you try to script for yourself, the one in which you're never hurt again. One problem is that our identities are all messed up; we don't know who we are and what we are.

In an attempt to counter your negative self-image, others may encourage you to see yourself in a story of self-love, self-reliance, and self-healing. But the identity that comes from that story is even darker disgrace and even more pain in the longer term because the self-made illusions about self cannot be maintained.

We should not construct our identities on shallow, wish fulfillment positive statements that we have no power to make a reality in our lives. The world will answer your questions of worth with affirmations of self-worth, self-esteem, and self-love. Your culture will tell you to first love yourself and then, and only then, can you rebuild a fractured identity and love others. Maybe you've heard the message that you can't truly love others until you learn to love yourself, and that a lack of self-worth is the basis of most psychological problems. These replies are insensitive to a suffering individual and do not answer the underlying problem of a distorted self-image. How do you receive or give love and affirmation when you believe that you are unlovable, dirty, worthless, impure, and corrupt?

Lewis Smedes describes the need for a renewed identity: "What I feel most is a glob of unworthiness. . . . What I need is a sense that God accepts me, owns me, holds me, affirms me, and will never let me go even if he is not too impressed with what he has on his hands."[8] Perhaps you've been living so long with the belief that your abuse has either defined you or left you without an identity at all.

There is another story different from the victim story and the self-affirmation story. God offers the redemptive story told in Scripture. The identity from that story is founded on grace in at least three specific ways.

Image of God

You are the image of God, which means that you have inherent dignity. You are not an unplanned accident: "All born for torment and for mutual death.... Tormented atoms in a bed of mud, devoured by death, a mockery of fate."[9] You were "fearfully and wonderfully made."[a] As the pinnacle of God's creation, human beings reveal God more wonderfully than any other creature. Man and woman were created like God, by God, for God, and to be with God.[b]

Being the image of God is a title of both dignity and humility. We are images *of God*, which is a point of significant dignity and challenges any negative distorted self-images. However, we are only *images* of God, not divine in any way of ourselves. Our dignity is derived from whom we image. This is a title of humility, which counters some of the lofty positive self-statements you may be tempted to apply to yourself.

People of God, Children of God

If you have faith in Christ, your identity is secure and robust. God calls you certain things that convey value. The "people of God" is one of the most significant. When God addresses the Israelites, he frequently says "my people." It is expressive of the covenant *hesed* relationship between God and his people: "I will be your God, and you shall be my people."[c] Being "my people" means that God chose them in his unilateral sovereign grace.[d] It also implies a community, as "people," obviously, is plural. Additionally, it means that these people belong to God as his possession[10] and that he is responsible for them and cares for them. In Exodus 19:5, God refers to his people as "my treasured possession."

Being a member of the people or family of God means that God

---

[a]Ps. 139:14.
[b]Gen. 1:26–27; 2:15.
[c]Ex. 6:7, 10:3; Lev. 26:12; Deut. 31:16; Jer. 7:23; 11:4; 30:22; Ezek. 36:28.
[d]Deut. 7:6.

accepts you: "The LORD takes pleasure in his people."[e] "Takes pleasure" literally means "accepts" and alludes to God's acceptance of propitiation offerings, which is based on the Day of Atonement sacrifices described in Leviticus 16.[11] It is a perfect picture of our relationship to God through Christ. We are accepted because God accepted Christ's sacrifice in our place on our behalf.

Being his people establishes your identity and worth: "Whoever touches you touches the apple of his eye."[f] "Touching" refers to "harmfully touching" or "plundering" God's elect people. This passage says it is tantamount to injuring God. "Apple of his eye" is a remarkable expression. It represents one of the most important and vulnerable parts of the body. To strike a blow at God's people is to strike one at God, wounding him in a most sensitive area. "Apple of his eye" describes something precious, easily injured, and demanding protection.

This intimacy of God's concern for his people is seen clearly in the declaration that you are a child of God if you trust in Christ.[g] This is, perhaps, the most amazing thing you can be called. This new identity is rooted in being adopted into God's family. Because you are adopted by God,[h] you are an heir of God and fellow heirs with Christ.[i] Another way of saying this is that you are a child of the promise.[j]

Paul writes that God "has blessed us in Christ with every spiritual blessing in the heavenly places."[k] There is simply no spiritual blessing that can compare with the glorious and gracious gift of adoption: "In love, [God] predestined us for adoption as sons."[l] This is why J. I. Packer calls adoption "the highest privilege that the gospel offers: higher even than justification."[12]

Understanding adoption is central for understanding your relationship with God.[13] A key passage that unpacks the meaning of adoption is Galatians 4:4–7:

> But when the fullness of time had come, God sent forth his Son, born of woman, born under the law, to redeem those who were under the

---

[e]Ps. 149:4.
[f]Zech. 2:8 NIV.
[g]1 John 3:1–2.
[h]Rom. 8:15.
[i]Rom. 8:17.
[j]Rom. 9:8.
[k]Eph. 1:3.
[l]Eph. 1:4–5.

law, so that we might receive adoption as sons. And because you are sons, God has sent the Spirit of his Son into our hearts, crying, "Abba! Father!" So you are no longer a slave, but a son, and if a son, then an heir through God.

We see in this passage that it takes the entire Godhead, the holy Trinity—Father, Son, and Holy Spirit—to complete our adoption. God the Father plans and initiates our adoption. Twice Paul says that God the Father "sent." At the fullness of time, the Father "sent" the Son into the world to redeem us and to secure our adoption and make us heirs. And the Father "has sent" the Spirit of Jesus into our hearts to seal our adoption.

Our adoption process began long ago. God the Father initiates and plans our adoption from eternity past.[m] Before the dawn of time, God the Father's heart of love was fixed upon you. The Father's adoption plan started in eternity past, and the blessings and joys that flow from this grace of adoption will continue throughout the endless ages of eternity. Then, in history, the Father sends both the Son and the Spirit to make our adoption happen.

The Father looked out at a world in rebellion against him. He saw the world filled with "children of wrath."[n] He saw children who had rejected him, walked away from him, turned their backs on him, and wanted nothing to do with him. And what is the Father's response? Out of his great love, he sends his one and only Son, his beloved Son, into the world to make "children of wrath" into "children of God"!

Because of the great love of God the Father, we are now children of God: "See what kind of love the Father has given to us, that we should be called children of God."[o] For this reason John Owen wrote: "The greatest sorrow and burden you can lay upon the Father, the greatest unkindness you can do to Him, is not to believe that He loves you."[14]

Paul applies this grace of adoption in order to undermine the performance mind-set that we are somehow more accepted by our Father by what we do, instead of because of who we are already in Christ. The Galatians were foolishly adding works of the law alongside faith in Christ as the way to be truly accepted by God. Paul labors to show that

---

[m]Ibid.
[n]Eph. 2:3.
[o]1 John 3:1.

we are accepted by God the Father by trusting in Jesus Christ, apart from any works. Because you are adopted, you are now "pitied, protected, and provided for" by your heavenly Father.[15] God adopted you and accepted you because he loves you. You didn't do anything to deserve his love. He loved you when you were unlovable. Remember this when you feel unlovable.

God the Son secures our adoption by redeeming us (Gal. 4:4b–5). God the Son came into this world as Jesus in order "to redeem those who were under the law, so that we might receive adoption as sons." The grace of the Son of God in the gift of adoption is simply staggering. The Son left his Father's throne above, took on human flesh, lived his entire life of perfect righteousness under the Law, and then died on the cross, redeeming us from the curse of the Law by becoming a curse for us, so that we might receive the adoption as sons.

Out of sheer grace, Jesus willingly endured being forsaken and abandoned by God the Father on the cross ("My God, my God, why have you forsaken me?"[p]), so that we might be accepted and adopted by God the Father. In addition to this, Paul makes clear both in this passage and in Romans 8:15–17, that if we are adopted, then we are also heirs of God and co-heirs with Jesus Christ, our elder brother. Everything that the Son owns we have coming to us as a future inheritance. He owns everything. He is the "heir of all things."[q]

Therefore, we have everything coming to us in the Son because we are co-heirs with him. "All things are yours, whether . . . the world or life or death or the present or the future—all are yours, and you are Christ's, and Christ is God's."[r] Our identity is secure. We were bought with the precious blood of Christ. And we have a glorious inheritance coming to us all because we have a new identity in him. We are now adopted as sons and daughters into the household of God, with all the rights and privileges of those who are children of God.

God goes one step further. God the Father has sent God the Spirit, "the Spirit of his Son," into our hearts, crying, "Abba! Father!" It is as if God the Father wanted to ensure that we actually believe, know, and have sealed onto our hearts that we are his children. It is not enough for it simply to be legally true that we are adopted. Like a good Father, God

---

[p] Matt. 27:46.
[q] Heb. 1:2.
[r] 1 Cor. 3:21–23.

continually assures us that we are his children. An adopted child might be, at times, suspicious that he is really and fully part of a family. In the same way, we often might doubt whether we have been truly accepted by God. God the Father wants to assure us that we are truly and fully part of the household of God. He wants you to know and believe that you are his child. So God sends the "Spirit of his Son," the "Spirit of adoption" into your heart to seal your new identity in your everyday experience.[s]

Jesus told his disciples: "I will ask the Father, and he will give you another Helper, to be with you forever, even the Spirit of truth. . . . You know him, for he dwells with you and will be in you. I will not leave you as orphans; I will come to you."[t] You are not an orphan alone in this world.

The Spirit of Jesus, the Spirit of sonship, the Spirit of adoption, the Holy Spirit of God was sent by the Father into your heart, crying "Abba! Father!" When you are suffering and the cry of your heart is "Abba! Father!" then the Holy Spirit is assuring you that you are God's child. You are not an orphan alone in this world. The Spirit is testifying in your spirit that you are a child of God. God is not against you. He is for you in Christ. He loves you. He is working all things together for your good and his glory.

This is the glorious new identity of every child of God. You are now a member of God's family.

Righteousness of God

God also uses shocking words and phrases to describe those who are his: redeemed and forgiven,[u] made righteous,[v] new creation,[w] God's workmanship,[x] reconciled to God,[y] saint,[z] chosen, holy, and beloved,[aa] child of light, not darkness,[ab] pure, blameless, glory of God,[ac] holy, blameless, and above reproach,[ad] and the righteousness of God.[ae]

---

[s]Rom. 8:15.
[t]John 14:16–18.
[u]Eph. 1:6–8.
[v]Rom. 5:1.
[w]2 Cor. 5:17.
[x]Eph. 2:10.
[y]2 Cor. 5:18.
[z]1 Cor. 1:2; Eph. 1:1; Phil. 1:1.
[aa]Col. 3:12.
[ab]1 Thess. 5:5.
[ac]Phil 1:10–11.
[ad]Col. 1:21–22.
[ae]2 Cor. 5:21.

Second Corinthians 5:21 is an amazing statement: "For our sake he made him to be sin who knew no sin, so that in him we might become the righteousness of God." Because of faith in Christ, you are the righteousness of God. This is imputation, which is ascribing characteristics to someone that they do not have by nature. Impute means to treat "as if." John Calvin writes: "Justification, moreover, we thus define: The sinner being admitted into communion with Christ is, for his sake, reconciled to God; when purged by his blood he obtains the remission of sins, and clothed with righteousness, just as if it were his own, stands secure before the judgment seat of heaven."[16]

Imputation is the crediting in our favor, from the standpoint of God, who is the source of all judgment, the perfect moral worth of Jesus. It also implies the humiliation of Jesus, by means of the transfer to him of the full burden of the disgraces we have done and those done to us.

The benefit of this is reconciliation and a new identity. In Colossians 1:21–22, we read an amazing promise: "And you, who once were alienated and hostile in mind, doing evil deeds, he has now reconciled in his body of flesh by his death, in order to present you holy and blameless and above reproach before him." Notice the words, "holy," "blameless," and "above reproach." These descriptive words are usually used to refer to Jesus Christ. But now, because of what Jesus Christ has done for us, paying the penalty of sins, we can now stand before God as we are declared holy, blameless, and above reproach.

By faith we are "in Christ" and as such we are seen as he is. His righteousness, holiness, and blamelessness are imputed to us.

Secure in Christ

If you are in Christ, your identity is deeper than any of your wounds. It is also found in Christ and founded on Christ, who is God, so your new identity is more secure and stable than any other identity that has been attributed to you.

This truth brings great relief, because you are not doomed to live as a victim. It doesn't eliminate your wounds nor silence your cry for deliverance or healing. But it does mean those wounds are not the final word on who you are. They don't enslave you and determine your life.

You can rest in the knowledge and assurance of your new identity because you did not earn it. It was achieved for you by God. Your identity is not only founded on being called an image of God, but even more so in the activity of Jesus on your behalf:

> Therefore when we say that the righteousness of Christ is imputed to us for justification and that we are just before God through imputed righteousness and not through any righteousness inherent in us, we mean nothing else than that the obedience of Christ rendered in our name to God the Father is so given to us by God that it is reckoned to be truly ours and that it is the sole and only righteousness on account of and by the merit of which we are absolved from the guilt of our sins and obtain a right to life.[17]

The difference between identity in Christ and anything else is huge. The difference is between resignation to a life as victim and its consequences versus living securely in Christ and all the grace that comes with it.

You do not have to fundamentally view yourself as the sum of your past experiences. There is another option. Martin Luther writes: "A Christian does not live in himself, but in Christ and in his neighbor. . . . He lives in Christ through faith, in his neighbor through love. By faith he is caught up beyond himself into God. By love he descends beneath himself into his neighbor. Yet he always remains in God and in his love."[18] His point is that you are neither made nor unmade by what others do to you or what you do. The heart of your identity rests in the hands of God. You are most properly yourself because God is in you and you are in God. Of course, what others have done to you marks you and shapes who you are, but it does not define you. God's love for you most fundamentally defines you.

Self-love and self-help do not work because we'll never peel back enough layers of ourselves to find the true self at the core that is pure and lovable. We need a bigger love to rescue us, one that overcomes the effects of the fall and restores to us the dignity that has been lost. We need a more solid foundation upon which to rebuild identities broken by abuse.

That bigger love is *hesed*, God's compassionate, faithful love expressed throughout the Bible for his people and perfectly reflected in the person and work of Jesus. Redemption doesn't only reconcile the fractured relationship between you and God, it makes you his.

First Corinthians 3 is a powerful passage about identity. Verse 9 calls you God's field and God's building. Verse 16 calls you God's temple. All these statements in 1 Corinthians 3 are about possession. Belonging to God means that you are valuable to God, that God is concerned about you, that God sees and knows you, and that God cares about you more than you do.

We are God's field, meaning that God owns us and cultivates us. We are God's temple. The temple is where God was most present, and God builds his temple. He will lay the foundation and make the jagged edges fit together masterfully. Notice his protection of his temple: "If anyone destroys God's temple, God will destroy him. For God's temple is holy, and you are that temple."[af]

First Corinthians 3 culminates with this declaration in verse 23: "You are Christ's, and Christ is God's." In other words, because you are in Christ, because he is your substitute, because he did the good you cannot do on your behalf, because he gave you his righteousness, because he died for your sins, you belong to God. He has his grip on you. He is not letting you go. In 1 Corinthians, Paul says twice "You were bought with a price."[ag]

Because your redemption is God's initiative, you are secure. Nothing can separate you from the love of God: "For I am sure that neither death nor life, nor angels nor rulers, nor things present nor things to come, nor powers, nor height nor depth, nor anything else in all creation, will be able to separate us from the love of God in Christ Jesus our Lord."[ah]

You are secure in God because you are his and he cannot disown himself. Despite the identity your experience of assault bestows to you, the identity God bestows to you is even more powerful. This is what Dietrich Bonhoeffer writes in "Who Am I?"—a poem he wrote in his prison camp cell awaiting execution. Notice his identity confusion and where he finds security.

> Who am I? They often tell me
> I stepped from my cell's confinement
> Calmly, cheerfully, firmly,
> Like a squire from his country-house.
> Who am I? They often tell me

[af]1 Cor. 3:17.
[ag]1 Cor. 6:19–20; 1 Cor. 7:23.
[ah]Rom. 8:38–39.

I would talk to my warders
Freely and friendly and clearly,
As though it were mine to command.
Who am I? They also tell me
I would bear the days of misfortune
Equably, smilingly, proudly,
Like one accustomed to win.
Am I then really all that which other men tell of?
Or am I only what I know of myself?
Restless and longing and sick, like a bird in a cage,
Struggling for breath, as though hands were
Compressing my throat,
Yearning for colors, for flowers, for the voices of birds,
Thirsting for words of kindness, for neighborliness,
Tossing in expectation of great events,
Powerlessly trembling for friends at an infinite distance,
Weary and empty at praying, at thinking, at making,
Faint and ready to say farewell to it all?
Who am I? This or the other?
Am I one person today, and tomorrow another?
Am I both at once? A hypocrite before others,
And before myself a contemptibly woebegone weakling?
Or is something within me still like a beaten army,
Fleeing in disorder from victory already achieved?
Who am I? They mock me, these lonely questions of mine.
Whoever I am, Thou knowest, O God, I am thine.[19]

He found his identity answer in the security of being God's. Because you are Christ's and Christ is God's, God accepts, owns, and affirms you. God will never let you go even when you think he may be unimpressed with you. That's because when you trust in who Jesus is and what he did, your identity is found in Christ.

The gospel changes our identity problem. Once we know how God sees us, we are free in our relationships with God, others, and ourselves. We don't have to keep the disguise going anymore. In order to have the cycle of disgrace broken, we need a God before whom we can put aside the disguises. When we trust in Christ, disgrace is halted and we can step onto the firm ground of God's acceptance and *hesed*.

You are more than what your assault experience tells you. If you are "in him," 2 Corinthians 5:21 calls you the "righteousness of God." The final word on you is not that you are a victim, but that you are the righteousness of God.

You don't have to live under illusions of your idealized self. You are not encouraged to suffer under the pain of feeling dirty and worthless. Because you are the righteousness of God, in the place of those feelings, peace, acceptance, and comfort might emerge.

You are not what your experience of assault calls you or what your perpetrator says about you. Also, you are not your positive self-statement. Based on your being in Christ by faith, you are the opposite of what your experience or perpetrator would say about you, and you are called way better than any positive self-statement you could imagine to apply to yourself.

You are Christ's, and Christ is God's. Therefore you can say the words of the psalmist in confidence: "This I know, that God is for me."[ai]

[ai]Ps. 56:9.

Barbara's Story

My name is Barbara. It has been a little over three years since I was last raped by my husband. From the beginning of our marriage he was controlling and mean, but never sexually abusive . . . until I got pregnant with our first child. I was put on bed rest at twenty-five weeks and told to refrain from sex for the duration of the pregnancy. My husband did not like this and told me it was my duty to have sex with him. He started questioning whether I loved him and enjoyed having sex with him.

I went along with his pleas and demands because I wanted to please him and prove my love. But as time went on I became annoyed and angry. I was pregnant and he didn't seem to care about me or the baby's well-being. Many nights I would wake up to him having sex with me. When I told him to stop or that I was in pain, he ignored my pleas, told me to be quiet, or argued that I was to be submissive. The abuse became more frequent and at times violent. He threatened to leave me if I didn't have sex with him when and how he wanted. He often misquoted Scripture to control me and verbally tore me apart with his mean and vindictive words.

I rationalized his behavior because he was insecure, abused as a child, and didn't grow up with a supportive and loving family. I felt sorry for him and believed his tears, apologies, and promises of change. For many years I didn't see what was happening as rape. Even though I resisted, said no, and pleaded with him to stop, I always thought that what transpired was the result of a communication problem (*Was I clear that I did not want to have sex tonight?*) or misunderstanding (*I told him I didn't want to, but perhaps I gave him the wrong signals?*). It was easier and less scary to believe those were the reasons rather than accept that my husband was raping me on a regular basis.

I felt betrayed that my husband would violate me like he did. Additionally, I felt abandoned by God and that I had disappointed him because I had failed as a wife. I was humiliated and ashamed that my marriage was falling apart and far from the picture-perfect image we presented to others. Shame and fear prevented me from reaching out to my closest friends for help. I even thought, "Who would believe that a husband would rape his own wife?" I became more and more isolated from everyone in my life because of shame, embarrassment, and fear of my husband if I were to say anything. From the outside everyone thought our lives were perfect, but I was living in hell.

I made every effort to be the model wife, mother, and homemaker, but inside I became numb as despair took over. I emotionally shut down in order to deal with the ongoing pain he caused. I walked around on eggshells every day never knowing what would set him off—my cooking, the laundry, the kids, the bills, my appearance. I blamed myself for a failed marriage and believed that if I was prettier, skinnier, a better cook, better in bed, or more outgoing that he would treat me better, love me more, stop hurting me, and start protecting me.

I feel like I should have known better than to marry him. I knew he got jealous easily, and I was often pressured for sex before we got married. I felt like I should have seen this coming and felt stupid for marrying him. This piled on even more shame and embarrassment. I blamed myself for what I was suffering. There were so many times when I wanted to cry out to God for help and understanding, but I didn't believe that he cared or would even listen to me. I had made a mess of my life and had to deal with it. I didn't see any way out.

But something changed inside of me when our daughter started puberty. I became fearful that he would start sexually abusing her, also. Then, one night while we were fighting, our daughter tried to break it up and he hit her. I knew it was only a matter of time before he started raping my daughter. I left that night with my three kids and moved in with my parents. We are now divorced and the children and I are safe from him.

My understanding of God as a loving Father who cares for me personally has developed over the years since the marriage ended. He is not a God who is disappointed in me, but a loving Father who sees the pain I have suffered, comforts me, and lets me know that he understands my shame and humiliation. I now see the freedom in not hiding my shame and suffering, and I'm now able to be honest about my brokenness and need before God and others. I only have this understanding and assurance because I have received grace and mercy through Jesus Christ.

My story is no longer steeped in shame because Jesus took it all and ended its grip on me with his death on the cross. Jesus died for me, a sinner who used to think that I had no need for him, especially when I was suffering. Because of his death and resurrection, I am no longer identified by the sins I have committed or by the sins that have been committed against me. Unlike my husband who did not love me as God intended, God is for me and loves me. God sees me as perfect, pure, righteous, and holy because of what Christ did for me.

I can now say truthfully that I am not responsible for my husband's behavior; he sinned against me. However, I still mourn the loss of the relationship and what it could have been. Occasionally, I have a tendency to hide from others in self-protection or act as if all is well when I am upset, lonely, scared, or angry. But by God's grace I am learning to trust him and others again. It is liberating when I am honest about my emotions and needs with God and with others. There is such joy in knowing that he is stronger than my shame and suffering. After years of rape, abuse, rejection, betrayal, and pain it is wonderful to have confidence in a Savior who conquered death so all that pain is not the end of my story. Because of Jesus I have a guarantee that one day in heaven I will not feel even a trace of shame, embarrassment, or rejection. I wait for his return.

6

Shame

Sexual assault is shameful for victims, and feelings of nakedness, rejection, and dirtiness are often associated with their assault. The feeling of shameful self-blame is often powerful and prominent for many victims. Jean-Paul Sartre accurately describes shame as "a hemorrhage of the soul" that is a painful, unexpected, and disorienting experience. Shame has the power to take our breath away and smother us with condemnation, rejection, and disgust.

Shame is a painfully confusing experience—a sort of mental and emotional disintegration that makes us acutely aware of our inadequacies, shortcomings, and is often associated with a shrinking feeling of failure.[1] Shame can be simultaneously self-negating and self-absorbed: "All day long my disgrace is before me, and shame has covered my face."[a]

What emerges from the core destructive perceptions of self are relational fears of rejection: "Shamed people feel exposed. Although shame doesn't necessarily involve an actual observing audience that is present to witness one's shortcomings, there is often the imagery of how one's destructive self would appear to others."[2] Shame is utterly isolating.

Shame can be particularly destructive if a victim feels stigmatized by withering, energy-draining feelings of worthlessness. Describing the suffering of shame, Dan Allender and Tremper Longman write: "To be covered in shame is to feel the self engulfed in something disgusting, even hideous. It may seem extreme, but the experience of shame feels like a prolonged, torturous death."[3]

Sexual assault victims have been personally violated, their sense of self trampled, their boundaries defiled. If you are a victim of assault, the desire to hide from others is understandable. Maybe in your self-loathing you inflict emotional or physical self-harm. Or in an effort to control your environment you concoct complicated eating regimens

---

[a]Ps. 44:15.

(eating disorders) or become compulsive in your behaviors. You feel guilty so you self-punish. You want to escape, so you drink or do drugs. Or you're cruel to others and sabotage relationships that should be places of refuge. Whatever the behavior, you're destroying your life and you know it.

While your experience may compel you to cry out to God, you may want to simply shut down emotionally. But if you minimize your abuse, you may find yourself stuck in a tragic rut of nameless shame. The effects of shame can be devastating, and amid your hurt and rejection, you may be confused about how God sees your sexuality. God may seem distant. Is he disgusted, hateful toward you, or completely uninvolved?

Perhaps you've turned your back on God, assuming he has already turned his back on you. In rebellion you have committed shameful sins, which have only intensified your problems. Or maybe you've simply accepted your shame as an unchangeable identity, and your life is now defined by what has been done to you. You shut down emotionally and live an isolated life to avoid ever being vulnerable or hurt again. Finally, you numb your pain through drugs, alcohol, sex, power, success, or whatever else enables you to stop feeling. You'll do whatever it takes to start feeling a measure of self-worth.

While escape, retreat, or hard living is a common response to shame brought on by sexual assault, there are other subtle means of escape including moral and religious overachievement. But trying harder to be a good Christian isn't the solution to your shame. This tactic is much more difficult to discern in yourself and in others. After all, being a good person is a virtue, right? But this pull-yourself-up-by-your-own-boot-straps mentality is simply a Christless self-salvation project wrapped in Bible-talk. And when you're unable to live up to your own (or someone else's) moral or religious standards, you will simply heap more shame upon yourself.

In light of the above-mentioned examples, it's clear that shame is a social-psychological experience, meaning it includes both a social dimension and a psychological dimension at the same time.[4] The social dimension of shame comes out in concern over how others see a victim in light of the perceived standards in a given community. The psychological dimension entails how one views self. Shame, then, is not just an internal feeling but also a reflection of expectations. It is as much an emotion as it is a mind-set or a perception about being a defective, exposed, and rejected person.

Shame is often poignantly experienced as internalized disgrace. We say this not to lay blame on victims for feeling shame but to point out the different dimensions of it. Once disgrace is internalized, their identity becomes associated with feelings of worthlessness, self-contempt, and inferiority.[5]

The belief that a victim should simply "get over" their shame through affirmations is erroneous and insensitive. Shame is a vicious cycle caught up in the dynamic between a victim's self-perception being shaped by things done to them that are in turn often reinforced by their community.[6] To be shamed is to be abased and dishonored, to be rejected from the community—especially when a victim isn't believed, is told to be silent, is blamed, or is not supported. To feel ashamed is to experience the pain of embarrassment, disapproval, and rejection.

Shame in the Bible

The Bible uses many emotionally charged words to describe shame: reproach, dishonor, humiliation, and disgrace. Additionally, there are three major images for shame in Scripture: nakedness, uncleanness or defilement, and being rejected or made an outcast. These images reflect the experiences of many victims regarding the effects of sexual assault.

Nakedness is the first core image of shame in the Bible. After they sinned, Adam and Eve realized they were naked and were ashamed. Shame gives the perception of being completely exposed and aware of being looked at. Regarding shame as exposure, Dan Allender and Tremper Longman write: "Shame is the traumatic exposure of nakedness. This is experienced when we feel the lance of a gaze (either someone else's or our own) tearing open the various cultural, relational, or religious coverings we put on. What is revealed, we feel, is an inner ugliness."[7] Biblical metaphors for shame combine exposure and disgrace such as stripping a woman naked[b] or the cutting of a man's clothing, especially so as to expose his body.[c]

The second major biblical image of shame is that of the outcast—being rejected and not belonging. Shame is connected to the notion of

---

[b]Ezek. 16:39; 23:26–30; Jer. 13:22.
[c]1 Sam. 24:4–6; 2 Sam. 10:4–5.

expulsion from the community of God's people. Expulsion from the camp presupposes the presence of God within the camp. The ground for expulsion of the impure was that God was with the camp,[d] and he was not willing to look upon any "shamefulness" or "defilement."[e]

Uncleanness is the third prominent image of shame. The book of Leviticus deals with this theme more than the rest of the Bible combined.[8] Cleanness symbolizes a right standing with God, and uncleanness indicates the opposite. In fact, according to Leviticus, merely coming in contact with that which was seen as unclean made one defiled. When the clean touched the unclean, they became unclean.[f]

The second and third images come together in the experience of the leper as an example of how shame can result from sin's effects even when they aren't committed by the one bearing shame. The cleanliness laws of Leviticus represent how sin contaminates everything it touches. For example, the leper is sent outside the Israelites' camp. Inside the camp one enjoyed belonging, communal life, and the presence of God at the tabernacle. Outside the camp was death: the waste from animal sacrifices, the scavenger animals, and lepers. The leper, according to Leviticus 13:45–46 (NIV), "must wear torn clothes, let his hair be unkempt, cover the lower part of his face and cry out, 'Unclean! Unclean!' . . . He must live alone; he must live outside the camp." There was no hiding even in exile.

In addition to the three images of shame throughout the Bible, there are also specific examples of shame caused by sexual assault, such as the assault of Dinah[g] and of Tamar.[h] Tamar experienced disgrace, violation, and reproach.[i] The description of her outward appearance in verse 19 is intended to show how she feels inwardly: "And Tamar put ashes on her head and tore the long robe that she wore. And she laid her hand on her head, and went away, crying aloud as she went." Ashes

---

[d]Num. 5:3; Deut. 23:14.
[e]Deut. 23:14.
[f]Throughout Scripture, there are numerous Hebrew and Greek words used to explain sin in terms of defilement. These are often translated into English as defilement, uncleanness, and filth (Jer. 2:23; Ps. 79:1; 106:39; Prov. 30:12). Some examples of the causes of uncleanness or defilement include: any sin (Ezek. 14:11), rape (Gen. 34:5, 13, 27), incest (Gen. 49:4; 1 Chron. 5:1), adultery (Lev. 18:20; Num. 5:20, 27–29), prostitution (Lev. 21:7–9, 14), bestiality (Lev. 18:23), witchcraft (Lev. 19:31), pagan syncretism (2 Chron. 36:14; Jer. 3:1–9; 7:30; 32:34; Ps. 106:38–39), murder (Lam. 4:13–14), and bitterness (Heb. 12:15).
[g]Genesis 34.
[h]2 Samuel 13.
[i]2 Sam. 13:13–22.

are a sign of humiliation and disgrace. She tears her special robe, a garment that symbolized her elevated social status. Tearing her clothing is an expression of her loss, lament, and dishonor. Putting her hand on her head is also an expression of shame. Jeremiah 2:37 uses the image of hands on the head to express shame. Because of her experience of shame, Tamar cried out, "Where could I get rid of my disgrace?"[j]

Similar examples of crying out because of shame or disgrace are found in the Psalms. Psalm 44 is a request for help for the disgraced: "All this has come upon us, though we have not forgotten you, and we have not been false to your covenant. . . . Awake! Why are you sleeping, O LORD? Rouse yourself! Do not reject us forever! Why do you hide your face? Why do you forget our affliction and oppression? For our soul is bowed down to the dust; our belly clings to the ground. Rise up; come to our help! Redeem us for the sake of your steadfast love!"[k]

There are four clear requests in this psalm: do not reject us, do not be hidden from us, remember our affliction and oppression, and come to our help. All of this is found in God's love for his people: "Redeem us for the sake of your steadfast love."

In this response to shame, there is anticipation for a time that God will respond in love for them and in power against their enemy. In Christ, this time has come.

God's Response to Your Shame

Jesus reveals the love of God for his people by covering their nakedness, identifying with those who feel or have been rejected, cleansing all their defilement, and conquering their enemy who shames them. In Philippians 4:19, Paul writes: "And my God will supply every need of yours according to his riches in glory in Christ Jesus." In 2 Peter 1:3, Peter writes: "His divine power has granted to us all things that pertain to life and godliness."

God's provision for you is comprehensive and founded on the gospel. God, who gave his own beloved Son to redeem you and make you his child, will not refuse to meet your needs. The "every need of yours" and "all things that pertain to life and godliness" promised in Christ most assuredly includes the removal of the shame that results from the

---

[j]2 Sam. 13:13 NIV.
[k]Ps. 44:17, 23–26.

sins done against you. This is what it means for God to be for you and for God to supply every need of yours.

In his ministry, Jesus brought grace to disgraced people. In the Gospels, especially in the Gospel of Luke, we learn that the good news Jesus brings is for all kinds of people, especially those who experienced shame—the lowly, marginalized, oppressed, the outsiders in society such as lepers and tax collectors.[l9] During his ministry, Jesus sought out one unclean outcast after another, touching them and making them clean. And while the specifics of your story may not be perfectly represented among the people Jesus ministered to, we can be sure that the hurting people he was in contact with most certainly had experiences of defilement and shame.

While Jesus' cross was the epitome of his identification with us in shame, his whole life and ministry displayed this:

> Jesus identified with the "poor." He was born and raised among the lower classes, associated with outcasts, and chose artisans, fisher folks, and tax collectors for his disciples. He belonged to the multitudes whom the religious leaders pronounced "accursed because they know not the law" (John 7:49). He identified with the socially excluded and despised and shared the stigma of their inferiority.[10]

Jesus actively pursued outsiders and outcasts, those who experienced shame.[m11]

Jesus purposely reached out to those who were rejected and considered "outside the camp" because they were considered "unclean"—morally, socially, or religiously. His solidarity with the shamed and excluded of his day led to the ultimate experience of shame—his crucifixion.

Christ Rejected, Defiled, and Outside the Camp

Jesus not only identified with the outsiders and unclean during his earthly ministry, but he also demonstrated solidarity with outsiders on the cross. Jesus endured the shame of crucifixion. He became a "man of sorrows" and "acquainted with grief." Jesus "was despised and rejected

---

[l]Luke 1:52–53; 4:18; 6:20–26; 14:4–11.
[m]See Luke 1:46–55; 4:16–21; 7:22–50; 15:1–32; 19:1–10.

by men" and his shame was such that he became "one from whom men hide their faces."[n]

The story of Jesus on the cross is a story of victimization and shame. He was sentenced to death in the most shameful manner possible—naked and on a cross outside the city gates. Crucifixion was for the scum of the earth, and Jesus voluntarily became a part of the dregs himself.

As the Romans put it, the crucified person was *damnation ad bestias*, meaning "condemned to the death of a beast." The purpose of the cross was to expose, display, and humiliate the condemned. The passion of Jesus was a ritual of humiliation. The cross was, and is, the way of shame in the eyes of the world. On the cross, Jesus felt shame but was innocent. He suffered the shame of others that was placed on him.

In Hebrews 11:26 and 13:13, the phrase "the reproach of Christ" is used regarding his crucifixion. This phrase originated from Psalm 69 (where "reproach" occurs in verses 7, 9, 10, 19, 20) and Psalm 89:50–51 (NASB). In fulfilling these verses, Christ exchanged the joy he should have had so he could share the hardship, shame, and reproach with the people of God.

In addition, the sufferings of Christ occurred, according to Hebrews, "outside the camp."[o] In Hebrews 13:12–13, Jesus is said to have suffered reproach "outside the gate" and "outside the camp." The phrase "bearing the reproach he endured" conveys the nuance of reproach, shame, and disgrace[p] because of the violence and abuse he endured.[12]

By describing the sacrifice of Jesus in this way, Hebrews 13 alludes to the cross in terms of the sacrificial offerings on the Day of Atonement.[q] The Day of Atonement was the climax of the Old Testament sacrificial system and was a day of great bloodshed. One goat was sacrificed, which was a substitute for the sinners who deserved a violently bloody death for their many sins. Then the high priest would take the second goat and lay his hands on the animal while confessing the sins of the people. This goat, called the scapegoat, was sent away to a solitary place or a remote area, literally to "a land of cutting off." This phrase refers to the fact that the place to which the goat was led was "cut off" from the camp so the animal had no chance of returning to Israel.[13] Throughout

---

[n]Isa. 53:3.
[o]Heb. 13:13.
[p]The NIV reads, "bearing the disgrace he bore" (Heb. 13:13).
[q]Leviticus 16.

Leviticus we find that to be excluded, or cut off, from the camp of Israel was to experience God's punishment for sin.[r]

Jesus fulfilled the sacrificial requirement of Leviticus 16:27 that the carcasses of the bull and goat sacrificed on the Day of Atonement be incinerated "outside the camp." According to Hebrews 13, the death of Jesus outside the gates of Jerusalem represents the definitive sin offering of the Day of Atonement. In his death, Jesus opened up for others access to God.

Additionally, the execution "outside the gate" involved the shame of exclusion from the sacred areas. Jesus was classified with the blasphemers who were to be stoned outside the camp.[s] The description of Jesus suffering death outside the camp brings out this element of shame. The people repudiated him, and his death appeared to seal his rejection as final. It was as an outcast that he offered his sacrifice to God.

The shame of expulsion from the camp presupposes the presence of God within the camp. The ground for expulsion of those who had become impure was that God was with the camp,[t] and he is not willing to look upon any "shamefulness" or "defilement."[u] However, after the golden calf incident in Exodus, God chose to demonstrate his presence "outside the camp."[v] The humiliation of Jesus and his death as an outcast show that God has again been rejected by his people and that his presence can be enjoyed only "outside the camp," where Jesus was treated with contempt and violence.

About the significance of Jesus' suffering in solidarity with those who are shamed and excluded, Martin Hengel writes:

> The earliest Christian message of the crucified messiah demonstrated the "solidarity" of the love of God with the unspeakable suffering of those who were tortured and put to death by human cruelty. . . . In the person and the fate of the one man Jesus of Nazareth this saving "solidarity" of God with us is given its historical and physical form.

---

[r]Lev. 7:20–27; 17:4, 9–14; 18:29; 19:8; 20:3, 5–6, 17–18; 22:3; 23:29.
[s]Lev. 24:10–16, 23.
[t]Num. 5:3; Deut. 23:14.
[u]Deut. 23:14. People became unclean in Leviticus by contacting what was unclean. When the clean touch the unclean, they become unclean. But when the holy touches that which is unclean it becomes clean. Defiled people need to be cleansed from the sin that defiled them, either as a victim of a sinner or as a sinner who victimized another. This is done through a vulnerable and intimate relationship with God and is explained in Scripture in various ways, such as an atonement (Lev. 16:30), a cleansing forgiveness (Jer. 33:8), a purifying fountain (Zech. 13:1), and Jesus' cleansing blood (1 John 1:7–9).
[v]Ex. 33:7–10.

In him, the Son of God, God himself took up the "existence of a slave" and died the "slave's death" on the tree of martyrdom (Phil. 2:8), given up to public shame (Heb. 12:2) and the "curse of the law" (Gal. 3:13) so that in the death of God life might win victory over death. In other words, in the death of Jesus of Nazareth God identified himself with the extreme wretchedness, which Jesus endured as a representative of us all, in order to bring us to the freedom of the children of God.[14]

Christ Despises Shame

Between the two passages in Hebrews regarding the reproach and shame of the cross is Hebrews 12:2: "Jesus . . . who for the joy that was set before him endured the cross, despising the shame, and is seated at the right hand of the throne of God."

This passage states that Jesus endured the cross and despised its shame. The word for "shame" carries the nuance of disgrace along with the shame associated with it. The way of the cross is to be understood as a public experience of humiliation, shame, and disgrace. The focus of verse 2 is Jesus' approach toward suffering in a way that entails shame and disgrace. Renouncing the joy that could have been his, he endured the cross, disregarding the shame associated with crucifixion. The phrase "despising the shame" underscores the horrific nature of crucifixion and Christ's utter humiliation in dying like a criminal in torment on the cross. In this, God identifies himself with an extreme expression of shameful disgrace.

"Despised" means to care nothing for, disregard, be unafraid of, or consider something not important enough to be concerned with when evaluated against something else. Cognitively, then, Jesus made an evaluation—an interpretation—based on his belief and trust in God and his delight in that joy before him; he was not controlled by the shame he endured.[15]

David A. DeSilva explains what it means for Jesus to have "despised the shame" of the cross:

Jesus despised the disgraceful reputation a cross would bring him in the eyes of the Greco-Roman world. His own vindication came afterward, when he "sat at the right hand of the throne of God" (Heb. 12:2). While in the public court of opinion, Jesus took the most disgraceful seat—on a cross—in God's court of reputation, Jesus was worthy of the highest honor. Jesus' own attitude toward the negative evaluation of the outside world was a pattern for believers who wished to follow him and share in his honor and victory: Because they have such a hope for honor from the higher court of opinion, namely, God's, the author may exhort them to disregard the opinion of unbelievers, who serve a lower court. The children of God may boldly assemble together for their common worship and show support for the socially disgraced and abused (Heb. 13:3; cf. 11:25–26), and go "outside the camp," as it were, to bear the reproach of Christ (Heb. 13:13). For the same Christ who suffered reproach but despised the shame will come a second time in judgment of those who reproached him and continue to dishonor and disgrace his sisters and brothers.[16]

Death by crucifixion was not only unbelievably painful, it was also considered shameful. F. F. Bruce describes the shame involved in crucifixion:

> To die by crucifixion was to plumb to the lowest depths of disgrace; it was a punishment reserved for those who were deemed most unfit to live, a punishment for those who were subhuman. From so degrading a death Roman citizens were exempt by ancient statute; the dignity of the Roman name would be besmirched by being brought into association with anything as vile as the cross.[17]

And yet even facing such extreme shame, Jesus still did not go back. The good news of the gospel is that Jesus endured the cross, disregarding the shame. The good news is that Jesus disregarded the shame of dying by crucifixion, and in doing so also took our shame upon himself.

Jesus willingly suffered the most shameful death and this exposed the extremity of sin's shameful consequences and the despicable character of our humanly devised shame. He "despis[ed] the shame." We can say that Jesus both shared our shame and bore our shame so that we can have freedom from its dread and power.

Christ the Conqueror

The death and resurrection of Christ is portrayed as the ultimate victory of the Son of God on behalf of his people. According to Martin Luther,

at the cross and through the resurrection, Jesus has won a victory for
his people:

> By His resurrection Christ won the victory over law, sin, flesh, world,
> devil, death, hell, and every evil. And this His victory He donated unto
> us. These many tyrants and enemies of ours may accuse and frighten
> us, but they dare not condemn us, for Christ, whom God the Father
> has raised from the dead is our righteousness and our victory.[18]

This is a cosmic warfare against a very real enemy, and it involves divine
self-sacrifice, but it is thereby triumphant over evil, with an eternal
victory.

God's response to shame is the costly but victorious conflict of God
himself, in Christ, with the forces of disgrace. In Colossians, Paul writes:

> And you, who were dead in your trespasses and the uncircumcision
> of your flesh, God made alive together with him, having forgiven us
> all our trespasses, by canceling the record of debt that stood against
> us with its legal demands. This he set aside, nailing it to the cross. He
> disarmed the rulers and authorities and put them to open shame, by
> triumphing over them in him.[w]

In other words, in dying on the cross Jesus disarmed the evil powers that stood against you. He nullified the charges that were brought
against you. He canceled your debts and paid the price for your redemption. These were all set aside and nailed to the cross. In his shameful
death, Jesus actually put your spiritual enemies to shame. The image
Paul uses is one of Jesus, the victorious warrior, leading a procession of
his captors, putting them to public ridicule and shame. Spiritual forces
are certainly in view regarding this passage. But you may also feel as
though the person who has defiled you has wielded power over you,
as well. Jesus has not only triumphed over the actual sin committed
against you and the power that it seems to hold over your head, he also
will conquer unrepentant sinners.

Not only does God heal your wounds, but he also defends you and
avenges the shameful things done to you. In the Psalms, a common
request regarding shame is that God would rescue his people from

---

[w]Col. 2:13–15.

shame and put their enemies to shame.[x] These psalms add the dimension of vindication regarding shame. Biblically, the path of honor often goes through the shame of another—both the shame of our enemy (ultimately Satan who was defeated and thus shamed at the cross) and the vicarious shame of the suffering servant of Isaiah 53 who was despised and rejected,[y] cut off from the land of the living,[z] and numbered among the trangressors.[aa]

In Psalm 109, David cries for God to act on his behalf against shame: "Help me, O LORD my God! Save me according to your steadfast love! Let them know that this is your hand; you, O LORD, have done it! Let them curse, but you will bless! They arise and are put to shame, but your servant will be glad! May my accusers be clothed with dishonor; may they be wrapped in their own shame as in a cloak!"[ab] He asks for his accusers to be clothed with dishonor. He does this because he knows that when God's people are being shamed, God rises up to act. The deliverance we long for is intimately tied up in not being put to shame: "In you [God] our fathers trusted; they trusted, and you delivered them. To you they cried and were rescued; in you they trusted and were not put to shame."[ac]

God is a God of irony. He chose for his Son to be born in shame, live his life in shame, and then die in the most shameful manner. Shame is evil's greatest weapon against God. But God takes the weapon of evil and uses it to mock and then destroy evil.[19]

The cross initially looks like the ultimate victory of shame. But the victory of shame and disgrace is short-lived because resurrection interrupts the celebration of evil and triumphs over shame by introducing hope. Disgrace has been made a shameful spectacle. It is triumphed over by the redemption of God's humiliation. Jesus endured the shame of the cross but also scorned it. He shamed shame and revealed God's love

---

[x]"O my God, in you I trust; let me not be put to shame; let not my enemies exult over me. Indeed, none who wait for you shall be put to shame; they shall be ashamed who are wantonly treacherous" (Ps. 25:2–3). "Let them be put to shame and dishonor who seek after my life! Let them be turned back and disappointed who devise evil against me" (Ps. 35:4). "Fill their faces with shame, that they may seek your name, O LORD. Let them be put to shame and dismayed forever; let them perish in disgrace" (Ps. 83:16–17). The psalmist's plea, "Let them be put to shame and confusion who seek my life! Let them be turned back and brought to dishonor who delight in my hurt!" (Ps. 70:2).
[y]Isa. 53:3.
[z]Isa. 53:8.
[aa]Isa. 53:12.
[ab]Ps. 109:26–31.
[ac]Ps. 22:4–5.

for, not rejection of, you. At the cross, Jesus triumphed over all of your enemies and put them to open shame. Jesus won the victory and leads a triumphal process.

If you have suffered disgrace, the weapons meant to harm you have been transformed and made a blessing through the cross. Calvin writes:

> Every good thing we could think or desire is to be found in this same Jesus Christ alone. For, He was sold, to buy us back; captive, to deliver us; condemned, to absolve us; He was made a curse for our blessing, sin offering for our righteousness; marred that we may be made fair; He died for our life; so that by Him fury is made gentle, wrath appeased, darkness turned into light, fear reassured, despisal despised, debt canceled, labor lightened, sadness made merry, misfortune made fortunate, difficulty easy, disorder ordered, division united, ignominy ennobled, rebellion subjected, intimidation intimidated, ambush uncovered, assaults assailed, force forced back, combat combated, war warred against, vengeance avenged, torment tormented, damnation damned, the abyss sunk into the abyss, hell transfixed, death dead, mortality made immortal. In short, mercy has swallowed up all misery, and goodness all misfortune. For all these things which were to be the weapons of the devil in his battle against us, and the sting of death to pierce us, are turned for us into exercises which we can turn to our profit. If we are able to boast with the Apostle, saying, O hell, where is thy victory? O death, where is thy sting? It is because by the Spirit of Christ, we live no longer, but Christ lives in us.[20]

At the cross cursing was transformed into blessing. Shame and disgrace were transformed into glory and grace.

Shame whispers lies that seduce you to believe that you are alone, rejected, and too stained for grace. Jesus' cross and resurrection proclaim the opposite.[ad] Instead of the whispered lies, his response to his people is singing and joy: "The LORD your God is in your midst, a mighty one who will save; he will rejoice over you with gladness; he will quiet you by his love; he will exult over you with loud singing."[ae]

[ad]Rom. 8:1.
[ae]Zeph. 3:17.

No More Shame

God understands your shame. God extends his compassion and his mighty, rescuing arm to take away shame. Jesus both experienced shame and took your shame on himself. Yet Jesus, of all people, did not deserve to be shamed. Still, he took on your shame, so it no longer defines you nor has power over you.

Perhaps the greatest fear of a person marked by shameful defilement is the fear of exposure. Consequently, they often labor to present themselves to others in the way that they wish they were instead of being honest about their brokenness and need. The answer for them is outlined by Jesus' best friend, John, who wrote, "But if we walk in the light, as he is in the light, we have fellowship with one another, and the blood of Jesus his Son cleanses us from all sin. If we say we have no sin, we deceive ourselves, and the truth is not in us. If we confess our sins, he is faithful and just to forgive us our sins and to cleanse us from all unrighteousness."[af]

Simply, John is stating that sin touches and affects everyone and confines life to the defiling darkness of shame, guilt, and isolation that either denies our woundedness or labors to hide it. Conversely, cleansing comes through living open and honest lives that bring our defilement into the light for Jesus and trustworthy Christian friends to see so that they can be the agents of healing and grace in our lives.

We saw that trust in self adds to shame. But trust in the Advocate shatters shame because it draws us to look beyond the hopelessness of the moment and gaze on the One whose strength and love are capable of pulling us out of the mire, cleaning us, and covering us. When shame exposes us, we can counter our penchant to hide in self-protection by hoping in our Advocate who will protect us and come to our defense. Confident hope increases gratitude. The light of gratitude melts shame in all its violent, furious self-hatred.[21]

It is Jesus' death on the cross that forgives our sins and cleanses the stains (resulting from sins we have committed and that have been committed against us) on our soul. The glorious result is a life purified of all unrighteousness, no longer defiled, but rather cleansed through a relationship with Jesus and his people because of his death on the cross to remove sin and its stain of filth. Because of the cross, we can be fully

---

[af] 1 John 1:7–9.

exposed, because God no longer identifies us by what we have done or by what has been done to us. If we trust in Jesus, God sees us as Jesus was: pure, righteous, and without blemish. We have been given the righteousness of Christ. We can't add to it or subtract from it. In Jesus, you are made completely new.

Brian's Story

When I began high school, I felt like I was on top of the world. As a freshman I was selected to play on the varsity baseball team, an honor not usually given to young newbies like myself. The intensified practice schedule and increased academic load caused my grades to slip and my parents to worry. My coach took me under his wing and promised my parents that he would make sure I gave my studies the deserved attention while remaining a key player on the team.

We'd meet at his house for tutoring sessions. I was so excited to be so close to the coach and that I got to go to his house. But after a few months, my excitement turned to dismay as our tutoring meetings became dark. After some superficial tutoring he'd started playing pornographic videos with me in the room while he masturbated in front of me. And then, eventually, he started masturbating me while watching the videos.

Sheer embarrassment kept me from telling anyone. While I knew what he has doing was wrong, it also felt good and pleasurable. I was utterly confused. I pretended that everything was fine, but inside I was beating myself up with guilt. I felt like I must have wanted it since I didn't stop him. Why was I allowing this to happen to me? I thought. I was too afraid to speak up because he threatened to cut me from the team if I said anything. My teammates would hate me if I reported this to the police because Coach would go to jail or at least be fired.

I was full of questions. What would my father think of me? Would people blame me or think I was gay? Would people make fun of me and my family if the secret got out? What would people at church think?

So I kept silent.

I became nervous and jumpy around everyone, always thinking that they had discovered my secret. I was so depressed and stressed that my life started to unravel. My grades plummeted and I became withdrawn and hostile toward my parents and friends. Also, any interest I had in baseball was gone, and my performance on the field suffered, despite my efforts to argue that everything was fine.

The abuse continued for another year until I dropped off the team just to get away from this man. I loved baseball, but it required being near the coach, and that felt suffocating and made me more and more anxious.

I felt gross about what happened to me, and I dreamed about it often. I was so confused about my sexual identity. Was I gay? Bisexual? I thought I must be if I let a man do that to me and enjoyed it. So, I became very promiscuous in high school and through my young adult years. I used women sexually to bolster my sexual identity. I used them the way my coach had used me. I already felt so dirty and guilty that I told myself it didn't matter anymore if I piled on more guilt.

I never told any of this to anyone before telling my wife. She could tell I was distant and cold when we were intimate. Our sex life was in shambles. She thought I was either committing adultery or uninterested in her, which killed me since intimacy with her was the only time that sex didn't make me feel guilty. And now even this goodness was tainted by darkness. So I told her everything that had happened to me and everything I had done in response to it. The burden of guilt was overwhelming.

There were lots of tears. I never felt more exposed and also loved than when she looked me in the eye and said, "You believe in Christ, therefore God forgives you for your sins. I forgive you, too. But you are not guilty for what your coach did to you. That was not your fault."

Her words were true, and I was comforted to know the difference between real and false guilt. For years, I had carried the burden of false guilt from the evil done to me. For the first time I realized the truth that I didn't cause that man to touch me. I didn't encourage or consent to what he did to me. I was not guilty for worrying about causing embarrassment to me and my family, which was the reason I did not report what happened. The truth is, my coach is guilty and I was his victim.

However, I actually felt the most guilt for how I responded to the sin done against me. I sinned against God in my bitterness and through promiscuity. I had always justified my outbursts because I felt betrayed and abused by someone I trusted. I felt like I had the right to do whatever I wanted, and it didn't matter what God wanted for me. I not only rebelled against God, but I also hurt others in an effort to regain control and power. But what I discovered is that all along I was running from the threat of judgment and exposure by either keeping others at a distance or under my control.

But my tactics weren't working because all I could feel was more self-contempt, anxiety, and fear. What I needed was God's forgiveness to completely remove my self-blame and judgment. I trusted in Christ for my salvation, but for some reason had never seen how it applied to this.

The night I talked to my wife, she helped me see how the gospel applied to my burden of guilt. Now I see that my freedom and forgiveness is based on the fact that at the cross, Jesus took on my sins and exchanged them with innocence and righteousness. Jesus reconciled me to God so that instead of viewing me as his enemy, one steeped in guilt, God saw me as having Jesus' pure and blameless righteousness. His sacrificing love is my only hope for peace to reign over me instead of guilt.

And when the haunt of guilt returns, I remind myself that I am forgiven because of Jesus' life, death, and resurrection. This good news that I needed so much for my past is a comfort each day, as well. Today, I still sin and I still need forgiveness. But now I return quickly to the cross to confess and receive grace and mercy. I received "grace upon grace" from Jesus (John 1:16).

7

Guilt

Many sexual assault victims feel deep guilt. This is frequently manifested in condemnation, judgment, and self-blame. Guilt is accompanied with the threat of judgment. And judgment is the root of fear, anxiety, stress, depression, chronic self-contempt, anxiety or panic attacks, self-hate, anger, and sometimes suicide.

Many victims heap upon themselves blame because they believe, at their cores, that perhaps they didn't do enough to stop the assault. Others may feel they are to blame as if they "brought it upon themselves" or somehow deserved to be assaulted. Or perhaps there is lingering guilt because they feel as if they were at the wrong place, at the wrong time, with the wrong people. Self-blame is also compounded in situations when victims obsess over whether they were dressed inappropriately at the time, if they were intoxicated, or simply "should have known better." Guilt is especially exacerbated in cases in which the victim felt aroused because of the sexual activity done to them during the assault.

Unfortunately, it's not uncommon for less than gracious responses to come from family and friends. When this happens, feelings of guilt are compounded. In addition, police, doctors, nurses, detectives, lawyers, or social workers may reinforce a victim's feeling that she or he "asked for it." Many victims believe that they could have or should have resisted more forcefully. The question of "why could I not stop the assault?" or the belief that "if I had only been smarter, stronger, or braver maybe it wouldn't have happened to me" intensifies the sense of guilt.

Furthermore, many victims feel guilty for embarrassing their family and community by opening up about their abuse and reporting it to the police. In some communities there exists a "culture of silence" whereby talking about a sexual assault, reporting perpetrators, or airing "family business" burdens victims even further.

If any of the above-mentioned feelings accurately portray your experience, it is very important for you to know that the assault was not your fault. The offender is guilty, not you. Nothing you did was "asking for it" and while you may feel guilty because you believe you could have somehow avoided the experience by acting differently, the offender is always at fault, never the victim.

Feelings of guilt and blame are often linked to the myths and misconceptions about sexual assault that prevail within our society, which frequently place the blame and responsibility on the victim rather than the offender. Dismantling these myths and misconceptions allows the guilt to rest appropriately on and solely with the offender.

Hear this: the assault was not your fault—not at all. This realization all by itself can bring great freedom and relief. Yet as soon as you move past this roadblock, you face the reality that the sin done against you is probably not the only reason you've felt guilty. Romans 3:23 says "all have sinned and fall short of the glory of God." You have sinned against God and others—both prior to your assault and in response to what happened to you. Sin corrupts us and we all have good reason to feel guilt and shame. But when feelings of guilt and shame collide with feelings of ambivalence brought on by the assault, your internal world can easily become very complicated and confusing. This is because the legitimate feelings of guilt and shame from your own sin can be very similar to the feelings of guilt and shame brought on by the assault. Guilt can be tricky. Don't confuse legitimate conviction of sin with a false sense of guilt for wrongs done against you.

While it is difficult to hear, you have sinned against God and others in your response to the sins done to you. And there are as many variations of this response as there are people. Maybe you have become hostile, critical, withdrawn, bitter, or self-righteous in an effort to stay in control and keep others at a distance. You've self-medicated in an effort to ease the pain. In the process you've become addicted to drugs, alcohol, food, exercise, or sex. These can be distraction techniques or expressions of self-destructive impulses. Perhaps you've become promiscuous in an attempt to harness what was used to harm you. Or maybe you despise sex and intimacy as a means of keeping the past pain, betrayal, and a sense of powerlessness at bay. Or maybe you turned to self-harm as a form of penance to "pay off" your guilt.

When you face the complicated, dark reality that you have sinned as a response to the evil done to you, you may feel disoriented and angry. You may be tempted to justify your sinful behaviors because of the harm, assault, mistreatment, loss, or betrayal you've experienced. You may feel as though no one can judge you because of the depth of pain you've already had to endure. But when seen through a cross-centered lens, this is simply one self-atonement strategy among many. If a faithful friend or pastor has pointed out this hard truth, you will likely feel deeply misunderstood and you may even want to end those relationships. Don't. You need forgiveness for your sins and freedom from guilt. The guilt you feel because of your sins is not merely a feeling or a personal problem—it is the reality of the human condition. God made us and requires us to be perfect.[a] However, because of original sin, we have all broken his commands and committed cosmic treason. R. C. Sproul writes:

> Sin is cosmic treason. Sin is treason against a perfectly pure Sovereign. It is an act of supreme ingratitude toward the One to whom we owe everything, to the One who has given us life itself. . . . The slightest sin is an act of defiance against cosmic authority. It is a revolutionary act, a rebellious act in which we are setting ourselves in opposition to the One to whom we owe everything. It is an insult to His holiness. We become false witnesses to God. When we sin as the image bearers of God, we are saying to the whole creation, to all of nature under our dominion, to the birds of the air and the beasts of the field: "This is how God is. This is how your Creator behaves. Look in his mirror; look at us, and you will see the character of the Almighty." We say to the world, "God is covetous; God is ruthless; God is bitter; God is a murderer, a thief, a slanderer, an adulterer. God is all of these things that we are doing."[1]

As sinners we are debtors who cannot pay our moral debts. Our debt is a failure to keep God's moral obligations. Sin is also the transgression of God's commands.[b] These transgressions can be committed in thought, word, and deed and can be due to a failure to do what God requires or

---

[a]Lev. 19:2; Matt. 5:48.
[b]Jesus, in Matt. 22:37–40, states, "You shall love the Lord your God with all your heart and with all your soul and with all your mind. This is the great and first commandment. And a second is like it: You shall love your neighbor as yourself. On these two commandments depend all the Law and the Prophets."

to actively doing what God prohibits. Also, our sin reflects not only external actions that violate God's laws, but it also reveals our internal motives, which are driven by inherent hostility toward God. After the fall, we are by nature and actions enemies of God.

Because of this guilt, most people seek grace. Yet in most places they encounter "shame, the threat of punishment, and a sense of judgment."[2] How are we to experience grace when deep down we feel disgrace? Our guilt comes because we have violated God's good and wise commands. For our sins, we are guilty and deserve being rejected and forsaken by God.

Grace to Sinners

The shocking message of grace is that Jesus was forsaken for us so we could be forgiven. This is powerfully expressed in two things Jesus said from the cross.

Jesus cries out from the cross: "My God, my God, why have you forsaken me?"[c] Jesus suffered the separation from God that we should have experienced. Jesus suffered on our behalf, in our place, and painfully endured relational separation from God so that we would not have to.[d] While the physical pain of the cross was excruciating and immense, the spiritual and relational pain must have been even greater.

The cost of sin is spiritual death[e] and relational separation from God.[f] Therefore, when Jesus cries out to the Father, he is expressing the unimaginable agony that is the proper penalty for our sins. This was a necessary step in God's ultimate plan of reconciling to himself sinners. John 3:16–17 answers Jesus' question: "For God so loved the world, that he gave his only Son, that whoever believes in him should not perish but have eternal life. For God did not send his Son into the world to condemn the world, but in order that the world might be saved through him." Why did God the Father temporarily abandon Jesus? Because he loves us and so he could forgive you.

Jesus also prayed from the cross: "Father, forgive them, for they

---

[c]Matt. 27:46; Mark 15:34.
[d]Second Cor. 5:21 (NASB) says, "He made him to be sin who knew no sin, so that in him we might become the righteousness of God." It seems that at some moment, when Jesus became sin on our behalf, God the Father, in a sense, turned his back upon the Son. It says in Hab. 1:13 that God is too pure to look upon evil. Therefore, when Jesus bore our sins in his body on the cross (1 Pet. 2:24), the Father, spiritually, turned away.
[e]Rom. 6:23.
[f]Isa. 59:2.

know not what they do."[g] As Jesus hung dying on the cross he prayed
for those who persecuted him. He did not pray for the good and the
innocent. He prayed for those guilty of doing sadistic things to him. His
prayer for them means there is nothing that you could ever do, or say, or
be, that would put you beyond the reach of Jesus' prayer. Nothing at all.

Ironically, Jesus' prayer is answered by his own death, which brings
the forgiveness of sins.[h]

The cross is the convergence of great suffering and divine forgiveness. Psalm 85:10 says that "righteousness and peace" will "kiss each
other." The cross is where that occurred, where God's demands, his
righteousness, coincide with his mercy. We receive divine forgiveness,
mercy, and peace because Jesus took our divine punishment, the result
of God's righteousness against sin.

On the cross, Jesus voluntarily and willingly bowed his head under
the power of sin and the curse of God. It is important that we understand that the Father did not do this to the Son. The Son and the Father
are doing this together. Jesus laid down his life as our substitute.[i] God is
submitting to God's own wrath for the sake of forgiving sinners.

J. Gresham Machen summarizes the significance of the cross for
sinners facing the awful fact of their guilt:

> The very point of the Christian view of the cross is that God does
> not wait for someone else to pay the price of sin, but in His infinite
> love has Himself paid the price for us—God Himself in the person
> of the Son, loved us and gave Himself for us; God Himself in the
> person of the Father, who so loved the world that He gave His only-
> begotten Son. . . . If you want to find an instance of true gratitude
> for the infinite grace of God, do not go to those who think of God's
> love as something that cost nothing, but go rather to those who in
> agony of soul have faced the awful fact of the guilt of sin, and then
> have come to know with a trembling wonder that the miracle of all
> miracles has been accomplished, and that the eternal Son has died
> in their stead.[3]

This is why the cross is the power of God to save you and forgive
you. If you trust in Christ, all your sins—past, present, and future—are

[g]Luke 23:34.
[h]Acts 2:38.
[i]Matt. 20:28; John 10.

forgiven. All of them. Also, threat of punishment, or sense of judgment, is canceled.

Declared Righteous

Because of the cross, God declares you righteous if you trust in Jesus.[j] He does this because he attributed your sin to Christ and his righteousness to you.[k] About this miraculous exchange, Martin Luther wrote:

> That is the mystery which is rich in divine grace to sinners: wherein by a wonderful exchange our sins are no longer ours but Christ's and the righteousness of Christ not Christ's but ours. He has emptied Himself of his righteousness that He might clothe us with it, and fill us with it. And He has taken our evils upon Himself that He might deliver us from them . . . in the same manner as He grieved and suffered in our sins, and was confounded, in the same manner we rejoice and glory in His righteousness.[4]

Reconciled

In addition to being declared righteous, you are also reconciled to God through the cross.[l] Instead of punishing you as the enemy of God, he gives you compassion and grace. You are now an adopted child of God and can call God *Abba*, an intimate title meaning father or daddy. Another image of reconciliation is marriage. Groom imagery in the Bible represents God in relation to his people.[m] Describing reconciliation with God, Ed Welch writes: "The gospel is the story of God covering his naked enemies, bringing them to the wedding feast and then marrying them rather than crushing them."[5]

Ransomed

On the cross, Jesus died to pay the ransom to free you from slavery to sin: "You were bought with a price."[n] About paying this ransom, John Calvin writes: "Having purposed to make atonement for sins, He put on our nature that we might have in our own flesh the price of our redemption."[6] God accomplished all he intended through his Son and gave

---

[j] Rom. 4:4–5, 13, 16; Eph. 2:8–10.
[k] 2 Cor. 5:21.
[l] Rom. 5:9–11.
[m] Hos. 3:4–5; Jer. 31:22; Ezek. 16:8.
[n] 1 Cor. 7:23.

everything in Jesus to get you. True grace is costly: "It is costly because it condemns sin, and grace because it justifies the sinner. Above all, it is costly because it cost God the life of His Son: 'ye were bought at a price,' and what has cost God much cannot be cheap for us. Above all, it is grace because God did not reckon His Son too dear a price to pay for our life, but delivered Him up for us."[7]

Confessing Sins

Because all who trust in Christ are declared righteous, reconciled with God, and ransomed from slavery to sin, you should be eager to confess your sins to be reminded of this good news. Romans 2:4 tells us that "God's kindness is meant to lead you to repentance." Read these two confessions of sin as examples of the comprehensiveness of confession and therefore the comprehensiveness of forgiveness:

> Most merciful God, we confess that we have sinned against you in thought, word, and deed, by what we have done, and by what we have left undone. We have not loved you with our whole heart; we have not loved our neighbors as ourselves. We are truly sorry and we humbly repent. For the sake of your Son Jesus Christ, have mercy on us and forgive us; that we may delight in your will, and walk in your ways, to the glory of your Name. Amen.[8]

> Almighty God, Father of our Lord Jesus Christ, maker of all things, judge of all men: We acknowledge and bewail our manifold sins and wickedness, which we from time to time most grievously have committed, by thought, word, and deed, against thy divine Majesty, provoking most justly thy wrath and indignation against us. We do earnestly repent, and are heartily sorry for these our misdoings; the remembrance of them is grievous unto us, the burden of them is intolerable. Have mercy upon us, have mercy upon us, most merciful Father; for thy Son our Lord Jesus Christ's sake, forgive us all that is past; and grant that we may ever hereafter serve and please thee in newness of life, to the honor and glory of thy Name; through Jesus Christ our Lord. Amen.[9]

Perhaps the best model of confession is from Jesus' parable of the tax collector's prayer: "God, be merciful to me, a sinner."[o] A longer version,

---

[o]Luke 18:13.

reflecting the same humility and acknowledgment of God's mercy is the following "Song of Penitence":

> O Lord and Ruler of the hosts of heaven, God of Abraham, Isaac, and Jacob, and of all their righteous offspring: You made the heavens and the earth, with all their vast array. All things quake with fear at your presence; they tremble because of your power. But your merciful promise is beyond all measure; it surpasses all that our minds can fathom. O Lord you are full of compassion, long-suffering, and abounding in mercy. You hold back your hand; you do not punish as we deserve. In your great goodness, Lord, you have promised forgiveness to sinners, that they may repent of their sin and be saved. And now, O Lord, I bend the knee of my heart, and make my appeal, sure of your gracious goodness. I have sinned, O Lord, I have sinned, and I know my wickedness only too well. Therefore I make this prayer to you: Forgive me, Lord, forgive me. Do not let me perish in my sin, nor condemn me to the depths of the earth. For you, O Lord, are the God of those who repent, and in me you will show forth your goodness. Unworthy as I am, you will save me, in accordance with your great mercy, and I will praise you without ceasing all the days of my life. For all the powers of heaven sing your praises, and yours is the glory to ages of ages. Amen.[10]

When you confess your sins and trust in Christ, God always has mercy on you, pardons and delivers you from all your sins, confirms and strengthens you in all goodness, and promises you everlasting life. First John 1:9 assures us: "If we confess our sins, he is faithful and just to forgive us our sins and to cleanse us from all unrighteousness."

The Heidelberg Catechism describes what this means regarding your guilt:

> Even though my conscience accuses me of having grievously sinned against all God's commandments and of never having kept any of them, and even though I am still inclined toward all evil, nevertheless, without my deserving it at all, out of sheer grace, God grants and credits to me the perfect satisfaction, righteousness, and holiness of Christ, as if I had never sinned nor been a sinner, as if I had been as perfectly obedient as Christ was obedient for me.[11]

Promises Guaranteed

God turned his wrath away from you and toward Christ on the cross. In the resurrection, God turns your eyes away from your sins and directs them to Christ. This means that the gospel is not just negatively stated—no more guilt, no more condemnation, no more wrath—but is also understood positively.[12] In Christ you are loved, accepted, innocent. You have assurance and confidence in relating to God.

The foundation of these promises to you in the gospel—the certification and guarantee of them—is that the Son of God bore in his body all your punishment, guilt, condemnation, blame, fault, and corruption, so all the benefits of his sacrifice are given to you freely.

Though you were a sinner, Christ Jesus loved you so much he died for you. This sacrificing love of God is your only hope:

> What love it is, that this holy God should give his Son—his only Son, his beloved—to suffer and die in the place of rebels. He gave him, not hoping he might be spared, but knowing that he would be despised, rejected, and killed. As he turned his face away from his Son in the blackness of Golgotha, he turned toward us—a people loaded with guilt, children given to corruption—and fulfilled those precious words "God so loved the world that he gave his only Son." A penal substitutionary understanding of the cross helps us to understand God's love, and to appreciate its intensity and beauty. Scripture magnifies God's love by its refusal to diminish our plight as sinners deserving of God's wrath, and by its uncompromising portrayal of the cross as the place where Christ bore that punishment in the place of his people. If we blunt the sharp edges of the cross, we dull the glittering diamond of God's love.[13]

About this kind of love, Søren Kierkegaard writes: "For love is exultant when it unites equals, but it is triumphant when it makes that which was unequal equal in love."[14] First John 4:10 says that you will know what love is when you understand that Jesus Christ laid down his life for you. God loves you now, right now. He doesn't love some future version of you that tries harder, is more obedient, that pays him back for your sins, or that proves that you deserve love. While you were a sinner he died for you because he loved you, and he still loves you now.

You have the assurance that you are fully known and fully loved, despite your faults and failings and irrespective of how badly others have treated you. You can approach God with confidence. Because Jesus has paid for your sins, you can come to God with confidence and confess all your sins. You can be honest about every sin and failure without fear because you know he is for you and will forgive you for Jesus' sake. Because he accomplished your redemption, guilt and sin have no right to condemn you. You may condemn yourself or others may condemn you, but for those who are in Christ there is now no condemnation:

> I cannot think little of sin, when I look at the cross of Christ. Would I know the fullness and completeness of the salvation God has provided for sinners? Where shall I see it most distinctly? Shall I go to the general declarations of the Bible about God's mercy? Shall I rest in the general truth that God is a God of love? Oh! no! I will look at the cross of Christ. I find no evidence like that. I find no balm for a sore conscience, and a troubled heart, like the sight of Jesus dying for me on the accursed tree. There I see that a full payment has been made for all my enormous debts. The curse of that law which I have broken has come down on One who there suffered in my stead. The demands of that law are all satisfied. Payment has been made for me, even to the uttermost farthing. It will not be required twice over. Ah! I might sometimes imagine I was too bad to be forgiven. My own heart sometimes whispers that I am too wicked to be saved. But I know in my better moments this is all my foolish unbelief. I read an answer to my doubts in the blood shed on Calvary. I feel sure that there is a way to heaven for the very vilest of men, when I look at the cross.[15]

He forgave you all your sins. Jesus' death cleanses your guilty conscience so you can now have confidence, rather than fear, in relating to God. This boldness in approaching God is the opposite of the fear of death, the guilt of sin, and expectation of judgment. The great reversal has taken place. Freedom has taken the place of bondage and judgment because Christ has taken the place of the guilty. Because there is no condemnation, you can have a clear conscience—love replaces darkness, joy replaces despair, and peace replaces fear.

While you have confidence now in approaching God, you can rest in the assurance that you are secure. You will never be rejected by God who calls you his. You are accepted. If you trust in Christ, then that is all you will ever hear! There is no more charge against you and no barrier between you and God.

You are accepted. Isn't that what you long to hear, especially when you know you don't deserve it and can't earn God's acceptance? Undeserved acceptance is a great way of explaining grace. It somehow changes guilt into assurance. Grace comes to you when you are weak, not strong. It's yours when you are in pain and restlessness. Grace floods you when you feel that your separation is deeper than usual. It runs to you when your disgust for your weakness and your lack of composure has become intolerable to you. Grace is already there when the longed-for progress does not appear, when the old compulsions reemerge, when despair destroys joy and courage. Grace is the wave of light that breaks into the darkness, and you hear God say: "Because of what my Son did, you are accepted. Once you had not received mercy, but now you receive mercy. You belong to me. Do not try to do anything right now. Do not seek for anything; do not perform anything; do not intend anything. Simply accept the fact that you are accepted!"

As you trust in Christ, may grace and peace overwhelm you instead of guilt. Instead of dealing with your real guilt by denial, escapism, resolutions, looking down on others, and obsessing, you are free to repent of your sins and receive forgiveness and blessing from God.

Mandy's Story

By the time I was twenty-one it seemed like sexual abuse, sexual assault, and sexual addiction would always somehow be a part of my life. But by that age I had found comfort knowing that I was the one in control of sex; it wouldn't be used against me, but rather I would use it to manipulate and toy with men the way I had been "toyed" with for years. But that sense of control was exposed as a lie the week before my twenty-second birthday. I was out dancing at a night club and after the bar closed I was invited into the VIP room. It was in that room where four or five men raped me and left me in tears on the floor. I was never in control.

For the next three years I remained emotionally disconnected from the event, numbing the pain with various types of escape like drugs, alcohol, and extreme behaviors. I became cold toward men. I left my childhood faith in Jesus, allowing my heart to become hardened and bitter against life and against God. After all, it seemed as though I had been abandoned by God anyway, so I relied on myself for comfort, protection, and direction.

But God had not abandoned me. In fact, he pursued me in a number of different ways. Eventually I was brought to my knees, crying out for him to explain himself! If it was true that he loved me, how could he let such harm befall me? I don't remember waiting for him to actually answer me. It was in Christian counseling that I found some solace in this idea: God did not want me to be raped, but he will use it to bring about something good. At the time, I accepted that as truth, and as I grieved over the rape and all the pain I endured, God was softening my heart, changing my desires, and redeeming many areas of my life. I figured that I had "gotten over it" and was healed.

But if I was to be truly honest, something seemed forced. When I would tell my story, there was still a disconnect between my head and my heart in acknowledging God in the midst of that horrific crime.

Even though it seemed my life was full of joy, there was still a lingering resentment toward the men who raped me. I did not feel angry toward them, but I refused to see them in my mind. They were the bad guys, my enemies. I wanted nothing to do with them. As time passed I believed that was where God wanted me, and I thought he even agreed with me. It was "us" against "them."

Then, seven years after the rape had passed, God said through some life circumstances that there was more to be done. I was reminded of the rape and God plunged me back into the pain, asking me to go deeper than I had gone before. I was terrified yet willing. The first time I asked him what he wanted to show me, he led me to Psalm 54 and told me that he is my vindication, that he knows my suffering, and that someday I will look upon my enemies in triumph. I felt comforted and validated. But he didn't leave it at that. He was also reminding me of his goodness, reminding me that he upholds my life, and that even in the midst of being raped he loved me and had good in mind for me. That's when I realized my greatest fear—could I really enter into the deepest part of this pain and still believe that God is good? Is it really possible to taste the searing agony of intense destruction and at the same time taste and see that the Lord is good? Would I trust him to find out? With apprehension and fear I slowly said, "Yes."

As I walked through each moment of that night, acknowledging the many ways I was harmed by those men, bringing into present reality what I had kept in a distant past, I cried out and God comforted me, showing me that even then I was in his hands. He held me in that deepest darkest moment, just as he holds me now. As he taught me to stop minimizing the pain associated with the rape, I began to see the fullness of the evil done against me. Progressively, as the magnitude of the evil grew in my awareness, it was amazing for me to realize that God is even bigger. His love encompassed that whole night. Following him through that dark valley and resting in his real promises rather than my own ideas became the true healing that I needed. I came to know the true God, sovereign over all, who is ultimately good. And I was his daughter, cherished and loved by him even in the midst of being raped.

When I reached that point, my heart was soft toward God, and I asked him what else he had for me. I remember driving to work saying, "Is there more, here?" And that's when it hit me. I saw their faces. I saw the men who raped me and felt a surprising compassion towards them. I began to cry out for them, "God save them." Just as I was an enemy of God in need of reconciliation, so they need to be reconciled by the blood of Christ. I wept for them for quite a while and still often find myself tearing up on their behalf, wishing that I could see them face-to-face and tell them of a great God who is bigger than their harmful acts of violence, who loves them to the point of crushing his own Son to deliver them from death. This forgiveness was a miracle. I have found freedom in loving them with the love of Christ. My anger, bitterness, resentment, escape, numbness, denial, self-pity, or any other response is not capable of removing their sin. Nothing but the blood of Christ will pay their debt.

And so I can look back on that night, recognizing the fullness of the pain God counted me worthy to suffer, and also look on it with the joy of knowing my God in a more intimate and magnificent way. It has become a mark of God's help in my life, a place where he ordained healing for me . . . and possibly even for those men. I would be overjoyed to someday raise our hands together in worship of the God who brings life out of darkness.

8

Anger

Sexual assault is unquestionably an evil, sinful act that understandably elicits anger. Deep in the hearts of victims, anger swells up against the perpetrator, their rage inflamed by suffering. Anger can be a natural and healthy response to sexual assault. While nearly all victims appropriately experience anger, most express it poorly or not at all.

Anger can evoke fear of being out of control and vulnerable. A powerful emotional force, anger is often used to conceal feelings of hurt, sadness, fear, and a threatened sense of security. Anger is not neutral. It can be confusing that the same word, "anger," reflects both a godly and appropriate response to evil and destructive feelings and acts. Anger felt by God and humans for the right reasons is good; the important factor is not who is feeling the anger but *why* it is felt. But when anger festers, it settles into bitterness and hostility, and becomes sinful, consuming, and destructive.

It is likely that you have been discouraged from expressing your anger. Most victims feel pressure from their families, society, or religion to ignore or suppress it. But suppression does not help anger to dissipate over time. Instead, anger turns into bitterness, hatred, and revengeful obsessions. In fact, unresolved or denied anger can become a destructive force that can tear your life apart through depression, anxiety, paralyzing fear, physical ailments, or symptoms of post-traumatic stress.[1] Anger holds you hostage and leaves you vindictive, addicted, embittered, immoral, and unbelieving.

Paradoxically, while you may feel pressure to suppress your anger, you may also be consumed by it. You can feel the adrenaline rush and your muscles clench as your mind races, your heart beating harder and faster. You want revenge against the person who harmed you. Amid your obsession, the people and things that really need your attention get swept aside as you fixate on your hatred for the perpetrator. And the longer anger consumes you, the harder it is to let go of the pride that comes with it. You feel justified. You truly have been wronged and the perpetrator should pay. Being consumed with anger slowly erodes the good and life-giving things in your life and starts to cloud your thinking about everyday situations that have nothing to do with why you are angry.

Ignoring your anger or being consumed by it probably makes you feel isolated from the people you love and who love you. Perhaps this is because you pick fights just because you want to be angry and have an opportunity to vent. Maybe you scream at a loved one even when they are not the object of your wrath. Anger can keep you from getting close to others who love and support you. It hinders you from opening up and sharing your feelings honestly. You may even push others away who don't want to listen to your complaining or who are intimidated by your hostility.

In an attempt to control your rage, maybe you've internalized your anger. Though no one would notice it on the surface, you silently loathe yourself or even go as far as to inflict self-harm like cutting. These are all examples of misdirected anger, which manifests in subtle and sophisticated ways by lashing out at others or shutting down emotionally. This is detrimental to relationships and can ruin them entirely, which further promotes your sense of isolation, distrust, and hostility.

When the appropriate feeling of anger turns into bitterness and hatred, it usually leads to an obsession with seeking vengeance. Bitterness and hatred are states of being characterized by intense animosity, hostility, reproach, vexation, or resentfulness; they are anger gone sour, an attitude of deep discontent that poisons your soul and destroys your peace. Though bitterness and hatred may dull the ache of desperation, hurt, fear, and vulnerability, you've fixed your focus outward rather than inward where the pain resides. These are very common, but rarely talked about experiences for victims of sexual assault.

The writer of Hebrews warns that bitterness can take root in your life and grow to "cause trouble and defile many."[a] Bitterness arises and sets in when you deny the anger you feel from the assault. Instead of crying out to God and dealing with how you really feel, you become consumed with sheer hatred for the perpetrator or ways to seek ven-

---

[a]Heb. 12:15 NIV.

geance. Locked in bitterness, you tend to hold grudges and are characterized by cynicism, implacability, vindictiveness, arrogance, hatred, and hostility.

You can spend years—even a lifetime—enslaved to bitterness, the consequences of which are adopting the character of the injured and helpless victim, with all the self-righteousness, resentment, and self-pity of that role. An unhealthy preoccupation with how you have been sinned against may be an attempt to justify your anger, gain sympathy, or gather allies in your efforts to seek revenge. In your bitterness, you might demand that others respond to your plight or pay the consequences.[2]

It is appropriate to be angry about the injustice, sin, violence, and evil you experienced. You have the right to be angry that you were violated, that perpetrators often get light sentences or none at all, that society often blames the victim, and that you feel vulnerable and afraid much of the time as a result of your assault. Scripture does not instruct Christians to suppress anger. However, it is where you go and what you do with your anger that must be examined. There is godly anger and sinful anger. Godly anger is healing and redemptive; sinful anger is ugly and vindictive as it gives way to bitterness and hatred.

Godly Anger—"Be Angry" (Ephesians 4:26a)

Despite popular misunderstanding, Scripture does not always describe anger as sin. As a matter of fact, the angriest person in the Bible is God. Isaiah 9:17 says that when he sees sin "his anger has not turned away."[b] The word "wrath" is used over six hundred times in reference to God's response to sin and evil. John 3:36 says that "the wrath of God remains on" those who do not believe in Jesus Christ. In Romans, Paul mentions God's anger over fifty times. Paul features the anger of God prominently in his letters: God's anger against sin and its effects is justified and displayed.[c]

That God is angry tells us something important: "Anger can be utterly right, good, appropriate, beautiful, the only fair response to something evil, and the loving response on behalf of evil's victims."[3] God's people can also express godly anger: "Be angry and do not sin."[d]

---

[b]NASB.
[c]Rom. 1:18; 2:5, 8; 3:5; 9:22; Eph. 5:6; Col. 3:6; 1 Thess. 2:16.
[d]Eph. 4:26.

This passage from Psalm 4:4 and quoted in Ephesians 4:26 shows that anger need not and should not be sinful. Legitimate anger should be felt and expressed in an appropriate manner. The fact that Paul distinguishes between anger and sin indicates that there is an anger that is not sinful. Anger at the evil done to you and the betrayal you experienced falls into the realm of godly anger.

God is angry and calls you to "be angry." God is angrier over the sin committed against you than you are. He is angry because what happened to you was evil and it harmed you. Godly anger is participating in God's anger against injustice and sin. To those who are ignoring their anger or settling for weak distortions such as bitterness or hatred, God invites you to participate in his anger for the sins done against you.

Not only are you *invited* to be angry at evil, but you are also *expected* to be angry. Because you are made in the image of God, you are a moral being. B. B. Warfield writes: "It would be impossible for a moral being to stand in the presence of perceived wrong indifferent and unmoved."[4] We are created with the capacity for anger at wrongdoing, as an expression of love for God and for those harmed by sin.

This is the opposite of denying, ignoring, or suppressing anger. Expressing godly anger with God is not a sin but is actually encouraged. In the Bible, there are many examples of godly anger in which anger is directed at the right objects.[e] Anger against sin or injustice is appropriate, good, and summoned by God.

God is angry at sin and at human oppression, a result of sin. It shows that he is the defender of the wronged. Every assault involves some form of injustice, and an injustice is any violation of God's design for life. Because he is holy and just, his anger is always legitimate:

> Yahweh can be angry because of human cruelty, or He can be angry exclusively because of the idolatry, rebellion, or pride of human beings. That Yahweh can be angry because of humans disregarding their common sense of justice demonstrates that He cares about how humans treat humans. . . . He is concerned about the lives of human beings and whether justice takes place among them. This concern is not merely a passive interest. He is angrily involved if the miscarriage of justice takes place.[5]

---

[e] Ex. 16:20; 32:19; Lev. 10:16; Num. 16:15; 31:14; Judg. 9:30; 1 Sam. 11:6; 2 Sam. 12:5; 13:21; Neh. 5:6; Jer. 6:11.

God loves what is good and hates sin. Because God loves, he's angry at what harms. Stanley Grenz writes: "We dare not confuse God's love with sentimentality. As the great lover, God is also the avenging protector of the love relationship. Consequently, God's love has a dark side. Those who spurn or seek to destroy the holy love relationship God desires to enjoy with creation experience the divine love as protective jealousy or wrath."[6]

Jesus was angry because of his great love for people: "Jesus burned with anger against the wrongs He met with in His journey through human life, as truly as He melted with pity at the sight of the world's misery: and it was out of these two emotions that His actual mercy proceeded."[7] He was angry when he encountered people who perverted the worship of God and contributed to or were calloused to the sufferings of others.

Mark 3:5 is the only passage where Jesus is clearly said to be angry. His anger was fueled by compassion for a man with a withered hand. Jesus' reason for anger fits the pattern for God's anger at sin, oppression, and injustice. Even when anger is not attributed to Jesus, there are times when it is implied.[f] Jesus felt godly anger about injustice and for God's honor. However, in his teachings, anger that divides and fosters personal hatred against another person is prohibited.

God's anger is a response to sin and rebellion. John Stott writes: "His anger is neither mysterious nor irrational. It is never unpredictable, but always predictable, because it is provoked by evil and evil alone."[8] At the same time, God is slow to anger and quick to forgive.[g] Our anger is similar to God's anger when it has the same cause and object. The problem often faced in our anger is that our standards are not God's. Thus, our anger is like God's in form, yet we do not have the character to feel it for the right reasons or to execute judgment in the right way.

Numerous psalms connect God's steadfast love and mercy to this loving wrath by which he does and will deliver his children from their sins and from those who harm them.[h] David Powlison argues: "We might fairly speak of the 'steadfast love/anger of the Lord,' of His 'lovingangerkindness.' The 'unfortunate, needy, and afflicted' who face the

---

[f]Matt. 3:7; 16:23; 18:6; 21:12; 23:2–36; Mark 8:33; 10:14; 11:15; 12:24–27; Luke 19:45; John 2:14–17.
[g]Isa. 48:9; Dan. 9:9; Rom. 9:22; 2 Pet. 3:9.
[h]Psalms 9–10, 37–40.

angry malice of others hope in the anger of God's love to make things right."[9] God's anger at the sins of our enemy is an object of faith in some psalms. Psalm 37 tells us we can trust God because God's anger will deal with evildoers. In Psalm 40, God's steadfast love/anger delivers us from our own sins and from those who hurt us.

God's anger now extends into the future, when God promises to end all suffering from others' sinfulness. This is the culmination of the theme of God's comfort for his afflicted people. God hates the way people hurt other people. In his steadfast love, God will deliver us from our enemies and destroy all causes of pain forever.

Sinful Anger—"And Do Not Sin" (Ephesians 4:26b–31)

God is the only one who is perfectly angry and is never sinfully angry. Because we are sinners, we frequently distort and confuse godly anger with our own desire for vengeance or control. This is why the general message of Scripture is that anger is a dangerous emotion that is most often destructive.[i] Most anger against another is not compatible with God's standards as the Bible does prohibit the thoughtless, unrestrained temper that often leads to rash, harmful, and irretrievable actions.

Ephesians 4:26 allows for anger. But it also warns against sinful anger—"and do not sin." Godly anger is permitted, and sinful anger is forbidden. And that which is forbidden is mentioned in Ephesians 4:31—bitterness, wrath, and anger that wills harm to another.

Sinful anger springs from malice and the desire to hurt people: "Anger can be utterly wrong, bad, inappropriate, ugly, a completely destructive response."[10] Sinful anger rebels against God and does harm. Godly anger loves God and loves doing good for people. Sinful anger feeds on itself and grows, making situations worse by responding to evil with evil, begetting more evil.

Godly, legitimate anger should not cause us to overlook the destructive force of anger. There is no question that sinful anger is seen as a destructive force in many Old Testament passages. It was the motivation behind the first murder as "Cain became very angry."[j] And the logical result of anger is reflected in Genesis 6:11—"The earth was filled

---

[i]Gal. 5:19–21; Col. 3:8; Eph. 4:31.
[j]Gen. 4:5 NASB.

with violence." Ungodly anger "harbors the hatred of Cain— it kills to make someone pay for exposure and pain."[11]

Close to but not synonymous with anger is hatred. Hatred is characterized by a general and long-standing negative evaluation of a person while anger is usually felt against a specific offense. Hatred is forbidden in many instances.[k] While hatred toward an individual is prohibited in some texts,[l] anger against them is not. Hatred which is long lasting and based on an overall negative quality is not to be felt against individuals, whom God made and loves. Anger that is often over a specific offense and is short-lived can be felt against an individual. "Anger must be directed toward destroying the problem, not toward destroying the person."[12]

God's anger is part of executing final judgment, which is his exclusive domain. Those harboring bitterness and hatred don't act as if God is concerned about their plight. Out of that false belief they often take matters into their own hands to seek justice. When one actively believes the distortion that anger is a catalyst simply for the self-satisfaction of seeing their perpetrator punished, God is displeased. Ungodly anger attempts to rectify the wrong done to us by empowering us to act instead of waiting vulnerably for God to do something.[13] It is not only a protection against harm; it is a taunt against God for apparently refusing to act on our behalf:

> Although our anger may be directed against others, ultimately we are directing our curses against God. Even when our anger is directed against inanimate objects, it is an attack against the Creator. We are furious at God for inequality. God seems to be either unable or unwilling to address injustice; sometimes it even feels as if He is on the side of evil, joining the assault against us. We want vengeance. The desire to violate is our repayment to God and others for the emptiness and harm that is not recompensed. It is an attack against an attack. And it will not be satisfied until the other is defeated, humiliated, and utterly annihilated.[14]

This sinful anger is now a given, after the fall, as we are hardwired for resentment and hatred for God and others.

Sinful anger creates vicious circles where evil begets evil. When our

---

[k]Lev. 19:17; Prov. 24:17; 25:21.
[l]Titus 3:3; 2 Thess. 3:14–15.

anger becomes punitive, out to get revenge, it is the opposite of godly anger that has a redemptive purpose of destroying ugliness in order to enhance what is good. Revenge does not heal; it only makes things worse: "Violence feeds on revenge; revenge, on violence."[15] The trouble with revenge is that it enslaves us as vengeance "acts in the form of reacting against an original trespassing, whereby far from putting an end to the consequences of the first misdeed, everybody remains bound to the process, permitting the chain reaction contained in every action to take its unhindered course."[16]

There is only one way out of this vicious cycle binding victim and perpetrator and perpetuating more violence:

> Repay no one evil for evil. . . . Beloved, never avenge yourselves, but leave it to the wrath of God, for it is written, "Vengeance is mine, I will repay, says the Lord." To the contrary, "if your enemy is hungry, feed him; if he is thirsty, give him something to drink; for by so doing you will heap burning coals on his head." Do not be overcome by evil, but overcome evil with good.[m]

God's vengeance makes the spiral of vengeance grind to a halt because the assurance that God will punish sin allows believers to freely love. You don't need to repay evil with evil because the Bible teaches that in the future God will take vengeance on his adversaries in such a horrific way that the violence of the Old Testament pales by comparison.[n] Because vengeance is God's, you don't have to be vengeful; you can love and forgive your enemy. As a matter of fact, if you don't forgive, you are usurping God's authority to act as judge.

You may be offended or shocked, and that would make sense since forgiveness is an outrage "against straight-line dues-paying morality."[17] But Christianity is not about karma; it is about grace. And this grace is sometimes shocking.

Love and Forgiveness (Ephesians 4:32–5:2)

We have seen that anger can be good and right. We've also seen that God uses anger for a redemptive plan, which is for grace to triumph. This

[m]Rom. 12:17–21.
[n]Matt. 23:33; Mark 9:43–49; Col. 3:6; Heb. 10:26–31; 2 Pet. 3:7, 10–12; Rev. 6:16–17; 11:18; 14:10–11, 19–20; 15:1–8; 16:1–21; 19:15.

doesn't mean we stop being angry at evil, but it does mean that we are to take seriously the Lord's Prayer: "Forgive us our debts, as we also have forgiven our debtors."[o]

Forgiveness means not taking vengeance into our own hands toward those who have sinned against us. Godly anger allows the offense to be seen as an issue between the offender and God. When someone sinned against you, they also sinned against God. Vengeance belongs to God, and he will repay.

Forgiveness means more than not being vengeful, it also means loving your enemies, and anyone who sins against you acts like your enemy: "But I say to you who hear, Love your enemies, do good to those who hate you, bless those who curse you, pray for those who abuse you."[p] To forgive is to love despite being sinned against. Miroslav Volf anchors forgiveness in love: God's love toward us, and then our love for others.[18]

We see this reflected in Ephesians 4:32–5:2, which calls us to extend forgiveness and love to others because that is what we receive from God: "Be kind to one another, tenderhearted, forgiving one another, as God in Christ forgave you. Therefore be imitators of God, as beloved children. And walk in love, as Christ loved us and gave himself up for us, a fragrant offering and sacrifice to God."

Receiving forgiveness and love from God through Christ is essential to understanding forgiveness. Because God forgave you for your sins, you are now free to forgive others. Jesus received God's anger and punishment so those guilty of cosmic treason would be forgiven. The gospel forgives and changes angry people into loving and forgiving people who are characterized by love, joy, peace, patience, kindness, goodness, faithfulness, gentleness, and self-control.

Grace is the miracle that causes change. It creates loving people who are empowered by the Spirit to do good in this world of hostility and evil. As sinners who have received mercy instead of wrath, we have the otherwise inexplicable capability simultaneously to hate wrong and to give love to those who do wrong. It is a miracle for a sinner to forgive another sinner. But this miracle is based on the prior miracle of God freely offering his Son to bear the wrath deserved by the guilty.

---

[o] Matt. 6:12. Also see Luke 11:4, "Forgive us our sins, for we ourselves forgive everyone who is indebted to us."
[p] Luke 6:27–28.

This is why Robert Cheong defines love and forgiveness as the "work of God." Cheong writes: "Love is a work of God on the human soul that compels one to give oneself to another, regardless of the cost, so that the other might love God more deeply. . . . Forgiveness is a work of God's love in the human soul that compels one to give oneself for another, despite being sinned against, so that the other might love God more deeply."[19]

What God did for us becomes the power to change. He forgave us. That opens up a relationship of love and a future of hope. Tenderheartedness flows from a heart overwhelmed with being loved undeservedly and being secured eternally. The command to be tenderhearted has more to do with what God has done for you than what your perpetrator did to you. You are not enslaved to your past.

When we forgive others their sins, we echo the forgiveness granted by a just and loving God who forgave our sins. Christ took upon himself God's fierce anger, which should have been poured out on us. As a result of Christ's sacrifice, for those who believe, God's anger is satisfied. As a result we rest in God's grace, enjoying his blessings free from the violence of his curses. God's one-way love toward us amid our sin undermines our bitterness and can prompt forgiveness of those who sin against us.

In repenting of your own sins—including the trespass of sinful anger—mercy and grace will flow into your life, making you merciful to others, even those who, like you, don't deserve it: "A pardoned soul is a monument of mercy."[20] If you've found the mercy of Jesus overflowing toward you for spectacular and fatal sins—cosmic treason—it is only natural for mercy to overflow toward others for their lesser, but still painful, sins against you. The more deeply you get to the heart of your participation in sin, the more you will understand with joy the mercy of God to you.

In the Psalms, those who cry out to God for justice are aware of their own guilt, that they are participants in the problem of evil, not just victims. For example, see Psalm 69:5: "O God, you know my folly; the wrongs I have done are not hidden from you." Crying out to God because of sins done to you will remind you that you are also guilty of sin, but have received forgiveness. And receiving forgiveness for your cosmic treason will undermine your bitterness for those who sinned against you and can prompt your forgiveness of them.

Mercy works to soften your heart. Jesus tells us to love our enemies[q] and pray for their well-being, which includes their repentance unto eternal life.[r] Mercy charges us to do persistent, straightforward acts of unmerited kindness.[s]

The command to forgive as you have been forgiven is repeated in the Bible.[t] Christian forgiveness demands that we take the initiative to forgive even before the evildoer has repented. Forgiveness from God frees us from the condemnation of our sins, compelling us to forgive others as we have been forgiven. Forgiveness is not contingent on the perpetrators repenting for their sins toward you. Our forgiveness of others is *unconditional*, even for unrepentant sinners.

Biblical forgiveness first involves a condemnation, accusation, or blame of some wrongdoing; second, it involves giving the gift of not counting the wrongdoing against the wrongdoer.[21] Therefore, when one receives forgiveness, one is first admitting to the guilt of the blame, and second, is receiving the gift of it no longer counting against him or her.[22] So in the case of an unrepentant sinner unwilling to accept the blame in the first place, the blame and condemnation remains on that person.[23] Forgiveness has been concretely granted but rejected. Because forgiveness has as a necessary starting point the condemnation of some evil, that condemnation remains upon the unrepentant sinner, even while the forgiver walks away having granted forgiveness.

Volf argues that forgiveness is not contingent on repentance, but he does link the two closely, making repentance *very* important: "Instead of being a *condition* of forgiveness, however, repentance is its necessary *consequence*."[24] If forgiveness is conditioned on the perpetrator's repentance, it once again places the victims under the control of their perpetrators and binds them to the destruction that bitterness and hatred bring.

Some have suggested that calling victims to forgive perpetrators may cause revictimization. That is certainly true when forgiveness is described in a simplistic, shallow, insensitive manner and not biblically defined. However, denying a victim the sense of freedom that only comes after biblical forgiveness has taken place, perpetuates the suffer-

---

[q]Matt. 5:44; Luke 6:27; 23:34; Acts 7:60.
[r]Luke 6:28.
[s]Rom. 12:20.
[t]Matt. 6:14–15; 18:21–35; Mark 11:25; Luke 6:37; 11:4; 17:3–4; Eph. 4:32; Col. 3:13.

ing caused by the initial assault because it allows the poison of hatred to continue to fester. To make forgiveness contingent on the perpetrator's repentance intensifies revictimization by stripping a victim of power and placing control back into the hands of the perpetrator. Not calling victims to forgive, or making forgiveness based on the evildoers' repentance, can imprison victims "in the automatism of mutual exclusion, unable to forgive or repent and united in a perverse communion of mutual hate."[25]

Many Christians mistakenly assume that forgiving someone who has hurt them means no longer feeling pain, anger, or a desire for revenge. Forgiveness does not mean that painful memories of the past are wiped away, nor does it mean that a desire for justice is ignored. Neither does forgiveness mean that the victim will not first feel a deep sense of anger and hurt for what has happened. In most, if not all, cases, real forgiveness cannot even be considered until those who have been assaulted have come out of the darkness of denial and have begun to feel the weight of wrongs committed against them. Forgiveness means a willingness and desire to cancel the debt that is owed to you because of the far greater kindness God has shown.[26] For the victim, forgiveness is not an event to be logged, but obedience to God and a freedom from bitterness that should be celebrated and nurtured.

Forgiveness is not a substitute for justice. As Volf writes: "Forgiveness is no mere discharge of a victim's angry resentment and no mere assuaging of a perpetrator's remorseful anguish, one that demands no change of the perpetrator and no righting of wrongs. On the contrary: every act of forgiveness enthrones justice; it draws attention to its violation precisely by offering to forego its claims."[27]

Forgiveness provides a framework in which the quest for properly understood justice can be fruitfully pursued. Only those who are forgiven and willing to forgive will be capable of relentlessly pursuing justice without falling into the temptation to pervert it into injustice.

Your forgiving the perpetrator is not sanctioning the violence they did to you. Forgiveness does not mean that you do not participate in activities that impose consequences on evil behavior such as calling the police, filing reports, church discipline, criminal proceedings, etc. You can forgive your abuser without the expectation of pretending the assault never happened.

In addition, dealing with anger and forgiveness does not need to be done alone. God's grace creates a community of grace, which is the church, and we bear each other's burdens.[u] Clearly, victims of sexual assault have been heavily burdened. They have suffered bodily harm, degradation, the sense of uncleanness, terrible fear, and the loss of self. When victims suffer, the community suffers with them.[v] Victims need to be comforted and supported, but they also need the full restoration of what they have lost. In this regard, the community of grace must support victims as they forgive perpetrators but also wisely call perpetrators to repentance.

There is a difference between forgiveness and reconciliation. Reconciliation, the restoration of relationship between parties, and forgiveness can happen independently. Forgiveness can happen spiritually and emotionally because of what Christ did on the cross and through the resurrection. But the promise of reconciliation is in the future. Forgiveness is a precondition for reconciliation.

Frequently, forgiveness is seen as simply an exercise in releasing bad feelings, ignoring past harm, and pretending all is well. Yet, forgiveness is just the opposite: "True forgiveness often deepens internal passion and sorrow. Yet it is a powerful agent in a process that can transform both the forgiver and the forgiven. It is a gift that pierces a hardened, defensive heart with rays of redemptive kindness."[28]

Forgiveness is not ignoring harm and acting as if nothing happened; it's the opposite. Forgiveness requires acknowledging the harm and calling it what it is—sexual violence, sin, evil—and calling the perpetrators what he/she/they are—evildoers and sinners. It also means acknowledging the consequence of God's judgment for the sins committed, and then not holding the charge against them. However, the perpetrator must deal with God at that point. The victim's forgiveness is not the declaration of God's forgiveness.

Forgiveness is costly for the victim, but it is not a naïve, foolish, simplistic, look-the-other-way pretense that all is well and parties should return to relating as they did before the assault. Forgiveness also does not mean that victims should feel like they need to prove their forgiveness by any interaction with the perpetrator. Forgiveness is something

[u]Gal. 6:2.
[v]1 Cor. 12:26.

the victim extends with or without the perpetrator's being aware of it. When possible, communication of forgiveness is best, but there are circumstances when this may not be possible or prudent: "Overlooking harm in order to achieve a sentimental but nonsubstantive peace actually encourages sin."[29]

Sadly, much revictimization can occur due to a simplistic rush to forgiveness, which masks an unwillingness to face complex layers of damage to the victim. Apart from victims encountering grace and having received forgiveness for themselves, demanding forgiveness toward others is simply a cruel burden to place upon them.

Though we must forgive, the only one who can ultimately forgive sins is "God alone."[w] Only God has the power and the right to forgive, and only God's forgiveness washes others clean of their wrongdoing and lifts the burden of guilt.

There is a double benefit of forgiving. First, we are commanded to forgive, and our obedience glorifies God. Thankfully, that which God commands he empowers you to actually do.[x] Second, the miraculous gift of forgiveness is also the best thing for the victim—it can release you from the anger, resentment, hatred, and bitterness that destroy you.[30] While forgiveness has been a topic reluctantly considered by sexual assault theorists,[31] the results from numerous studies suggest that forgiveness is helpful in the counseling of victims.[32] Forgiving provides greater reduction in the long-term symptoms associated with the sexual assault experience and improved overall functioning. It promotes more effective living, reductions in long-term effects of sexual assault, improved well-being, improved marital satisfaction, and improved relational skills.

The God of the Oppressed

You are invited by God to cry out for him to do what he has promised to do: destroy evil and remove everything that harms others and defames God's name. For example, God promises that "the way of the wicked will perish."[y] When evil presses in, prayer pleads for God to make it so.

The Psalms show us that rage belongs before God—the rage of the oppressed over injustice belongs in the presence of a just God who is

[w]Mark 2:7.
[x]Phil. 2:13.
[y]Ps. 1:6.

the God of the oppressed. In the light of God's justice, the oppressed will also see their sinfulness and violation against God and need for forgiveness. In the presence of God our rage over injustice may give way to forgiveness. In the presence of God, you know you deserve the wrath of God while you cry out your need for mercy. That anger at your sin eventually produces repentance, hope, and faith. In Psalm 40, God's steadfast love and anger deliver you from both your own sins and from those who hurt you.

Anger is more than just a stage to get through, "it is an act of profound faith to entrust one's most precious hatreds to God, knowing they will be taken seriously."[33] Anger expressed to God is the cry of the weak one who trusts the strong One, the hurting person who trusts the One who will make it all better.

In the Bible, God is One who stands with the vulnerable and powerless and speaks judgment against those who choose to use their power in ways that harm others. The strong unjustly use force and deceit to take from the weak. The oppressors think that no one cares and no one will interfere with their plans. But God's interest in the abuse of power is not mild. Nor is he at all resigned to injustice in a fallen world. The strong's unjust use of power meant to abuse the weak strikes at the very core of God's holy heart. Many passages in the Bible speak out on the issue of violence and God's attitude toward those who repeatedly use violence.[z]

God's wrath is a source of positive hope for the victim. You know that God loves you and will destroy the evil that has harmed you. God is the refuge of his people and shows steadfast love by destroying those who "strike terror."[aa] The wrath of God is often presented not as something to fear, but as something on which to set your hopes, as the consolation, refuge, and deliverance of God's suffering people.

Because vengeance is God's, you are free from the exhausting hamster wheel of vindictive behavior. Victims can trust God to make all wrongs right so they can get on with their lives and not fixate on bitterness and hatred. In this regard, the wrath of God is a central piece of the hope of God's people.

You never have to stop longing for God to deliver you from evil. The Bible closes with the plea, "Come, Lord Jesus!"[ab] This is a request that

[z]Ps. 11:5; 37:9; Zeph. 1:9; Mal. 2:16.
[aa]Ps. 10:18.
[ab]Rev. 22:20.

the Jesus of Revelation will come to remove all evils and destroy death, Satan, all causes of tears, and all sin.

The Bible links hope in God with a willingness to wait.[ac] To wait is to have confidence that God will bring justice. He will satisfy the depths of our desire, but in his time and not ours.

[ac]Ps. 27:14; 33:20; 130:5.

Nicole's Story

As a teenager, I struggled with my body image, and I hated what God created. When I was sixteen, people in church introduced me to a thirty-something-year-old married woman from our church who had a long battle with anorexia and bulimia.

Early in our friendship, I initially felt understood in my struggle. However, her validation of my thoughts and feelings toward my body only solidified the deception that Satan was trying to enslave me with. Soon after our friendship began, this woman began to manipulate me emotionally. Soon her manipulation became very strong. She told me that she was the only one who could really understand and help me. After knowing each other for a year, she molested me for the first time.

I was devastated.

She told me that I couldn't tell anyone because people would think I was a lesbian. She said that if anyone found out, her life would be ruined. She cried and told me how much she needed me, how lost she would be without me, and she even used Scripture to validate the way she felt. She promised never to do it again, but the cycle of molestation, lies, and emotional and spiritual manipulation repeated itself over two years like a nightmare I couldn't wake up from.

I wasn't a child when all this happened. In fact, I was a teenager. I was ridden with guilt and shame. I told myself that I should have known better and that somehow, what was happening must have been my fault. I hated every part of it yet felt completely powerless to break free. It seemed there was no way out. I tried countless times to break away, but she lured and guilted me back. My purity and femininity had been stolen.

I was finally able to break free and ended all communication, risking what felt like everything. Several years later, God blessed me with a godly husband. But I elevated him to be my savior. I believed that marrying a man who loved God and had committed his life to serving as a pastor and engaging in God-honoring sex would finally break the bonds of hopelessness. I wanted to bury any remaining despair, but my heart only opened up for further despair. God created marriage and sex, but he did not create them to replace him.

I cannot fully describe the despair, disillusionment, and shame that overwhelmed me. I felt utterly hopeless. It wasn't until several years later that I was able to break the silence and share with people I trusted what had happened to me. However breaking the silence did not put an end to my despair, and human validation offered no real hope.

Not only had sexual sin been committed against me, but this woman had heaped deception and darkness upon my life, and I was left feeling hopeless for years. She grossly misrepresented Christ to me by misquoting Scripture and using it as a weapon to keep me enslaved to her evil desires. If God was on her side, I thought, I wanted absolutely nothing to do with him. I was separated from the very One who would be my hope and bring healing. I also hated church. If God's people could do such unspeakable evil, the last thing I wanted was fellowship with them. I was sickened by testimonies of people who spoke of God's love. So I turned inward where despair and shame were my only companions.

I feasted on lies for years, which led to deeper hopelessness. The only relief I could imagine was death. I felt like my identity was broadcast on my forehead, as though everyone I encountered saw the words: damaged, filthy, worthless, lesbian, adulterer, broken, and beyond repair. This despair and shame had a numbing effect on my soul. There were times when I felt deep depression and brokenness.

I cried lots of tears. Then at other times, I felt nothing. In these moments I wanted tangible pain, so I would cut my arms and legs just to feel something. I wanted relief. I longed for real hope. I hungered for a savior.

God did not allow me to be put to shame or to die in despair. He lovingly and triumphantly broke through the deception and death intended by my abuser and by the Evil One. I cried to the Lord and he heard me. He delivered me from my distress. The Lord is close to the brokenhearted and saves those who are crushed in spirit (Ps. 34:17–18).

The cross is the very essence of my deliverance from despair and shame. The cross is not just an abstract theological symbol or a reminder of a time in history. The freedom that the cross brings is real. My Savior is real and alive today. My enemy has been defeated at the cross. Evil and death have no sting. Christ defeated them and has all authority over them (Col. 2:13–15).

I gave the enemy all power to tell me who I was. Deception bred hopelessness and despair. I was so engulfed in despair that I did not even realize how deceived I was. Because my Savior lives and my enemy is defeated, I have hope. I have hope! I have tasted freedom from shame and despair. And I now walk in the truth of who my Savior is and who I am because of my Savior.

My identity does not come from within me in my brokenness, shame, victimization, or pain. My identity is in Christ. What hope that brings! When I look to myself, I find very limited hope. But Jesus Christ died for me. He fully paid the price for all of my sin, and I don't have anything to add. He took all of my shame and hopelessness upon himself on the cross and exchanged my shame and despair for hope. I don't have to strive to find hope. Instead, hope is in the very person of my Savior.

I believe God mourned as I cut my flesh to bring relief. He summoned me to hear his truth. He brought me to his cross, and yet I chose to live in deception. I ignored the bright light of his hope. I didn't believe it could possibly be true . . . for me. But this is the glorious truth: Jesus died to save me from myself and to redeem me from the heinous sin committed against me. He felt the weight of my sin, shame, and despair so that I could feel the weight of his forgiveness, love, and hope.

Until I am finally face-to-face with Jesus, I will continue to be tempted to despair. I will be lured to forsake the hope of my Savior. I will be reminded of my sin, the sin committed against me, and the brokenness it caused in my life. I will be tempted to respond to my husband as if he is my enemy. In some moments I will succumb to temptation, and in other moments I will walk in the authority and freedom of Jesus, as I bring to mind the finished work of the cross. And one glorious day, I will be face-to-face with my Savior. I will be perfect as he intended me to be, and I will fall to my knees to worship him who died for me. My hope will finally, fully be realized.

9

Despair

Despair is the most commonly reported symptom of sexual assault. Feeling that you lost something, whether it's your innocence, youth, health, trust, confidence, or sense of safety can lead to despair. For those who have experienced the evil of sexual violence, it's likely that you've had an encounter with despair and depression.

Depression adds seemingly inescapable weight to the existential experience of despair: "Depression is the heavy cloud of hopelessness settling over our confidence and hope. You can be suddenly depleted of hope and feel your weakness so heavily that it seems to express the whole truth about your life. It becomes all you believe about yourself."[1]

The terrible experience of being powerless and vulnerable during an assault often leads to hopelessness. For some victims, feelings of hopelessness and helplessness come and go, while for others these feelings deepen into despair. When the feelings of powerlessness are internalized, self-hatred and self-pity intensify to the point of despair.

Despair invades all areas of life, depriving victims of motivation and sense of purpose. If you've experienced the exhaustion of despair, you've often wondered how you can make it through another day just managing day-to-day life. You might find yourself frequently crying over the seeming hopelessness of the present and what the future may hold. You may feel totally alone, as if no one cares, and abandoned without help. In addition to the emotional and mental agony of fear, anxiety, self-hatred, and even recurring thoughts of death or suicide, despair may manifest physically in the form of lethargy, change in appetite and sleep, indecisiveness, unexplained aches or pains, or other physical indications of stress. Since despair is so painful, many victims "seek to avoid awareness of it as much as possible, purposely but unconsciously perpetuating their self-deception."[2]

Despair is the total absence of any sense of hope, accompanied by a feeling of powerlessness. Despair deadens our hearts to the hope that we will be rescued, redeemed, and relieved of suffering. Despair refuses to hope. William Styron writes: "It may be more accurate to say that despair . . . comes to resemble the diabolical discomfort of being imprisoned in a fiercely overheated room. And because no breeze stirs this cauldron, because there is no escape from this smothering confinement, it is entirely natural that the victim begins to think ceaselessly of oblivion."[3]

Despair often leads to hatred of desire. Desire is aroused, but hope is disappointed, and the soul is consequently deadened through despair. After all, when there is nothing you can do to change the suffering, the natural response is to simply give up. The risk of hope is too great. It seems easier to quit trying and become numb than to have hope dashed again and again. Will you ever receive the support or belief from your family and friends? Will you ever feel safe in new relationships, or should you withdraw and hide? In your loneliness, it seems as though no one cares whether you live or die.

Despair refuses to dream that there's hope amid the valley of the shadow of death; it refuses the agonizing pangs of uncertainty, loss, and the irrepressible desire for redemption. It seems better to kill hope rather than face the agony of remembering and pondering God in the midst of suffering.

Despair is the enemy of hope: "Despair looks at the world and notes it emptiness—the lack of true relational intimacy, the utter blackness of death. It concludes that life is not worth it. This is the core of all forms of destructive despair: abandonment, loss, the death of desire, and a subsequent refusal to hope."[4] Hope is what propels us into the future. When hope is lost, life becomes mechanical, rote—seeing each day as nothing more than a repetition of what came before.

Hope

Is there any reason to believe that there is healing available now and hope for the future? Will it ever get any better? Or do you wonder, is the pain you are feeling right now all there is and will be?

There is hope. Rather than being simply a desire for a particular outcome that is uncertain, hope is characterized by certainty in the

Bible.[a] Hope is sure because God is behind the promise, and he has provided faithfully in the past to his people.[b] The hope you need right now borrows from God's faithfulness in the past and anticipation of it in the future.

The basis you have for hope is the resurrection of Jesus from the dead. Peter bases hope on the resurrection: "According to his great mercy, he has caused us to be born again to a living hope through the resurrection of Jesus Christ from the dead, to an inheritance that is imperishable, undefiled, and unfading, kept in heaven for you, who by God's power are being guarded through faith for a salvation ready to be revealed in the last time."[c] Similarly, hope and resurrection are closely linked in Ephesians. "The hope to which [God] has called you" is based on God's "great might that he worked in Christ when he raised him from the dead."[d]

Why does the resurrection give you hope if you trust in Christ? First, by his resurrection, Jesus conquers all your enemies: Satan, sin, hell, death, and the grave. Second, the resurrection is a guarantee of your future resurrection to eternal life.

Conquering through Suffering

Because of Jesus' resurrection, all threats against you are tamed if you trust in Christ. Jesus conquered death, so death and evil done to you is not the end of the story and you can have hope. In the book of Revelation, one of the key themes is conquering through suffering. This theme is evident in the number of the occurrences of the verb "to conquer" in the book.[e] John describes amazing promises to Christians, addressing the promises specifically to those who "conquer":

• To the one who conquers I will grant to eat of the tree of life, which is in the paradise of God. (2:7)

• The one who conquers will not be hurt by the second death. (2:11)

• To the one who conquers I will give some of the hidden manna, and I will give him a white stone, with a new name written on the stone that no one knows except the one who receives it. (2:17)

---

[a] Heb. 6:13–20.
[b] Heb. 3:6; 6:15; 10:23.
[c] 1 Pet. 1:3–5. Also see verse 21.
[d] Eph. 1:18–20.
[e] John uses the verb "to conquer" 17 times: Rev. 2:7, 11, 17, 26; 3:5, 12, 21; 5:5; 6:2; 11:7; 12:11; 13:7; 15:2; 17:14; 21:7.

- The one who conquers and who keeps my works until the end, to him I will give authority over the nations. (2:26)

- The one who conquers will be clothed thus in white garments, and I will never blot his name out of the book of life. I will confess his name before my Father and before his angels. (3:5)

- The one who conquers, I will make him a pillar in the temple of my God. Never shall he go out of it, and I will write on him the name of my God, and the name of the city of my God, the new Jerusalem, which comes down from my God out of heaven, and my own new name. (3:12)

- The one who conquers, I will grant him to sit with me on my throne, as I also conquered and sat down with my Father on his throne. (3:21)

How will these staggering promises come to pass? How will they conquer amid affliction and persecution? How will they find the strength to endure and overcome against all odds? John provides the answer: they will conquer by looking by faith to the One who has already conquered, Jesus Christ. We read in Revelation 5:5–6:

> And one of the elders said to me, "Weep no more; behold, the Lion of the tribe of Judah, the Root of David, *has conquered*, so that he can open the scroll and its seven seals." And between the throne and the four living creatures and among the elders I saw a Lamb standing, as though it had been slain.

John describes Jesus as the kingly Lion and the meek Lamb who has conquered all of his and our enemies. Jesus has conquered his enemies through his suffering and death on the cross, and yet he is also one who has been slaughtered. Jesus is "the faithful witness, the firstborn of the dead, and the ruler of kings on earth," and he is the one "who loves us and has freed us from our sins by his blood and made us a kingdom, priests to his God and Father."[f] We reign with him because he died and freed us and made us a kingdom for his glory.

This truth should be a strong encouragement to you in the middle of suffering. You follow a crucified Redeemer who by his death and resurrection has conquered death and Hades. Death and hell are no longer enemies that ought to produce fear in you. Jesus says: "Fear not, I am

---

[f]Rev. 1:5–6.

the first and the last, and the living one. I died, and behold I am alive forevermore, and I have the keys of Death and Hades."[g]

This image of the conquering Christ who prevailed through suffering can give you hope. In being united to Christ, you, too, will conquer as you look through the eyes of faith to the one who has accomplished everything on your behalf through his death and resurrection. It is for this reason that John writes in Revelation 12:11: "And they have conquered him by the blood of the Lamb and by the word of their testimony, for they loved not their lives even unto death."

Making All Things New

Because Jesus rose from the dead, he ascended to heaven and is "making all things new."[h] What Jesus' resurrection began will find its completion in the new creation. The new heavens and the new earth described in Revelation 21:3–5 is a picture of perfection:

> Behold, the dwelling place of God is with man. He will dwell with them, and they will be his people, and God himself will be with them as their God. He will wipe away every tear from their eyes, and death shall be no more, neither shall there be mourning, nor crying, nor pain anymore, for the former things have passed away. . . . Behold, I am making all things new.

God will be with us; he will bring peace and we will be perfected in the new creation. Disgrace is replaced by grace. Anxiety will give way to peace. Sam Storms writes:

> There will be nothing that is abrasive, irritating, agitating, or hurtful. Nothing harmful, hateful, upsetting, or unkind. Nothing sad, bad, or mad. Nothing harsh, impatient, ungrateful, or unworthy. Nothing weak, or sick, or broken, or foolish. Nothing deformed, degenerate, depraved, or disgusting. Nothing polluted, pathetic, poor, or putrid. Nothing dark, dismal, dismaying, or degrading. Nothing blameworthy, blemished, blasphemous, or blighted. Nothing faulty, faithless, frail, or fading. Nothing grotesque or grievous, hideous or insidious. Nothing illicit or illegal, lascivious or lustful. Nothing marred or mutilated, misaligned, or misinformed. Nothing nasty or naughty,

[g]Rev. 1:17–18.
[h]Rev. 21:5.

offensive or odious. Nothing rancid or rude, soiled or spoiled. Nothing tawdry or tainted, tasteless or tempting. Nothing vile or vicious, wasteful or wanton! Wherever you turn your eyes you will see nothing but glory and grandeur and beauty and brightness and purity and perfection and splendor and satisfaction and sweetness and salvation and majesty and marvel and holiness and happiness. We will see only and all that is adorable and affectionate, beautiful and bright, brilliant and bountiful, delightful and delicious, delectable and dazzling, elegant and exciting, fascinating and fruitful, glorious and grand, gracious and good, happy and holy, healthy and whole, joyful and jubilant, lovely and luscious, majestic and marvelous, opulent and overwhelming, radiant and resplendent, splendid and sublime, sweet and savoring, tender and tasteful, euphoric and unified! Why will it be all these things? Because we will be looking at God.[5]

Because of the resurrection, your eyes can be fixed forward on the new creation, something wholly different—and better than broken life in the here and now. Jesus is the first of that new creation, has already given you new birth into that new creation, and promises to complete it in you, making you gloriously, perfectly like him.[i]

Revelation 21:4 describes the promise of your peace and restoration: "He will wipe away every tear from their eyes, and death shall be no more, neither shall there be mourning, nor crying, nor pain anymore, for the former things have passed away." This is what your completed restoration will look like when all cause for sorrow is removed forever. Your restoration will take time. And it may be painful to realize that your healing takes longer than you anticipated. But one thing is certain: if you belong to Jesus, the same Spirit of God that resurrected him from the dead resides in you.[j] Your redemption is as certain as his resurrection.[6]

Present Sufferings, Future Glory (Romans 8:18–39)

We've discussed, at length, our future hope. But what does the resurrection mean for you, in the midst of suffering right now? We will investigate Romans 8:18–39 for an answer. This passage is one of the most

---

[i]1 Cor. 15:23; 2 Cor. 5:17; Phil. 1:6; 1 John 3:2.
[j]Rom. 8:11.

hopeful passages about the future and simultaneously one of the most realistic about present sufferings.

Not Worth Comparing

In Romans 8:18, Paul makes an amazing claim: "For I consider that the sufferings of this present time are not worth comparing with the glory that is to be revealed to us." He says your current sufferings will seem slight when compared to the glory that will be revealed. This is not to deny suffering. Paul concedes that suffering is painfully real. But in comparison to glory, suffering looks different because it is dwarfed by the grandeur of glory awaiting believers. It is important to see that rather than minimizing suffering, Paul is actually maximizing glory.

Paul boldly states that those who trust in Jesus are the adopted children of God who will receive a great inheritance. The statement about our suffering in verse 18 is in the context of ten references to us being the adopted children of God—six times in verses 14–17 and four times in verses 19–23.

The imagery of adoption means that you are not *naturally* a child of God, but that you have *become* one because of Christ. Isn't this what you need to hear in the middle of your despair? Being a child of God indicates warmth as well as confidence to call on God as a father who is able and ready to help.

Your adoption combats the cruel notion that you should feel uncertain concerning your status with God. Being the adopted child of God summarizes the message of the Bible: that God is merciful, loving, and patient, that he is faithful and true, and that he keeps his promises. All the promises of God were fulfilled in the gift of his only begotten Son, that according to John 3:16 "whoever believes in him should not perish but have eternal life."

If your future is based on Christ, you can have hope that your present sufferings are not the final cries in an empty universe. Instead, your cries are the prelude of joy at the final redemption. Through Christ, God has secured your eternal life and salvation. Because of that you can have hope; God is not done with you. Philippians 1:6 says: "And I am sure of this, that he who began a good work in you will bring it to completion at the day of Jesus Christ."

Holy Spirit

In Romans 8:23–27, Paul encourages you by drawing your attention to the support you have in the midst of suffering. You do not face despair or trouble in isolation because God sent his Holy Spirit to comfort you:

> We ourselves, who have the firstfruits of the Spirit, groan inwardly as we wait eagerly for adoption as sons, the redemption of our bodies. For in this hope we were saved. Now hope that is seen is not hope. For who hopes for what he sees? But if we hope for what we do not see, we wait for it with patience. Likewise the Spirit helps us in our weakness. For we do not know what to pray for as we ought, but the Spirit himself intercedes for us with groanings too deep for words. And he who searches hearts knows what is the mind of the Spirit, because the Spirit intercedes for the saints according to the will of God.

Paul admits clearly that God's children "groan inwardly" under the pressure of suffering. The pain and darkness can be so much that we "do not know what to pray for as we ought." But the Spirit is with us. Instead of arguing against "groaning," Paul does the opposite and says the Spirit groans even deeper: "the Spirit himself intercedes for us with groanings too deep for words." The Holy Spirit feels your pain and bears your burdens before the Father. When you are discouraged to the point that you are speechless, the Spirit cares and speaks for you. The Spirit is with you in your suffering.

God's Sovereignty

In addition to the gift of the Spirit, Paul encourages us by pointing us to the plan of God. Romans 8:28 tells us that God has a plan for our troubles; he will use them for our good: "And we know that for those who love God all things work together for good, for those who are called according to his purpose."

Notice how this divine plan is all-encompassing. *All* things—not *some* or *most*—work together for your good. But no matter how discouraging the despair, you know something that gives hope. God has a plan to turn despair into blessings. He's so merciful, creative, and sovereign that he uses everything, no matter what it is, for your ultimate good.

Because of God's plan for you, you can have hope. The world may be a place of suffering, and Paul will not deny that. But rather than only lamenting that, he directs your gaze in hope toward the future. That is why you can groan in expectation; it is both out of suffering and out of expectation that he will not let you remain suffering forever.

If God can turn the murder of his Son, the ultimate travesty of justice, into the redemption of the world, how much more can he use things in your life for your ultimate good? If he can turn murder into salvation, you can be confident that he can transform and use things in your life.

In Romans 8:29–30, Paul lists things God's determined for us. He does this to assure us that God is absolutely unwavering in his desire to bring good out of our suffering: "For those whom he foreknew he also predestined. . . . And those whom he predestined he also called, and those whom he called he also justified, and those whom he justified he also glorified." When we understand these aspects of God's plan, we can rest assured that God is fully determined to work all things for our good.

Before the universe was created, God gave individual and personal attention to you. From the infinite recesses of eternity, God cared for you with tender love and affection. God settled ahead of time the direction your life would take. Your trajectory is not toward destruction and disgrace but toward healing and grace. Your future is not open to the winds of random change. All those in Christ had their futures absolutely determined before the world even existed.

Surprisingly, Paul says we are "glorified." Notice that it is past tense. From God's eternal perspective you have already been glorified. Your full redemption is not something that hangs in the balance of future events. You are secure and your glorification is as good as done. This is why Article 17 of the 39 Articles of Faith says that predestination and election is "full of sweet, pleasant, and unspeakable comfort." When you grasp how God's unchanging eternal decrees secure your future, you can hold on to hope even when the time "in between" becomes very difficult. God does not immediately turn every event of suffering into a blessing, but eventually everything that happens, without exception, will be for your good.

This perspective on the sovereignty of God can free you to breathe a sigh of relief and thanksgiving instead of despair. Because God's plan for you is never to allow anything to separate you from his love, you can face the worst of the world's uncertainties with great confidence:

> What then shall we say to these things? If God is for us, who can be against us? He who did not spare his own Son but gave him up for us all, how will he not also with him graciously give us all things? Who shall bring any charge against God's elect? It is God who justifies. Who is to condemn? Christ Jesus is the one who died—more than that, who was raised—who is at the right hand of God, who indeed is interceding for us. Who shall separate us from the love of Christ? Shall tribulation, or distress, or persecution, or famine, or nakedness, or danger, or sword? As it is written, "For your sake we are being killed all the day long; we are regarded as sheep to be slaughtered." No, in all these things we are more than conquerors through him who loved us. For I am sure that neither death nor life, nor angels nor rulers, nor things present nor things to come, nor powers, nor height nor depth, nor anything else in all creation, will be able to separate us from the love of God in Christ Jesus our Lord.[k]

Since God did not spare his own Son, but gave him up for us all, God will most surely, most certainly, without any doubt or any possibility of failure, provide for us: "The wonder is not only that God the Father gave His Son but that He did so in this way, by sacrificing the one He loved. It is astonishing that He gave the Beloved for those who hated Him. See how highly He honors us. If even when we hated Him and were enemies He gave the Beloved, what will He not do for us now?"[7]

Because God's plan for you is so certain, you can face the worst difficulties, the most terrifying enemies, and the most devastating ordeals with confidence. You do not merely survive your trials; you are "more than a conqueror" because absolutely nothing will be able to separate you from the love of God in Christ.

Redemptive Sorrow

Godly despair is the groan of the Holy Spirit, and while you may see no explanation for your pain, he knows there is an answer and lovingly communicates your pain to a sovereign God who listens. Your God is

[k]Rom. 8:31–39.

strong and he, not the evil done to you, will have the final say about you. That hope animates "groans within ourselves" that everything will someday be renewed. We will be delivered from all sin and misery. Every tear will be wiped away when evil is no more.

So we groan in pain because the painful is still painful. But we also groan in hope because we know what is to come. Hope is a positive expectation for something in the future as opposed to despair that sees only pain and hardship.[8] Biblically, hope has the power to encourage in the present because it is based on sure future expectations. Gabriel Marcel wrote, "Hope is a memory of the future."[9] This side of glory, we will not be fully redeemed and satisfied, but sorrow opens the heart to the desire for the hope of redemption to be fully realized.

PART THREE
Grace Accomplished

10

Sin, Violence, and Sexual Assault

In this chapter, we will explore what God says in Scripture about sexual assault and its effects. But before doing that, we must investigate what the Bible says about sin, evil, and violence. This is important because sexual assault is a result of sin, evil, and violence. Evil and sin work to infuse disgrace and violate peace. Sexual assault is a powerful means of achieving such destructive effects.

In the Beginning

The Bible begins with God, the sovereign, good creator of all things: "In the beginning, God created the heavens and the earth."[a] God's creative handiwork, everything from light to land to living creatures, is called "good."[b] But humanity, being the very image of God, is the crown of God's good creation ("behold, it was very good"[c]). As the pinnacle of God's creation, human beings reveal God more wonderfully than any other creature—as they were created to be like God,[d] by God,[e] for God,[f] and to be with God.[g]

In Genesis 1:26, God says "Let us make man in our image."[1] In the very beginning, our Creator gave us a remarkable title: he called us the image of God. This reveals the inherent dignity of all human beings.

To fully understand what "image of God" means, we need to look at the context of Old Testament history. Moses, the author of Genesis, and his Israelite readers understood these words because they lived in a world full of images. The most dominant images in the cultures of the

---

[a]Gen. 1:1.
[b]See the sevenfold use of "good": Gen. 1:4, 10, 12, 18, 21, 25, 31.
[c]Gen. 1:31.
[d]Gen. 1:26.
[e]Gen. 1:27.
[f]Gen. 2:15.
[g]Gen. 2:15.

ancient Near East were those of kings. Kings throughout the ancient world made images of themselves and placed them in various locations in their kingdoms. The pharaohs of Egypt, the emperors of Babylon, and the rulers of other empires used images of themselves as a way to display their authority and power. This custom of Moses' day helped him understand what was happening when God called Adam and Eve his image. Just as human kings had their images, the divine King ordained that the human race would be his royal image. Put simply, the expression "image of God" designated human beings as representatives of the supreme King of the universe.[2]

Immediately after making the man and woman, God granted them a special commission: "And God blessed them. And God said to them, 'Be fruitful and multiply and fill the earth and subdue it and have dominion over the fish of the sea and over the birds of the heavens and over every living thing that moves on the earth.'"[h] This verse contains five commands: "be fruitful," "multiply," "fill," "subdue," and "have dominion." These decrees reveal our most basic human responsibilities.

It was God's design that humanity should extend the reign of God throughout the world. This involves two basic responsibilities: multiplication and dominion. First, God gave Adam and Eve a commission to multiply: "Be fruitful . . . multiply . . . fill." Their job was to produce so many images of God that they would cover the earth. Second, God ordered them to have dominion over the earth: "fill . . . subdue . . . have dominion." Adam and Eve were to exercise authority over creation, managing its vast resources on God's behalf. Having dominion means being good stewards of creation and creators of culture—not dominating.[3]

Richard Pratt argues that multiplication and dominion are deeply connected to our being the image of God. To explain this, he describes the ancient Near Eastern context:

> Many kingdoms in the ancient Near East stretched for hundreds of square miles. The kings of these empires were powerful leaders, but the sizes of their domains presented serious political problems. . . . Ancient kings simply could not have personal contact with all regions of their nations. They needed other ways to establish their authority. Many rulers solved this problem by erecting images of themselves at key sites throughout their kingdoms. They produced numerous

---

[h]Gen. 1:28.

statues of themselves and endowed their images with representative authority. . . . When citizens saw the images of their emperor, they understood to whom they owed their allegiance. They knew for certain who ruled the land.[4]

Moses described the twofold job of humanity against this historical background. To be sure, God had no problem filling the earth with his presence, but he chose to establish his authority on earth in ways that humans could understand. Similar to how ancient emperors filled their empires with images of themselves, God commanded his images to populate the landscape of his creation. In the command to "multiply," God wanted his images to spread to the ends of the earth. Just as an emperor conferred authority on his images, God commanded his likeness to reign over the world. His command to "have dominion" is God giving humans authority to represent him in his world.[5]

Shalom and Violence

In Genesis 1 and 2, we see that God's plan for humanity was for the earth to be filled with his image bearers, who were to glorify him through worship and obedience. This beautiful state of being, enjoying the cosmic bliss of God's intended blessing and his wise rule, is called *shalom*. One scholar writes, "In the Bible, *shalom* means *universal flourishing, wholeness, and delight*—a rich state of affairs in which natural needs are satisfied and natural gifts fruitfully employed, a state of affairs that inspires joyful wonder as its Creator and Savior opens doors and welcomes the creatures in whom he delights. Shalom, in other words, is the way things ought to be."[6]

Shalom means fullness of peace. It is the vision of a society without violence or fear: "I will give peace (*shalom*) in the land, and you shall lie down, and none shall make you afraid."[i] *Shalom* is a profound and comprehensive sort of well-being—abundant welfare—with its connotations of peace, justice, and the common good. While it is "intertwined with justice," says Nicholas Wolterstorff, it is more than justice. In *Until Justice and Peace Embrace*, Wolterstorff argues that *shalom* means harmonious and responsible relationships with God, other human beings, and nature. In short, biblical writers use the word *shalom* to describe

---

[i] Lev. 26:6.

the world of universal peace, safety, justice, order, and wholeness God intended.[j7]

Genesis 3 records the terrible day when humanity fell into sin and *shalom* was violated. Adam and Eve violated their relationship with God by rebelling against his command. This was a moment of cosmic treason. Instead of trusting in God's wise and good word,[k] they trusted in the crafty and deceitful words of the Serpent.[l] In response, the Creator placed a curse on our parents that cast the whole human race into futility and death. The royal image of God fell into the severe ignobility we all experience.[8]

This tragic fall from grace into disgrace plunged humankind into a relational abyss. Paul Tripp writes:

> What seemed once unthinkably wrong and out of character for the world that God had made now became a daily experience. Words like falsehood, enemy, danger, sin, destruction, war, murder, sickness, fear, and hatred became regular parts of the fallen-world vocabulary. For the first time, the harmony between people was broken. Shame, fear, guilt, blame, greed, envy, conflict, and hurt made relationships a minefield they were never intended to be. People looked at other people as obstacles to getting what they wanted or as dangers to be avoided. Even families were unable to coexist in any kind of lasting and peaceful union. Violence became a common response to problems that had never before existed. Conflict existed in the human community as an experience more regular than peace. Marriage became a battle for control, and children's rebellion became a more natural response than willing submission. Things became more valuable than people, and they willingly competed with others in order to acquire more. The human community was more divided by love for self than united by love of neighbor. The words of people, meant to express truth and love, became weapons of anger and instruments of deceit. In an instant, the sweet music of human harmony had become the mournful dirge of human war.[9]

God's good creation is now cursed because of the entrance of sin.[m10] The world is simply not the way it's supposed to be. The entrance of sin

---

[j]Isa. 32:14–20.
[k]Gen. 2:16–17.
[l]Gen. 3:1–5.
[m]Gen. 3:14–24.

into God's good world leads to the shattering of *shalom*. Sin, in other words, is "culpable shalom-breaking."[11]

Evil is an intrusion upon *shalom*. The first intrusion was Satan's intrusion into God's garden, which led to Adam and Eve's tragic disobedience—the second intrusion. When sin is understood as an intrusion upon God's original plan for peace, it helps us see the biblical description of redemption as an intrusion of grace into disgrace or light into the darkness of sin or peace into disorder and violence. Just as sin and evil are an intrusion on original peace, so redemption is an intrusion of reclaiming what was originally intended for humans: peace.

Sin wrecks the order and goodness of God's world. Sin is the "vandalism of shalom."[12] Plantinga writes: "God hates sin not just because it violates his law but, more substantively, because it violates shalom, because it breaks the peace, because it interferes with the way things are supposed to be. God is for shalom and *therefore* against sin. In fact, we may safely describe evil as any spoiling of shalom, whether physically, morally, spiritually, or otherwise."[13]

Regarding this dimension of sin, Plantinga writes: "All sin has first and finally a Godward force. Let us say that *a* sin is any act—any thought, desire, emotion, word, or deed—or its particular absence, that displeases God and deserves blame. Let us add that the disposition to commit sins also displeases God and deserves blame, and let us therefore use the word *sin* to refer to such instances of both act and disposition. Sin is a culpable and personal affront to a personal God."[14]

God's image-bearers were created to worship and obey him and to reflect his glory to his good creation. According to G. K. Beale, "God has made humans to reflect him, but if they do not commit themselves to him, they will not reflect him but something else in creation. At the core of our beings we are imaging creatures. It is not possible to be neutral on this issue: we either reflect the Creator or something in creation."[15] After the fall, humankind was enslaved to idolatry (hatred for God) and violence (hatred for each other). Sin inverts love for God, which in turn becomes idolatry, and inverts love for neighbor, which becomes exploitation of others. Instead of worshiping God, our inclination is to worship anything else but God. Idolatry is not the ceasing of worship. Rather, it is misdirected worship, and at the core of idolatry is self-worship.

Instead of loving one another as God originally intended, fallen humanity expresses hatred toward their neighbors. Sin perverts mutual love and harmony, resulting in domination and violence against others.[16] Both the vertical relationship with God and the horizontal relationship with God's image-bearers are fractured by the fall. Evil is anti-creation, anti-life, and the force that seeks to oppose, deface, and destroy God, his good world, and his image-bearers. Simply put, when someone defaces a human being—God's image-bearer—ultimately an attack is being waged against God himself.

The foundational premise of the Bible after Genesis 3, therefore, is that this fallen world, particularly fallen humanity, is violent.[17] The cosmic war begun by the Serpent in Eden, described in Genesis 3, produces collateral damage in the very next chapter. Immediately after the fall, there is a radical shift from *shalom* to violence, as the first murder takes place in Genesis 4. After God shows regard to Abel's worshipful offering, Cain responds by raging against God and murdering his brother.[n] The downward spiral of humankind and the constant spread of sin continued as God's blessing is replaced by God's curse.[o]

Violence is sin against both God and his image-bearers. In our hatred for God, we hoard worship for self and strike against those who reflect God's glory. Cornelius Plantinga explains: "Godlessness is anti-shalom. Godlessness spoils the proper relation between human beings and their Maker and Savior. Sin offends God not only because it bereaves or assaults God directly, as in impiety or blasphemy, but also because it bereaves and assaults what God has made."[18]

A portion of the Old Testament is a catalog of cruelty. Widespread violence and the appalling evil of fallen humanity are recorded in detail on nearly every page of the Hebrew Bible:

> Acts of reprobate violence explode from the pages of the Old Testament as evil people perform unspeakable acts: Children are cannibalized (2 Kings 6:28–29; Ezek. 5:10; Lam. 2:20), boiled (Lam. 4:10), and dashed against a rock (Ps. 137:9). During the Babylonian invasion, Zedekiah is forced to watch his sons slaughtered, after which his own eyes are gouged out (Jer. 52:10–11). Pregnant women are ripped open (2 Kings 15:16; Amos 1:13). Other women are raped (Gen. 34:1–5; 1 Sam. 13:1–15; Ezek. 22:11); one of them is gang raped to the point of death

---

[n]Gen. 4:4–5, 8.
[o]The word "curse" occurs five times in Genesis 3–11: 3:14, 17; 4:11; 5:29; 9:25.

(Judg. 19:22–30). Military atrocities are equally shocking. We read about stabbings (Judg. 3:12–20; 2 Sam. 2:23; 20:10) and beheadings (1 Sam. 17:54; 2 Sam. 4:7–9). These are normal military atrocities. More extraordinary cases involve torture and mutilation: limbs are cut off (Judg. 1:6–7), bodies hewed in pieces (1 Sam. 15:33), eyes gouged out (Judg. 16:21; 2 Kings 25:7), skulls punctured (Judg. 4:12–23; 5:26–27) or crushed by a millstone pushed from a city wall (Judg. 9:53). Two hundred foreskins are collected (1 Sam. 18:27), seventy heads gathered (2 Kings 10:7–8), thirty men killed for their clothing (Judg. 14:19). Bodies are hanged (Josh. 8:29), mutilated and displayed as trophies (1 Sam. 31:9–10), trampled beyond recognition (2 Kings 9:30–37), destroyed by wild beasts (Josh. 13:8; 2 Kings 2:23–24) or flailed with briers (Judg. 8:16). Entire groups are massacred (1 Sam. 22:18–19; 1 Kings 16:8–14) or led into captivity strung together with hooks through their lips (Amos 4:2).[19]

Sin and Sexual Assault

We have seen how violence is a bitter fruit of the fall and is, without question, a "vandalism of shalom." In biblical thinking, we can understand neither *shalom* nor sin apart from reference to God. David confesses to God, "Against you, you only, have I sinned and done what is evil in your sight, so that you may be justified in your words and blameless in your judgment."[p] Despite committing adultery with Bathsheba and orchestrating the murder of her husband, Uriah, David can write that he has sinned against God "only."[q] David's sins against other human beings were also, in the ultimate sense, transgressions committed against God himself. According to Plantinga, "Shalom is God's design for creation and redemption; sin is blamable human vandalism of these great realities and therefore an affront to their architect and builder."[20]

Sexual assault is a vandalization of *shalom*. It can influence how victims feel about themselves, how they understand connections and boundaries with others, and ultimately, how they relate to God. Throughout the Bible, the conception of sexual assault is that it has devastating emotional and psychological consequences for the victim.[r]

Sexual violence uses sex as a weapon of power and control against

---

[p] Ps. 51:4.
[q] See 2 Samuel 11.
[r] Deut. 22:25–29; Judg. 19:22–25; 20:5; and 2 Sam. 13:12, 22, and 32 are a few places where sexual coercion is depicted in the Bible.

others. Sex is the means by which we fulfill our calling of multiplying and taking dominion. It is noteworthy that the very means of fulfilling God's plan for humanity is now a tool for violence toward other images of God. In *shalom*, sex was also a reflection of unity and peace between man and woman. It is a picture of two becoming one.

God meant for sexual feelings, thoughts, and activity to give pleasure and build intimacy in marriage. Satan understands the importance of what God has designed, and sexual assault is one of his chief means of destroying it. Sexual abuse creates in the victim's mind a tragic and perverse linkage between sex, intimacy, and shame. When someone is sexually violated, one of the most creative and intimate of human experiences—sexuality—is transgressed by violence and subjugation.

Sex, the very expression of human union, intimacy, and peace, becomes a tool for violence after the fall. Plantinga writes: "The story of the fall tells us that sin corrupts: it puts asunder what God had joined together and joins together what God had put asunder. Like some devastating twister, corruption both explodes and implodes creation, pushing it back toward the 'formless void' from which it came."[21] Violence is also the outworking and fruit of idolatry as humans have inherent dignity as the image of God. One scholar notes:

> The Old Testament records some horrific incidents of sexual violence: when people are alienated from God, depravity and violence are inevitable. Biblical stories of rape are infrequent but vivid, including the story of Dinah's rape and the resulting sexual retaliation by her brothers (Genesis 34), the abuse to death of the Levite's concubine (Judges 19) and Amnon's rape of his sister Tamar (2 Samuel 13:1–21). In a similar vein are pictures in the prophetic books of the ravishing of wives and virgins as the aftermath of a nation's being conquered (Isaiah 13:16; Lamentations 5:11; Zechariah 14:2).[22]

Sexual violence distorts this beautiful act of union, pleasure, calling, and worship. God intended humankind to "be fruitful and multiply,"[5] spreading divine image-bearers throughout his good world. This multiplying of offspring and exercising of dominion was to happen through the God-ordained sexual union between man and woman, husband and wife, in the context of marriage: "Therefore a man shall

---

[5]Gen. 1:28.

leave his father and his mother and hold fast to his wife, and they shall become one flesh. And the man and his wife were both naked and were not ashamed."[t]

This peaceful, loving relationship was shattered by the entrance of sin into the world. Instead of unashamed intimacy and trust, there is shame and mistrust. Instead of grace, there is disgrace. Hatred toward other divine image-bearers, not love, characterizes human life after the fall:

> As soon as human rebellion and self-assertiveness reared their ugly heads, shame, guilt and self-consciousness took over. Pathetic attempts at self-concealment (Gen 3:7) are replaced by God's own provision of covering (Gen 3:21). Henceforth nakedness was unnatural. Clothing is God's covering, his divine gracious response to human rebellion. Being unclothed thus becomes a metaphor for being exposed to the judgment of God.[23]

A foundational element of paradise—sexual innocence in community—has been spoiled by the treachery of sexual assault. Sexual assault is uniquely devastating precisely because it distorts the foundational realities of what it means to be human: embodied personhood is plundered, sexual expression is perverted and used for violence, intrapersonal trust is shattered, and disgrace and shame are heaped on the victim.

Sexual assault is one of the most frequent and disturbing symbols of sin in the Bible. It is a complete distortion of relationship, a mockery and devastation of the original intent of being made for relationships with God and others. References to sexual violence is a way that God, through the biblical authors, communicates that sin has progressed so far that sex, an expression of union, peace, and love, is now used as a tool for violence.

The betrayal of creation and the refusal of any sense of covenantal relationship, sexual assault physically, emotionally, culturally, and structurally wounds the victim. Sexual assault is not just a criminal, physical, and psychological act; it is also a spiritual act in which the connectedness of humans with one another and with God is violated and broken, and the reality of defilement, guilt, terror, shame, alienation, and separation can take years to be made whole again.

---

[t]Gen. 2:24–25.

Sin names the reality of sexual assault, and assault in turn symbolizes sin and its destructive effects. The Bible speaks about the reality and effects of sin in various ways: disease, burden, debt, and defilement. Sexual assault is another way to speak of sin, in both its reality and effects. Sexual assault both names and symbolizes that sin is not only something that is done to us but also carries the effects of defilement, woundedness, and terror.

Sin is broken relationships with God, self, and others, and sexual assault signifies, even as it causes, brokenness and disruption. Sexual assault reminds us of the double-sidedness of so much sin: it is both personal and cultural. Sexual assault is an individual act of violence, one person against another. But it's also cultural: it is used as a weapon in warfare,[24] and it's an epidemic in nearly all cultures.[25]

There appears to be a societal impulse to blame traumatized individuals for their suffering. Alexander McFarlane and Bessel van der Kolk suggest that doing otherwise would threaten our cherished conceptions that the world is essentially just and that persons are free, self-determining, and basically good individuals responsible for their destinies:

> Society becomes resentful about having its illusions of safety and predictability ruffled by people who remind them of how fragile security can be. Society's reactions [to traumatized people] seems to be . . . in the service of maintaining the beliefs that the world is fundamentally just, that people can be in charge of their lives, and that bad things only happen to people who deserve them.[26]

In short, we sacrifice those who suffer so we can maintain our illusions of autonomy and safety.

The distress caused by sexual assault can be described well by Simone Weil's term "affliction." An event constitutes "affliction" if it has uprooted and attacked someone in all dimensions: physically, psychologically, and socially. Since affliction involves "social degradation or the fear of it in some form," it can be argued that one of the factors involved in affliction includes some form of interpersonal neglect or harm.[27] If victims were offered sufficient social support, they could be spared from the kind of suffering that constitutes affliction.

Marie Fortune describes sexual assault four different ways. First, it is a bodily sin. Sexual assault is a violation of bodily boundaries of personal space and distorts one's sense of body image. Second, sexual assault is a sin against relationship, violating the command to love one's neighbors as oneself. Third, it is a sin betraying trust and destroying relationships between victims and those who should have cared for them but instead caused them harm. The consequence of this sin is that it creates barriers of trust for victims in their future relationships. Fourth, it is a sin against not only the victims but also the community surrounding those victims.[28]

It is obvious that sexual assault is a sin against another human involving physical, psychological, and emotional violation through the commission of a nonconsensual sexual act imposed through coercion, intimidation, force, domination, and violence. Such an act entails not only a violation of the physical boundaries of the body, but also a denial of the victim's will or agency—one dimension of being the image of God.

Through sexual assault, the assailant aims to reduce the victim to a nonperson. Because the assault is bodily, it is sexed, and the scope of its harm includes the very personhood of the victim. The dominance inherent in an act of sexual assault, by which the assailant forces his/her incarnate will on the victim, is a hierarchical structure in which the victim's difference from the assailant is stamped out, erased, and annihilated.[29]

This aspect of sexual assault involves the violation of the victim both bodily and mentally. By constraining the victim and disregarding, disbelieving, or deliberately acting contrary to her or his desires, the transgressor undermines the victim's sense of personhood.[30] Such acts of violence often result in emotional trauma for the victim, which is manifest in a sense of helplessness, loss, vulnerability, shame, humiliation, and degradation.[31] A particularly evil effect of sexual assault is that some victims not only feel a sense of radical disgrace, but also participate in their own self-destruction.[32] The self-hatred, defilement, and guilt they experience cause them to act out self-destructively.

Violence ensnares the psyche of the victim and propels its action in the form of defensive reaction. This is one of the most insidious aspects of violence. In addition to inflicting harm, the practice of evil keeps re-creating a world of violence, either against others or oneself.

Evil generates new evil as evildoers fashion victims in their own ugly image. In addition to being a sin against others, sexual assault is also a sin against God because the blessing of sexuality is used to destroy instead of build intimacy. It is an attack against his image in his imager-bearers. The ability of sexual assault to obscure internal and external relationships makes it a cosmic affront to the Creator and the order of his creation.[u][33] Sexual assault is a sin against God because it violates his most sacred creation, human beings made in his image.

There are explicit passages calling sexual assault sin—a violation of God's law. Deuteronomy 22:25–29 addresses nonconsensual sexual acts and shows concern for the welfare of the violated woman. In Deuteronomy 22:25–27, the perpetrator is put to death by stoning, and it is stressed in the text that the woman is innocent of any wrongdoing and that no harm should come to her.[34]

In addition to these and other biblical texts calling sexual assault sin, there are also depictions of sexual acts that the Bible characterizes as sexual assault resulting in emotional trauma. These passages are 2 Samuel 13, Hosea 2:1–13, Jeremiah 13:20–27, and Ezekiel 16 and 23. They demonstrate an understanding that such acts of sexual assault result not only in emotional trauma for the victim, but also in humiliation and a debilitating loss of sense of self. These passages depict sexual assault as deeply traumatizing and resulting in devastating emotional and psychological consequences for the victim.

The Bible says that sexual assault is wrong, should not be done, and is not something the victims should experience. It also claims that God sees, knows, and cares about this sin and its effects, and has acted to redeem people from its effects.

Transgression against God and Victim

Far from being a peripheral issue in the Bible, sexual assault is clearly depicted as sin against God and neighbor, mentioned frequently throughout the Bible, and referred to as a symbol of how badly sin has corrupted God's good creation.

The Bible confirms the effects of sexual assault we described in chapter 3. On what the Bible says about sexual assault, Hilary Lipka

---

[u]Gen. 6:1–3.

writes: "A comprehensive study that includes all biblical texts reveals that there is evidence not only of a core conception of rape, but also an understanding that sexual violence is devastating for the victim, resulting in emotional trauma and a debilitating loss of sense of self."[35]

We have seen in this chapter that sexual assault is a sin against the victim and a sin against God. However, it is very difficult in the Bible to distinguish the difference between the transgression against the victim and the transgression against God. It is so difficult that some scholars assert that there is no distinction between these two aspects of transgression. Sexual assault is always a sin against the victim and God because all crimes are depicted as sins, that is, violations of God's will and the reflection of his glory in others.[36]

The victim's experience of assault is not ignored by God, minimized by the Bible, or outside of the scope of healing and hope found in redemption. God's response to evil and violence is redemption, renewal, and re-creation. Evil and violence are not the final word. They are not capable of creating or defining reality. That is God's prerogative alone. However, evil and violence can pervert, distort, and destroy. They are parasitic on the original good of God's creation. In this way evil serves as the backdrop on the stage where God's redemption shines with even greater brilliance and pronounced drama. What evil uses to destroy, God uses to expose, excise, and then heal.[37]

God's redemption imparts grace and brings peace. We turn to God's redemption in the next two chapters.

11

Grace in the Old Testament

In the previous chapter, we saw the effects of the vandalism to *shalom* as generally expressed in violence and as it is specifically expressed in sexual violence. While the fall brought a curse upon creation, God did not leave his image-bearers to rot under its effects forever without hope of rescue. Before the fall, Adam and Eve were "both naked and unashamed." Post-fall, however, nudity is sheer vulnerability. More than polite embarrassment, shame implied the danger of physical exploitation and humiliation. We see this as Adam's shame soon festers into Noah's exploitation.[1] Nakedness and exploitation mark the earliest characters in Genesis and are traced throughout as a symbol of the depth of the effects of sin.

Originally, Adam and Eve were naked without shame,[a] enjoying open harmony with each other and God. Post-fall, however, they recognized that they were naked and ashamed—no longer holy and righteous. They were morally defiled because of sin.

From the very beginning, God made provisions through establishing sacrifices to deal with guilt from sin. After Adam and Eve disobeyed, they realized they were guilty and tried to cover themselves with fig leaves. God replaced their leaves with garments made from animal skins. Bible scholars refer to this as the first sacrifice in the Bible. A life had to be sacrificed before Adam and Eve were clothed.

E. J. Young, an Old Testament scholar, writes, "It would also appear that this act of God in the taking of animal life laid the foundation for animal sacrifice."[2] In this passage we see the pattern for all salvation history. God took a sacrificial animal (probably a lamb), slew it before the eyes of Adam and Eve, and wrapped the skins about their naked bodies. At that time, God gave them instructions about sacrifice and

---

[a]Gen. 2:25.

the covering of sins. The animal was God's gift. He furnished the skins to cover Adam and Eve. Since his first covering of guilt and shame, God has always provided his people with adequate covering for them to stand before him.[3]

God did not desert them to the futility of sin's harsh dominion. Even before covering them, God declared a plan to redeem them from sin and death: "And I will put enmity between you and the woman, and between your offspring and hers; he will crush your head, and you will strike his heel."[b] This declaration is about the hope for redemption, but notice the violence it involves—enmity, crushing, and striking.

Martin Luther called Genesis 3:15 the "proto-evangelion"—the first gospel announcement and promise concerning Jesus Christ. At first glance, a curse against God's enemy—the Serpent—may not seem like amazing grace. But this verse reveals God's plans to redeem humanity by his victory over Satan. The Serpent will continue to trouble Eve's descendants, constantly nipping at their heels, but one day the offspring of Eve will crush Satan's head in glorious victory.

This redemptive plan has unfolded through the history of the Old Testament and was fulfilled in the cross and resurrection of Jesus Christ. The New Testament tells us that this wondrous destiny is ultimately realized in Christ, the greatest child of Eve. In his death, Christ destroyed Satan: "Since therefore the children share in flesh and blood, he himself likewise partook of the same things, that through death he might destroy the one who has the power of death, that is, the devil."[c]

When Christ rose from the dead he gained victory over death: "'Death is swallowed up in victory.' 'O death, where is your victory? O death, where is your sting?' The sting of death is sin, and the power of sin is the law. But thanks be to God, who gives us the victory through our Lord Jesus Christ."[d]

The final victory over Satan and the curse of death will occur when God's redeemed people inherit the new heavens and new earth. As Paul told the Romans, "The God of peace will soon crush Satan under your feet."[e] Christ will lead his people to glory even as Adam led us into death.

---

[b]Gen. 3:15 NIV.
[c]Heb. 2:14.
[d]1 Cor. 15:54b–57.
[e]Rom. 16:20.

Although Christ's ultimate victory over the grave is a future event, God in his grace has not deserted the human race to the horrors of futility and death. The testimony of Scripture is clear. Christ is the climax of a long historical process. God granted rich blessings in the exodus, the Day of Atonement, and the prophetic promises of the Messiah. He paved a way for his fallen image-bearers to receive foretastes of the restoration and dignity Christ will give to his people.

The Bible attests again and again to God's persistence and desire for the redemption of his people: "God wants shalom and will pay any price to get it back. Human sin is stubborn, but not as stubborn as the grace of God and not half so persistent, not half so ready to suffer to win its way."[4]

God expresses grace to his people in his willingness to suffer for the sake of *shalom*: "Before the Fall the experience of wholeness flowed naturally from unhindered fellowship between Adam and Eve and between them and God. Afterward the experience of wholeness with God requires the grace of God . . . because of violence within and without."[5]

Separation from God and one another is a feature of the fallen order, whereas union with God and others is an essential feature of the gospel. Moving forward, we will explore the Bible for the unfolding themes of violence and redemption—or disgrace and grace.

Violence after the Promise

After the fall, the human capacity to injure others is consistently greater than the ability to show neighborly love. The raging cataract of violence that fills the pages of the primeval history in Genesis reaches a culmination in the flood narrative (Gen. 6:9–8:22): "The LORD saw that the wickedness of man was great in the earth, and that every intention of the thoughts of his heart was only evil continually."[f] Instead of the original "good" creation, we read that God's world was "corrupt in God's sight, and the earth was filled with violence."[g]

It was "violence" that intruded upon and violated God's creation (Gen. 6:11, 13) and pained his heart.[h] The "violence" and corruption (Gen. 6:11) refer to cruelty, oppression, and moral perversion. Stephen Dempster writes: "The world has become a frightful place under the rule of sin. The magnificent creation that once elicited the seven-fold

[f]Gen. 6:5.
[g]Gen. 6:11.
[h]Gen. 6:6.

'it is good' has become a house of horrors. The creation is being raped by a humanity engaging in widespread evil."[6] In response to this, God determines to un-create his fallen creation through the judgment of the flood (Gen. 6:7, 17).

Redemption and the Flood

Even on this dark canvas of violence shine the bright colors of God's merciful redemption. God graciously spares Noah, who found grace and favor in his eyes (Gen. 6:8), but after the flood, we still read of the negative effects of sin. Even amid God's blessing of Noah we find the effects of the curse still remain.

The Flood as a Divine Re-Creation

Genesis 1–3	Genesis 9
God blesses humankind: "Be fruitful and multiply and fill the earth" (1:28).	God blesses Noah: "Be fruitful and multiply and fill the earth" (9:1).
God plants a garden for humans to enjoy (2:8).	Noah plants a vineyard / orchard (9:20).
Adam and Eve eat of the fruit and become naked (2:25; 3:6–7).	Noah eats the fruit of his vineyard and becomes naked (9:21).
Adam and Eve cover the shame of their nakedness (3:7, 21).	Shem and Japheth cover the shame of Noah's nakedness (9:23).
A curse (3:14–19).	Blessing and a curse (9:25–27).

If the flood is an act of divine "de-creation" against human rebellion and sin, it is also an act of divine "re-creation" because of God's original good purpose. According to Paul Williamson,

> The climax of the flood narrative is best understood in terms of a "re-creation"—a restoration of the divine order and God's visible kingship that had been established at creation. . . . The earth is made inhabitable by the separation of the land from the water (Gen. 8:1–3; cf. Gen. 1:9–10). Living creatures are brought out to repopulate the earth (Gen. 8:17–19; cf. Gen. 1:20–22, 24–25). Days and seasons are reestablished (Gen. 8:22; cf. Gen. 1:14–18). Humans are blessed by God (Gen. 9:1; cf. Gen. 1:28a), commanded to "Be fruitful and multiply, and fill the earth" (Gen. 9:1b, 7; cf. Gen. 1:28b), and given dominion over the animal kingdom (Gen. 9:2; cf. Gen. 1:28c). God provides humanity—

made in his image (Gen. 9:6; cf. Gen. 1:26–27)—with food (Gen. 9:3; cf. Gen. 1:29-30).[7]

The message of the flood narrative is clear. Even in this fallen world, God can make all things new. Human depravity cannot stop God's steadfast love from blessing, saving, and restoring all those who trust in him. Despite the actions of sinful people, God's will is accomplished. His good purposes cannot be thwarted. This is seen clearly in the Genesis 9 narrative: immediately following the flood, God makes a covenant with Noah and his offspring (Gen. 9:8–11).

Noah, much like Abraham after him, represents a new beginning for humanity through God's gift of the covenant. Williamson writes: "The glue that binds all the biblical covenants together is God's creative purpose of universal blessing. Each of the subsequent covenants simply takes us one step closer towards the realization of that divine goal."[8] The redemption of God's people is rooted in God's covenantal faithfulness, his enduring steadfast love or *hesed*. *Hesed* is God's lovingkindness—"the consistent, ever-faithful, relentless, constantly pursuing, lavish, extravagant, unrestrained, one-way love of God."[9] It is often translated as covenant love, loving-kindness, mercy, steadfast love, loyal love, devotion, commitment, or reliability. In the Bible, God describes himself as having an overwhelming and abundant "steadfast love and faithfulness" toward his people. *Hesed* and grace describes God's goodness, love, mercy, and kindness toward his people without regard to their deeds and in spite of what they deserve.[10]

Hesed is the foundation for God's redemption and is seen throughout the entire Bible, especially in the psalms.[i] The most repeated phrase used in praising God—"his steadfast love endures forever"—includes the idea of God's covenantal faithfulness, even if the word *hesed* is not present.[j] This means that the foundation of faith in God is God's enduring love for his people.

God's love moves him to compassion for his people. God's acts of redemption are motivated by his love and compassion. He *feels* his people's suffering.[k] God's love implies his jealousy for his people as he pours out wrath on their sin and the sin that is done against them.

---

[i]Ps. 44:26; 92:1–2; 103:17–18; 106:44–45; 143:12.
[j]Ps. 92:12; 106:1; 107:1; 118:1; 136:1–26; 1 Chron. 16:34; 2 Chron. 20:21.
[k]Ps. 103: 9–14; Jer. 3:19; Jeremiah 30 and 31; Isa. 14:1; 49:14–16; 54:7–8; 63:16; 66:16; Hos. 11:8–9.

Redemption and the Exodus

Violence and redemption meet again in the exodus, the greatest divine act of salvation in the Old Testament. According to Dempster, "the story of the Exodus is the central salvation event in the Old Testament. The account of the liberation of a band of Hebrew slaves from horrific oppression in Egypt is the event that shaped virtually everything in the biblical imagination."[11]

The exodus brings three redemptive themes together: God compassionately responding to his people by freeing them from their bondage, atoning for sins in the Passover, and fighting against their enemy. These are all based on his promise to be their God and for them to be his people (Ex. 6:7; 25:8; 29:45–46).

The violence and redemption narratives in Exodus occur because of God's *hesed* for his people. This is clearly proclaimed in Exodus 34:6–7: "The LORD, the LORD, a God merciful and gracious, slow to anger, and abounding in steadfast love and faithfulness, keeping steadfast love for thousands, forgiving iniquity and transgression and sin, but who will by no means clear the guilty." It's precisely because of his *hesed* for his suffering people that God violently conquers their enemy.

Redemption and grace are central to understanding the themes of the exodus. Dempster writes: "Exodus language becomes the grammar used to express future salvation. Whether it is Hosea speaking of Israel going up from the land (Hos 1:11), Isaiah of leading the people through the sea again (Isa 11:15), Micah of Yahweh leading an exodus of crippled and outcasts (Mic 4:6–7), Jeremiah of a new covenant (Jeremiah 31–34), the Exodus language of salvation is the way Israel construed its understanding of the future. . . . Without this Exodus grammar it becomes virtually impossible to understand the language of the Bible."[12]

The narrative begins with God's people languishing in Egypt, enslaved to a murderous dictator,[l] and seemingly abandoned by their God. Yet God is "merciful and gracious, slow to anger, and abounding in steadfast love (*hesed*) and faithfulness."[m] And at their time of greatest need, God heard Israel's desperate cries for help. The covenant had not been forgotten: "Israel groaned because of their slavery and cried out for help. Their cry for rescue from slavery came up to God. And God heard

---

[l] Ex. 1:22.
[m] Ex. 34:6.

their groaning, and God remembered his covenant with Abraham, with Isaac, and with Jacob."[n] In this passage, God shows more personal knowledge of his people, more compassion for those suffering, and more faithfulness to his promises to his people, than any one of them could muster for themselves. Redemption focuses on God's love (*hesed*) and not self-love.

The author of Exodus makes an explicit connection back to the God of the patriarchs. This means that God is a covenant-keeping God. He is the God of the patriarchs, "the God of Abraham, the God of Isaac, and the God of Jacob."[o] God "remembered" his covenant pledge to Israel, just as he had also graciously "remembered" Noah,[p] Abraham,[q] and Rachel,[r] in their times of greatest distress. This covenantal "remembrance" is intended to produce hope: "Israel's presence in Egypt is no product of chance. The Israelites in Egypt are to view their present suffering and oppression in light of God's larger, unchanging picture. God chose a people for himself and brought them down into Egypt. He will bring them out again."[13]

In spite of major opposition from Pharaoh and "in the midst of the horrific genocide in Egypt, a child is born that is preserved from the holocaust. Moses is saved from the water and will eventually save his people from the water."[14] Moses, God's chosen deliverer, escapes death by being placed in an ark (same Hebrew word used for Noah's ark[s]) in the Nile River.[t] So the deliverance of Moses from the deadly waters not only looks back to God's redemption of Noah but it also foreshadows a greater saving work yet to come in the exodus narrative when God saves his people at the Red Sea.

In the exodus, God is depicted as a divine Warrior, completely sovereign and mighty to save. This story of God's people being delivered from the hands of their oppressors is filled with violence. This is a continued unfolding of the Genesis 3:15 promise. D. G. Reid writes:

> God's conquest of the Egyptian army in the Exodus event shapes an archetypal image of salvation in the Bible. It is a portrait of divine and

---

[n] Ex. 2:23–25.
[o] Ex. 4:5; cf. 3:16.
[p] Gen. 8:1.
[q] Gen. 19:29.
[r] Gen. 30:22.
[s] Gen. 6:14.
[t] Ex. 2:1–10 KJV.

redemptive violence in which God shows himself to be a divine warrior, superior to the powerful gods of Egypt (Exod. 15) and overthrowing the proud and mighty on behalf of the weak and the oppressed. Yet the Genesis story of Israel's descent into Egypt is fraught with violence within the patriarchal family (Gen. 37:12–36; *cf.* also Gen. 38; 49:5).[15]

However, this image of God's greatness and strength is not what the narrator focuses his attention on in the beginning of the story. The Lord, the God who keeps his covenant, is merciful and compassionate. In Israel's bleakest hour, amidst genocidal oppression, God mercifully remembers his covenant promises and draws near to his people.

> Not only does God *hear*, God also *sees*. And out of hearing and seeing, God *knows* the suffering of the people. These three words are repeated: first the narrator uses them in Exodus 2:24–25, and then God affirms them of himself in Exodus 3:7: "I have indeed *seen* the affliction of my people in Egypt. I have *heard* their outcry because of their slave-masters, and I *know* their sufferings."[16]

The Almighty sympathizes with the groans of his people. Another scholar writes, "God is not such a transcendent being as to be exalted above engagement with people. . . . God gets involved with their suffering."[17]

After remembering his gracious promises to Abraham, God responds by calling Moses to be the chosen deliverer of his covenant people.[u] God says to Moses:

> I have surely seen the affliction of my people who are in Egypt and have heard their cry because of their taskmasters. I know their sufferings, and I have come down to deliver them out of the hand of the Egyptians and to bring them up out of that land to a good and broad land, a land flowing with milk and honey. . . . And now, behold, the cry of the people of Israel has come to me, and I have also seen the oppression with which the Egyptians oppress them. Come, I will send you to Pharaoh that you may bring my people, the children of Israel, out of Egypt.[v]

God's rescue mission begins as Moses returns to Egypt and confronts Pharaoh. But instead of releasing the enslaved people of Israel,

---

[u]Ex. 3:1–4:31.
[v]Ex. 3:7–10.

the king of Egypt increases their labor.[w] Yet, the cruelty of Pharaoh proves no match for the omnipotent mercies of the Creator who commands Moses to declare to all of Israel:

> I am the LORD, and I will bring you out from under the burdens of the Egyptians, and I will deliver you from slavery to them, and I will redeem you with an outstretched arm and with great acts of judgment. I will take you to be my people, and I will be your God, and you shall know that I am the LORD your God, who has brought you out from under the burdens of the Egyptians. I will bring you into the land that I swore to give to Abraham, to Isaac, and to Jacob. I will give it to you for a possession. I am the LORD.[x]

God then performs ten devastating plagues upon Egypt.[y] The culminating plague takes the life of every Egyptian firstborn son and persuades the hard-hearted Pharaoh to finally release his captives.[z] The purpose of these plagues was not to destroy but, rather, to display.[aa] God displays his righteous judgment against the hostile powers opposed to his people and his good purposes. He also demonstrates his magnificent saving power to all the earth.[ab] The plundering of Egypt,[ac] the parting of the Red Sea,[ad] and the destruction of Pharaoh's pursuing army[ae] inspire a song of praise for the triumphant God of Israel:[af] "Your right hand, O LORD, glorious in power, your right hand, O LORD, shatters the enemy."[ag] Out of sheer grace, God responded to the cries of his needy people and saved them to the uttermost.

According to Christopher Wright,

> In the exodus God responded to *all* the dimensions of Israel's need. God's momentous act of redemption did not merely rescue Israel from political, economic, and social oppression and then leave them to their own devices to worship whom they pleased. Nor did God

---

[w]Ex. 5:1–18.
[x]Ex. 6:6–8.
[y]Ex. 7:1–12:36.
[z]Ex. 12:29–32.
[aa]See Ex. 9:16; Isa. 19:16–25.
[ab]Rom. 9:17.
[ac]Ex. 12:35–36.
[ad]Ex. 14:1–22.
[ae]Ex. 14:23–31.
[af]Ex. 15:1–21.
[ag]Ex. 15:6.

merely offer them spiritual comfort of hope for some brighter future in a home beyond the sky while leaving their historical condition unchanged. No, the exodus effected real change in the people's real historical situation and at the same time called them into a real new relationship with the living God. This was God's total response to Israel's total need.[18]

Later biblical writers reflect upon the exodus as the paradigm of God's gracious salvation. Isaiah 43:1–3 reads as a poem of remembrance of God's redemption:

> Fear not, for I have redeemed you; I have called you by name, you are mine. When you pass through the waters, I will be with you; and through the rivers, they shall not overwhelm you; when you walk through fire you shall not be burned, and the flame shall not consume you. For I am the LORD your God, the Holy One of Israel, your Savior.

At the heart of the exodus lies God's costly and saving grace. And the pinnacle of this grace is the Passover.

Passover

Right before God delivered his people from their bitter bondage in Egypt through the exodus, he instituted a sacrifice—the Passover.[19] According to Dempster, "the Passover is the *climax* in a titanic battle that is waged between the God of Israel and the gods of Egypt."[20] This battle reflects the original conflict between God and Satan in Genesis 3:15—the proto-evangelion.

According to God's instruction to Moses, every Israelite household was to select a year-old, unblemished, male lamb and slaughter it at twilight.[ah] Morris notes that the "animal was to be roasted whole and eaten that night, together with bitter herbs and bread made without yeast."[21] God tells Moses, "They shall take some of the blood and put it on the two doorposts and the lintel of the houses in which they eat it.... The blood shall be a sign for you, on the houses where you are. And when I see the blood, I will pass over you, and no plague will befall you to destroy you, when I strike the land of Egypt."[ai] Only those who are

---

[ah]Ex. 12:5, 6, 21.
[ai]Ex. 12:7, 13.

covered in the blood of the lamb would be saved. "The Passover lamb functioned as a penal substitute, dying in the place of the firstborn sons of the Israelites, in order that they might escape the wrath of God."[22] The shedding of blood averted divine punishment. Moses believed God's promise. He walked by faith. And he was spared. "By faith he [Moses] kept the Passover and sprinkled the blood, so that the Destroyer of the firstborn might not touch them."[aj]

In this one act of bloody sacrifice, through the slaying of a spotless lamb, God's people were protected from his wrath and consecrated to his holiness. The celebration of the Passover was to remain an annual reminder to Israel of the greatest act of redemption in their storied history. Successive generations were to remember what God had done in their midst: "And when your children say to you, 'What do you mean by this service?' you shall say, 'It is the sacrifice of the LORD's Passover, for he passed over the houses of the people of Israel in Egypt, when he struck the Egyptians but spared our houses.'"[ak]

Dempster notes that this is the "second time in the larger storyline that a firstborn son is spared by the spilling of sacrificial blood (cf. Genesis 22). The narrative awaits a time when such a son will not be so fortunate, but whose spilled blood will save the world, not just a nation."[23]

Redemption and the Day of Atonement

God's presence with his people is a theme that can be traced in the Bible from cover to cover, all the way from Eden[al] to the new heaven and the new earth.[am] Not surprisingly, it is also a major theme in Exodus. During their wilderness wanderings, the Lord went ahead of Israel and guided the nation with a pillar of cloud by day and a pillar of fire by night.[an] God also manifested his holy presence on Sinai at the giving of the law.[ao]

Yet God's holy presence is problematic when sinful people draw near to him. Morris notes: "Approach to God was a tricky business in the days of Moses and Aaron. On the one hand it was the greatest of blessings and nobody wanted to be without God's promised presence. . . . But

---

[aj]Heb. 11:28.
[ak]Ex. 12:26–27.
[al]Genesis 2–3.
[am]Revelation 21.
[an]Ex. 13:21–22.
[ao]Exodus 19.

on the other hand God was awe inspiring and powerful. To approach him in the wrong way might be disaster."[ap][24]

How can a holy and righteous God dwell in the midst of a sinful and unclean people? The resolution to this problem comes in the book of Leviticus where we learn that the "relationship between a holy God and a sinful people can be maintained by sacrifice."[25] And the central sacrifice in the book of Leviticus is the Day of Atonement.

The Day of Atonement was the climax of the Old Testament sacrificial system and was a day of great bloodshed in which the gravity of humanity's sin could be seen visibly. Because of its importance, it eventually became referred to simply as "the Day."

The primary section in Scripture concerning the Day of Atonement appears in Leviticus 16–17. This passage functions as the center of the book of Leviticus, which itself is the center of the Pentateuch:

> [Leviticus 16] is like a hinge for the whole book of Leviticus. It brings to a climax all the preceding chapters about priestly duties in relation to sacrifice and to the diagnosis and treatment of uncleanness. The Day of Atonement provided an annual opportunity to "wipe the slate clean" by cleansing both the sanctuary and the people of all the defilements that had not been noticed and dealt with routinely. Fixed in the annual calendar exactly six months after the spring Passover, which celebrated the unique historical event of Israel's redemption, it provided the ongoing means of cleansing God's redeemed people so that he could continue to dwell among them.[26]

On this day, and on this day alone, the high priest would enter the Holy of Holies to atone for the sins of Israel in order to avert the holy wrath of God for the sins of the past year and to remove their sin and its stain from them. Two healthy goats without defect were chosen. They were therefore fit to represent sinless perfection.

The first goat was a propitiating sin offering. The high priest slaughtered this goat, which acted as a substitute for the sinners who deserved a violently bloody death for their many sins. Atonement and blood sacrifice are wedded in the book of Leviticus: "For the life of the flesh is in the blood, and I have given it for you on the altar to make atonement for your souls, for it is the blood that makes atone-

---

[ap]See Lev. 10:1.

ment by the life."[aq] Commenting on this verse, David Peterson writes: "Atonement here is not simply a matter of removing guilt or defilement by purging, but averting the wrath of God by offering the life of a substitute."[27] The substitutionary nature of the sacrifice is clear.

Then the high priest, acting as the representative and mediator between the sinful people and their holy God, would take the second goat and lay his hands on the animal while confessing the sins of the people. This goat, called the scapegoat (i.e., escape goat) would then be sent away to die in the wilderness away from the sinners, symbolically expiating or removing the sins of the people by taking them away. "The goat shall bear all their iniquities on itself to a remote area, and he shall let the goat go free in the wilderness."[ar]

The scapegoat was sent away to a solitary place or a remote area, literally to "a land of cutting off." "Throughout Leviticus we find that to be excluded, or cut off, from the camp of Israel was to experience God's punishment for sin (e.g. Lev. 7:20–27; 17:4, 8–14; 18:29; 19:8; 20:3, 5–6, 17–18; 22:3; 23:29). The clear implication is that the goat is depicted in 12:22 as suffering this fate."[28]

Propitiation and Expiation

The slaughtered goat diverts the wrath of God from the people to the goat. This is called propitiation. The scapegoat achieves purity and cleanliness for the people as it removes the guilt and shame of sin. This is expiation. The sacrifices of the Day were designed to pay for both sin's penalty and sin's presence in Israel. The shedding of blood and the sending off of the scapegoat were meant to appease God's wrath against sin and to cleanse the nation, the priesthood, and even the sanctuary itself from the taint of sin.[as] This day speaks of the Lord's gracious concern both to deal fully with his people's sin and to make them fully aware that they stand before him, accepted and covered irrespective of all iniquity, transgression, and sin.[at]

Propitiation is "an offering that turns away the wrath of God directed against sin."[29] Expiation removes sin and its effects because sin is "canceled out by being covered over."[30]

[aq]Lev. 17:11.
[ar]Lev. 16:22.
[as]Lev. 16:30.
[at]Lev. 16:21.

Expiatory views of atonement focus on sacrifices as the way to free people of sin and its defilement. Propitiatory understandings of atonement present sacrifices as the appeasement of divine wrath. The symbolism of two goats on the Day of Atonement indicates that both concepts are essential in the OT imagery of atonement. The sacrificial system of the OT is presented as God's design for satisfying the just judgment of God but also for removing the guilt of sin from those for whom sacrifices are made.[31]

In both cases the ultimate goal of the atonement was to restore the relationship between the covenant God and his covenant people. "Sacrifice was the means of making the unholy pure again and restoring fellowship in the presence of a holy God who cannot tolerate the presence of sin and uncleanness. In other words, sacrifice was the means by which the central blessing of the covenant—communion between Yahweh and his people—was ensured and maintained."[32] The way of communion with God was through sacrifice. But the oft-repeated offerings for sin under the old covenant pointed to a greater sacrifice, a perfect sacrifice that was yet to come.

Redemption and the Suffering Servant

The vision of an ultimate atoning sacrifice is literally personified in the prophetic vision of Isaiah 53. This passage paints a portrait of the suffering servant who is subjected to unjust violence for the sake of and in the place of others. Through substitutionary violence, the suffering servant brings *shalom* to sinners:

> He was wounded for our transgressions; he was crushed for our iniquities; upon him was the chastisement that brought us peace, and with his stripes we are healed. All we like sheep have gone astray; we have turned—every one—to his own way; and the LORD has laid on him the iniquity of us all.[au]

The suffering servant becomes, himself, a sin offering, so that sinners might be healed and forgiven. The suffering servant, the righteous one, through the anguish of his soul, bears the iniquities of his people, in order that they might be counted righteous before God.

[au]Isa. 53:5–6.

The "servant of the Lord" is described in Isaiah's four so-called "servant songs."[av] While the first three servant songs are often interpreted as referring collectively to the nation of Israel, the final song describes an individual. And not just any individual, but the Messiah.[33]

In the fourth servant song, the identity of the servant is most certainly an individual who suffers *in place of* others. The servant endures violence *on behalf of* and *for* others. The sinless servant becomes a substitute *for sinners*:

> The Servant is explicitly said to suffer "for" others. The substitutionary character of his suffering is highlighted by the repeated contrast in Isaiah 53:4–6 between *he, his,* and *him* on the one hand, and *we, us, we all,* and *us all* on the other. The original Hebrew text underlines this even more forcefully by an emphatic use of personal pronouns. . . . A similar use of pronouns is found in verse 11, "their iniquities—*he* will bear them," and in verse 12, "for *he*—the sins of many, he bore them." All of this serves to underline the simple fact that the Servant, who is distinct from God's people, suffered in their place, as their substitute.[34]

Few passages in the Old Testament weave together more redemptive images and themes than this final servant song in Isaiah 52:13–53:12. Cole summarizes the saving work of the suffering servant:

> The servant sprinkles the nations, an idea with sacrificial overtones (Isa. 52:15). He takes on our infirmities and carries our sorrows (Isa. 53:4). He is pierced for our transgressions, crushed for our iniquities, and bears our punishment (Isa. 53:5). He substitutes for others. But in so doing he brings peace (*shalom*, Isa. 53:5). His wounds heal (Isa. 53:5). All this when we mistakenly thought it was God who was afflicting him for his iniquities (Isa. 53:6). He suffers for the sins of others, not his own. He is like a sacrificial lamb going to slaughter (Isa. 53:7). His conduct is exemplary (Isa. 53:7). Experiencing violence, he returns none (Isa. 53:9). He even intercedes for the transgressors (Isa. 53:12). He bears our iniquities and in fact bears the sins of many (Isa. 53:11–12). He becomes a guilt offering (Isa. 53:11). This is the offering that wipes out guilt (cf. Lev. 5:1–19; Num. 5:8; 1 Sam. 6:3–8). . . . His faithfulness leads to triumph (Isa. 53:10–12).[35]

[av]Isa. 42:1–4; 49:1–6; 50:4–9; 52:13–53:12.

The suffering of this servant is a violent affair. The servant "had done no violence" yet he substituted himself and bore in his own body chastisement that brings peace to others. Reid writes:

> Isaiah articulates a new and powerful vision of redemption in which violence is absorbed and transformed. In Isaiah 52–53 the heralding of Israel's divine warrior returning to bring Zion's deliverance (Isa. 52:7–12), suddenly gives way to a description of a suffering servant of Yahweh (Isa. 52:13–53:12). This representative servant figure, who has "done no violence" (Isa. 53:9), suffers violence on behalf of Israel, even to the extent of being "stricken by God, smitten by him, and afflicted" (Isa. 53:4). His triumph and exaltation (framing the passage in Isa. 52:13 and 53:12) is not a consequence of violent warfare but of his pouring out his life unto death (Isa. 53:12).[36]

The servant dies for the sins of the people and is "cut off out of the land of the living."[aw] Yet, he "shall see his offspring" and the Lord "shall prolong his days."[ax] This servant, "the righteous one," will justify and "make many to be accounted righteous."[ay] In order to procure these blessings, the servant endures unspeakable evil. "From beginning to end, the passage emphasizes the appalling horror of what the Servant endured—far beyond what has ever been borne by any other human being."[37] He is a "man of sorrows, and acquainted with grief."[az]

Yet this servant not only has solidarity with humankind. The servant, while distinguished from the Lord in Isaiah 53, is also accorded divine status by the phrase "high and lifted up" in Isaiah 52:13: "Behold, my servant shall act wisely; he shall be *high and lifted up*, and shall be exalted."[38] This Hebrew phrase only appears three other times in the Old Testament, all of them in Isaiah,[ba] and in each case they refer to the Lord. Alan Groves notes, thus "Yahweh's own lips declared that the servant was to be identified with Yahweh himself."[39]

So this passage is chiefly about the atoning work of a human/divine figure who will make "an offering for guilt."[bb] This phrase refers unmistakably to the guilt offerings described in Leviticus 5–7 as the atoning

---

[aw]Isa. 53:8.
[ax]Isa. 53:10.
[ay]Isa. 53:11.
[az]Isa. 53:3.
[ba]Isa. 6:1; 33:10; 57:15.
[bb]Isa. 53:10.

sacrifice for sins. "By using the same word here Isaiah plainly intends to ascribe the same significance to the suffering Servant. Isaiah 53:10 thus anticipates something that will become explicit in the New Testament: the animal sacrifices of Leviticus are ultimately fulfilled in the sacrificial death of a person."[40]

Restoring *Shalom*

The Old Testament prophets are filled with images of a time when God would put things right again, and when *shalom* would be finally and permanently restored to God's creation.[bc] Plantinga writes:

> The prophets dreamed of a new age in which human crookedness would be straightened out, rough places made plain. The foolish would be made wise, and the wise, humble. They dreamed of a time when the deserts would flower, the mountains would run with wine, weeping would cease, and people could go to sleep without weapons on their laps. People would work in peace and work to fruitful effect. Lambs could lie down with lions. All nature would be fruitful, benign, and filled with wonder upon wonder; all humans would be knit together in brotherhood and sisterhood; and all nature and all humans would look to God, walk with God, lean toward God, and delight in God. Shouts of joy and recognition would well up from valleys and seas, from women in streets and from men on ships. The webbing together of God, humans, and all creation in justice, fulfillment, and delight is what the Hebrew prophets call *shalom*.[41]

The restoration of *shalom* is frequently united to the coming of the Messiah, the long-awaited deliverer, prophesied throughout the Old Testament. The hope of *shalom* was the hope of Israel. And the hope of Israel was the only hope for the world. According to the book of Isaiah, the hope of Israel was clearly embodied in the messianic child of Isaiah 9 and the suffering servant of Isaiah 53. This figure, the messianic child and the suffering servant of Isaiah, is one in the same: a suffering Messiah who brings *shalom*.

> For to us a child is born, to us a son is given; and the government shall be upon his shoulder, and his name shall be called Wonderful Coun-

---

[bc]Isa. 2:2–4; 11:1–9; 32:14–20; 42:1–12; 60; 65:17–25; Joel 2:24–29; 3:17–18.

selor, Mighty God, Everlasting Father, Prince of Peace [Heb. *shalom*]. Of the increase of his government and of peace [Heb. *shalom*] there will be no end, on the throne of David and over his kingdom, to establish it and to uphold it with justice and with righteousness from this time forth and forevermore. The zeal of the LORD of hosts will do this.[bd][42]

Note, again, Isaiah 53:5: "But he was wounded for our transgressions; he was crushed for our iniquities; upon him was the chastisement that brought us peace [Heb. *shalom*], and with his stripes we are healed."

The New Testament writers clearly understand this suffering servant, this bringer of peace, to be Jesus of Nazareth. Isaiah 53 is directly quoted seven times in the New Testament as referring to Jesus Christ,[be] and alluded to over thirty-four times.[43] In his perfectly sinless life and his substitutionary atoning death, Jesus secured salvation for sinners and brought them *shalom* with God.

Jesus Christ came into this violent world that was shattered by sin, and he suffered a violent death at the hands of violent men in order to save rebellious sinners, rescuing them from divine wrath, and supplying them with divine peace, mercy, grace, and love. The sinless one suffered disgrace in order to bring sinners grace. The light of heaven entered into the darkness of this world. "The people dwelling in darkness have seen a great light, and for those dwelling in the region and shadow of death, on them a light has dawned."[bf]

In our survey of the Old Testament, we have seen that the Scriptures do not avoid the issue of violence. "The Bible is not a 'nice' book that hides the sordid side of life. The Bible is a book of thoroughgoing realism. The Bible's stories of violence demonstrate the depths of depravity to which the human race descends. Paradoxically, though, the nadir of depravity represented by biblical stories of violence is also the climax of the Bible's story of redemption. The violence of the cross is the pivot point of redemption."[44]

And it is the cross of Jesus Christ, the pivot point of redemption, to which we now turn our attention.

[bd]Isa. 9:6–7.
[be]Matt. 8:16–17; Luke 22:37; John 12:38; Acts 8:32–35; Rom. 10:16; 1 Pet. 2:22–25.
[bf]Matt. 4:16; cf. Isa. 9:2.

12

Grace in the New Testament

We have already focused on the radical shift from peace and *shalom* to violence and sin. We have seen that God's desire to restore peace and bring redemption is expressed throughout the entire Old Testament by tracing the themes of violence (disgrace) and redemption (grace). Now we will see how they converge on the cross of Jesus Christ:

> An entire episode of human history is sealed with the narrator's judgment that "the earth was filled with violence" (Gen. 6:11). The biblical logic of redemption, viewed through the canonical lens of the incarnation and the cross, allows no other course for its plot line than to run the gauntlet of human violence. But the outcome is a divine and dramatic resolution of violence, and the world-transforming power of the gospel.[1]

The cross is God's attack on sin and violence; it is salvation from sin and its effects. The cross really is a coup de grace, meaning "stroke of grace," which refers to the deathblow delivered to the misery of our suffering:

> Jesus' submission to the violence of the cross demonstrates God's will to absorb in the Son the wrath that is due to Israel and the world. Jesus' prayer to the Father from the cross, "forgive them, for they do not know what they are doing" (Luke 23:34; cf. Acts 7:60 NIV), memorably expresses the commandment to love one's enemies even as they perpetrate their violence. The cross embodies Jesus' victory over violence and is the climax of the biblical story of violence.[2]

In the cross God is not revealed in the power and glory, which natural reason can recognize as divine, but in the very opposite of divinity, in human disgrace, poverty, suffering and death, in what seems to be weakness and foolishness.

God's desire for *shalom* and his response to violence culminates in the person and work of Jesus Christ. The life, death, and resurrection of Jesus fulfills redemption themes from the Old Testament: the Passover sacrifice in Exodus, God in Exodus as the divine Warrior protecting his people by conquering their enemy, the sacrifices of propitiation and expiation in Leviticus 16, and the suffering servant whose suffering brings peace. This good news of the Bible is that in Jesus Christ, the God-man, our Creator has become our Redeemer.

This astounding reality is the best part of the good news. For this reason, the gospel of Jesus Christ occupies the central place in the New Testament, as the message of first importance.[3] The heart of this message concerns the person and the work of Jesus Christ, that is, who Jesus is and what he has accomplished by his life, death, and resurrection.[4]

Tim Keller explains the scope and goal of the good news:

> The "gospel" is the good news that through Christ the power of God's kingdom has entered history to renew the whole world. When we believe and rely on Jesus' work and record (rather than ours) for our relationship to God, that kingdom power comes upon us and begins to work through us. Through the person and work of Jesus Christ, God fully accomplishes salvation for us, rescuing us from judgment for sin into fellowship with him, and then restores the creation in which we can enjoy our new life together with him forever.[5]

To better understand that Jesus is the fullness of God's plan to redeem humanity, restore *shalom*, and replace disgrace with grace, we will look at who Jesus is and what he has done.

Who Jesus Is—God with Us

Like Genesis, the Gospel of John begins in the beginning.[a] John 1:1–3 tells us: "In the beginning was the Word, and the Word was with God, and the Word was God. He was in the beginning with God. All things were made through him, and without him was not any thing made that was made." From the very outset of his Gospel, John shines the spotlight on the Son of God, Jesus Christ. Christ is the eternal Word of God,[b]

---

[a]Gen. 1:1 and John 1:1.
[b]John 1:1.

who was eternally with God,[c] and who was the agent through whom all things were created by God.[d]

The highlight of John's prologue comes in 1:14 when he writes: "And the Word became flesh and dwelt among us, and we have seen his glory, glory as of the only Son from the Father, full of grace and truth." According to John, the eternal, divine Son of God, the one who made all things, became flesh. In Jesus, God became a man and lived on the earth that he created. God took on flesh, which is the meaning of "incarnation." In Jesus, "the whole fullness of deity dwells bodily."[e] In Jesus Christ, the invisible God has become visible: "No one has ever seen God; the only God, who is at the Father's side, he has made him known."[f] Therefore, God the Son makes known God the Father.

John goes on to say that our Creator has become our Redeemer. The Son of God came in the flesh in order to make possible the salvation of sinners: "He came to his own, and his own people did not receive him. But to all who did receive him, who believed in his name, he gave the right to become children of God, who were born, not of blood nor of the will of the flesh nor of the will of man, but of God."[g]

The divine Son of God has come into the very world he created on a rescue mission to save sinners from the wrath of God, condemnation, sin, and sin's effects. The rescue mission of Jesus is a key theme in each Gospel account, but particularly in the Gospel of John.[6] This rescue is described as light intruding into the darkness: "The light shines in the darkness, and the darkness has not overcome it."[h] Jesus Christ, who called himself "the light of the world,"[7] entered into the darkness of this world to bring light and eternal life to sinners who are dwelling in the darkness of their rebellion and sin: "The people dwelling in darkness have seen a great light, and for those dwelling in the region and shadow of death, on them a light has dawned."[i]

Between his two claims to be the light of the world,[j] Jesus heals a blind man. The miracle of giving sight to the man born blind demonstrates the purpose of Jesus' ministry. It illustrates Jesus' power to bring

---

[c]John 1:2.
[d]John 1:3.
[e]Col. 2:9.
[f]John 1:18.
[g]John 1:11–13.
[h]John 1:5.
[i]Matt. 4:16; see also Isa. 9:2.
[j]John 8:12; 9:5.

his light to those in darkness. Where darkness, death, and decay had reigned, Jesus breaks in with light, liberation, and love.

A picture of this comes from Robert Louis Stevenson, the author of *Treasure Island*, who lived in Scotland in the nineteenth century. As a boy, his family lived on a hillside overlooking a small town. Robert was intrigued by the work of the old lamplighters who went about with a ladder and a torch, lighting the streetlights for the night. One evening, as Robert stood watching with fascination, his nurse asked him, "Robert, what in the world are you looking at out there?" With great excitement he exclaimed: "Look at that man! He's punching holes in the darkness!"[8]

The light of the world has entered into the world's darkness in order to punch holes in it and bring those who dwell in darkness into the dawn of his grace and truth. None of this would be possible apart from Christ's incarnation. But, in addition to rescuing us, the incarnation also means that God is present with us: "[God] comes for you, in the flesh, in Christ, into suffering, on your behalf. He does not offer advice and perspective from afar; he steps into your significant suffering. He will see you through, and work with you the whole way. He will carry you even *in extremis*."[9]

The Gospel of Matthew introduces Jesus as the long-awaited deliverer of God's people. In the narrative of Jesus' birth, Matthew quotes Isaiah 7:14, an Old Testament prophecy about the coming Messiah who would save his people from their sins: "All this took place to fulfill what the Lord had spoken by the prophet: 'Behold, the virgin shall conceive and bear a son, and they shall call his name Immanuel.'"[k] Matthew tells us that "Immanuel" is a Hebrew name that is translated "God with us." Even though "Immanuel" is used only two times in the Bible,[l] we have seen that the idea of God's dwelling with humankind, his gracious presence with his people, spans the entire story of redemption. *Hesed*, God's covenantal love, is a repeated theme throughout both testaments: "I will live among them and walk among them, and I will be their God and they will be my people."[m] So the hope of a Savior is found in this person called "Immanuel." And that person is Jesus.

---

[k] Matt. 1:22–23.
[l] Isa. 7:14; 8:8.
[m] Gen. 17:8; Ex. 6:7; 25:8; 29:45–46; Lev. 22:33; 26:11–12; Deut. 4:20; 7:6; 14:2; 29:13; 1 Kings 6:13; Zech. 2:10; Jer. 7:23; 11:4; 24:7; 30:22; 31:33; 32:38; Ezek. 11:20; 14:11; 36:28; 37:23, 27; Matt. 1:22–23; and 2 Cor. 6:16.

While the Gospel of Matthew begins by saying that Jesus is "God with us," the rest of the book details what Jesus did while he was on earth.[10] At the end of Matthew, Jesus issues a glorious promise: "Behold, *I am with you* always, to the end of the age."[n] Matthew's Gospel begins with the prophecy that the Savior would be "Immanuel, that is, 'God with us,'" and it ends with Jesus' promise to his disciples: "I am with you always." In other words, the Gospel of Matthew tells us that the way God will be *with his people* is through a relationship *with his Son*, Jesus Christ.

What Jesus Has Done

Our knowledge of the life and ministry of Jesus Christ comes almost entirely from the four New Testament Gospels. These books detail what Jesus taught and what Jesus did during his three-and-a-half-year ministry in and around Jerusalem.[11] However, the central emphasis of these books is the atoning death and triumphant resurrection of Jesus. According to Mark Driscoll, "In total, the four Gospels, which faithfully record his life, devote roughly one-third of their content to the climactic final week of Jesus' life leading up to the cross."[12] With such an overwhelming emphasis on the atonement, on the redemptive suffering of Jesus Christ, the Gospels have been often described as crucifixion narratives with extended introductions.

The New Testament is brimming with descriptions of what God did for us through the cross of Christ:

> Jesus is presented as having paid the penalty for sin (Rom. 3:25–26; 6:23; Gal. 3:13). He died in place of sinners so that they might become God's righteousness (2 Cor. 5:21). He redeemed sinners through his blood (Eph. 1:7). He paid the price for sinners to go free (1 Cor. 6:20; Gal. 5:1). He won the victory over death and sin, sharing with believers the victory (1 Cor. 15:55–57) that he paraded in spectacular fashion by his cross (Col. 2:15). Peter's statement captures well the means and importance of Jesus' ministry of atonement: "He himself bore our sins in his body on the tree, so that we might die to sin and live for righteousness; by his wounds you have been healed" (1 Pet. 2:24).[13]

A central way that these Gospel narratives describe the way God has dealt with sin is often called penal substitutionary atonement.[14] On the

---

[n]Matt. 28:20, emphasis added.

cross, Jesus took our place and bore the wrath that we deserved: "The doctrine of penal substitution states that God gave himself in the person of his Son to suffer instead of us the death, punishment and curse due to fallen humanity as the penalty for sin." [15]

Jesus Paid Our Ransom

First, to free us from bondage, Jesus paid our ransom on the cross. In the Gospel of Mark, Jesus foretells his death three times in detail.[o] After these predictions, Jesus says to his disciples in Mark 10:45, "For even the Son of Man came not to be served but to serve, and to give his life as a ransom for many." In other words, Jesus would serve and take the low place, humbling himself to die on the cross as a "ransom for many." In his death, Jesus paid the ransom price of his life as a substitutionary payment in the place of sinners.[16]

The New Testament writers frequently borrow the language of the Old Testament to describe the redemption secured by Jesus. Mark, in using the idea of a "ransom," is borrowing from the Old Testament imagery connected with the exodus.[17] During his transfiguration, Luke tells us that Jesus "appeared in glory and spoke of his *departure* [literally "exodus"], which he was about to accomplish at Jerusalem."[p18] Just like Moses, Christ would lead his people out of bondage. But Christ's deliverance would far surpass the work of Moses.[19]

Ransom is a major dimension of God's redemptive plan revealed in Scripture. According to theologian John Murray:

> The language of redemption is the language of purchase and more specifically of ransom.... Ransom presupposes some kind of bondage or captivity, and redemption, therefore, implies that from which the ransom secures us. . . . Redemption applies to every aspect in which we are bound, and it releases us into a liberty that is nothing less than the liberty of the glory of the children of God.[20]

In his letter to the Colossians, Paul says that we ought to give "thanks to the Father, who has qualified you to share in the inheritance of the saints in light. He has delivered us from the domain of darkness and transferred us to the kingdom of his beloved Son, in whom we have

---

[o]Mark 8:31; 9:31; 10:33–34.
[p]Luke 9:31, emphasis added.

redemption, the forgiveness of sins."[q] Paul contrasts the condition sinners found themselves in apart from the gospel. We were in the "domain of darkness." We were citizens of Satan's dark kingdom. But in Christ, because of the cross, Paul says we have been brought out of this deadly kingdom into the life and light of the kingdom of God's beloved Son.

Bible scholar N. T. Wright notes that Paul borrows the salvation vocabulary of the exodus: "This is Exodus language. Just as the children of Israel were brought out of slavery under Pharaoh and were established as God's free people, so now, by the preaching of the gospel, people everywhere can be transferred from the grip of the powers into the kingdom of Jesus."[21] All those who have trusted in Christ and have been saved by him are partakers of a kingdom that includes the glorious inheritance of the saints in light.

This inheritance is described elsewhere as "imperishable, undefiled, and unfading, kept in heaven for you."[r] All of these spectacular blessings were purchased by Christ's redemption. This redemption has at its heart, the forgiveness of sins: "You were ransomed from the futile ways inherited from your forefathers, not with perishable things such as silver or gold, but with the precious blood of Christ, like that of a lamb without blemish or spot."[s]

Peter, like Paul, saw the work of redemption purchased by Christ, to be a new exodus: "But you are a chosen race, a royal priesthood, a holy nation, a people for his own possession, that you may proclaim the excellencies of him who called you out of darkness into his marvelous light. Once you were not a people, but now you are God's people; once you had not received mercy, but now you have received mercy."[t]

Jesus Bore Our Curse

Jesus not only paid our ransom; Jesus also bore our curse. According to Paul, "Christ redeemed us from the curse of the law by becoming a curse for us—for it is written, 'Cursed is everyone who is hanged on a tree.'"[u] Christ became our curse-bearer on the cross: "When Jesus emptied the cup of God's wrath, He endured the ultimate limit of the Law's curse. Christ became a

---

[q] Col. 1:12–14.
[r] 1 Pet. 1:4.
[s] 1 Pet. 1:18–19.
[t] 1 Pet. 2:9–10.
[u] Gal. 3:13.

curse for us. Literally, He became a curse in our place as our substitute. He experienced the full fury of the curse that we should have experienced."[22]

Part of the curse that Jesus bore for sinners was the God-forsakenness that he endured during the final hours of his crucifixion. According to Mark's Gospel: "And at the ninth hour Jesus cried with a loud voice, 'Eloi, Eloi, lema sabachthani?' which means, 'My God, my God, why have you forsaken me?'"[v]

J. I. Packer comments about this passage:

> On the cross Jesus lost all the good that he had before: all sense of his Father's presence and love, all sense of physical, mental, and spiritual well-being, all enjoyment of God and of created things, all ease and solace of friendship, were taken from him, and in their place was nothing but loneliness, pain, a killing sense of human malice and callousness, and a horror of great spiritual darkness.[23]

While the physical pain was excruciating, this paled in comparison to the mental and spiritual sufferings Jesus endured on Calvary. "What was packed into less than four hundred minutes was an eternity of agony."[24]

Christ endured the curse for us, and we receive all of heaven's spiritual blessings in him.[w] According to Jerry Bridges, "We should never cease to be amazed that the One who established the Law and determined its curse should Himself ransom us from that curse by bearing it in our place."[25] Bearing our curse, Jesus fulfilled the promise of the suffering servant, who is also identified as the "man of sorrow" in Isaiah 53. "Jesus suffered the indignity of accusation and condemnation and the shame of crucifixion. His was the tortured soul in Gethsemane, the torn flesh at Calvary. And as thick darkness enveloped the whole land, it was He who was pierced for our transgressions and crushed for our iniquities; His was the punishment that brought us peace; His were the wounds that wrought our healing."[26]

Jesus Was Our Propitiation and Expiation

In Romans 3:21–26, Paul describes how God has completely and justly dealt with our sins and condemnation in a way that perfectly accords with his righteousness:

---

[v]Mark 15:34.
[w]Eph. 1:3.

> But now the righteousness of God has been manifested apart from the law, although the Law and the Prophets bear witness to it—the righteousness of God through faith in Jesus Christ for all who believe. For there is no distinction: for all have sinned and fall short of the glory of God, and are justified by his grace as a gift, through the redemption that is in Christ Jesus, whom God put forward as a propitiation by his blood, to be received by faith. This was to show God's righteousness, because in his divine forbearance he had passed over former sins. It was to show his righteousness at the present time, so that he might be just and the justifier of the one who has faith in Jesus.

God's wrath is his holy hostility toward sin and his just anger towards anything that violates his holiness. It is his righteous reaction against unrighteousness. God's holy and righteous wrath should be justly poured out on all of humanity. According to Packer: "The wrath of God is as personal, and as potent, as his love; and, just as the bloodshedding of the Lord Jesus was the direct manifesting of his Father's love toward us, so it was the direct averting of his Father's wrath against us."[27]

In Christ, God has made a way possible for both his grace and his righteousness to be displayed in the salvation of sinners. God did this by putting Christ forward as a "propitiation by his blood."[x] According to John Murray, the doctrine of propitiation is precisely this:

> That God loved the objects of His wrath so much that He gave His own Son to the end that He by His blood should make provision for the removal of His wrath. It was Christ's so to deal with the wrath that the loved would no longer be the objects of wrath, and love would achieve its aim of making the children of wrath the children of God's good pleasure.[28]

The book of Hebrews also emphasizes both the propitiation and expiation that Jesus secured through his work as both high priest and sacrifice. The imagery that Christ was "made ... sin" for us[y] and that he "bore our sins"[z] matches the role of both goats on the Day of Atonement—the one sacrificed as a sin offering and the one that carried

---

[x]Rom. 3:24–25.
[y]2 Cor. 5:21.
[z]1 Pet. 2:24.

off the confessed sins of the people. In his death, "the LORD has laid on him the iniquity of us all."[aa] In Psalm 51:1–2 we read: "Have mercy on me, O God, according to your steadfast love; according to your abundant mercy blot out my transgressions. Wash me thoroughly from my iniquity, and cleanse me from my sin!"

The Day of Atonement was a foreshadowing of Jesus, the Lamb of God who takes away the sins of the world, and our great High Priest who is able to sympathize with us in our weaknesses. These great images of the priest, slaughter, and scapegoat are all given by God to help us more fully comprehend Jesus' bloody sacrifice for us on the cross. Jesus' fulfillment of the Day of Atonement is why we are forgiven for and cleansed from our sins. Regarding the centrality of sacrifice for atonement, Charles Spurgeon writes: "Many pretend to keep the atonement, and yet they tear the bowels out of it. They profess to believe in the gospel, but it is a gospel without the blood of the atonement; and a bloodless gospel is a lifeless gospel, a dead gospel, and a damning gospel."[29] Jesus Christ fulfills and accomplishes forever what the two goats symbolized. The Old Testament sacrifice of animals has been replaced by the perfect sacrifice of Christ.[ab] Christ paid sin's penalty.[ac] He redeemed us,[ad] paying the price that sets us free.[ae] He turned away God's wrath[af] and reconciled believers to God[ag] so we can be forgiven for our sins and cleansed from all unrighteousness.[ah]

First John 1:9 refers to propitiation and expiation: "If we confess our sins, he is faithful and just to forgive us our sins and to cleanse us from all unrighteousness." Elsewhere in 1 John, the work of Jesus is said to "cleanse us from all sin"[ai] and to be "the propitiation for our sins."[aj]

Salvation by Substitution because of Love

In Romans 5:6–11, Paul describes how the salvation of sinners is not only by propitiation but also by substitution. That is, Jesus Christ became

---

[aa]Isa. 53:6.
[ab]Heb. 9:26; 10:5–10; 1 John 2:1–2; 4:9–10.
[ac]Rom. 3:25–26; 6:23; Gal 3:13.
[ad]Eph. 1:7.
[ae]1 Cor. 6:20; Gal. 5:1.
[af]Rom. 3:25.
[ag]Eph. 2:16.
[ah]1 John 1:9.
[ai]1 John 1:7.
[aj]1 John 2:2.

a substitute and died in our place for our sins. At the cross, God, once and for all time, demonstrates his love for us. God provides evidence through action of his love for sinners: "God shows his love for us in that while we were still sinners, Christ died for us."[ak] Notice the tense of the verb: "God *shows*." The death of Christ in the past proves today, tomorrow, and for all time that God loves us. The death of Christ is a timeless proof of God's love. Throughout the endless ages of eternity forgiven sinners will sing the glories of the Lamb who was slain for them on Calvary. The cross is the supreme display of God's love.

The cross is not only the public display of God's righteousness[al] but also of God's love.[am] And Paul makes clear in this passage that there is no love that has ever been that can compare to the dying love of Christ for sinners. Paul's words "Christ died for us" in 5:8 are even more amazing when you observe how he has described "us." In the context, the "us" is described as "weak,"[an] "ungodly,"[ao] "sinners,"[ap] and "enemies."[aq] This is astounding. While we were helpless, ungodly, wicked, sinners, and enemies of God, Christ died *for* us.

Christ died in place of his enemies. He died in our place for our sins. Paul says this in another way in Romans 4:25: Jesus "was delivered up for our trespasses." In other words, Jesus was handed over for our sins. This was only possible because Jesus didn't have any sins: "For our sake he made him to be sin who knew no sin, so that in him we might become the righteousness of God."[ar]

Salvation and Obedience

The work of Jesus was not just his death on the cross, but also his perfect life. His death accomplished the forgiveness of our sins and removed the guilt and stain of sins securing assurance of eternal life. Our sins were imputed (attributed) to Christ, and he died the death of a sinner. However, his righteousness was imputed to those who have faith in Christ.

Francis Turretin explains the significance of Christ's obedience:

[ak]Rom. 5:8.
[al]Rom. 3:21.
[am]Rom. 5:8.
[an]Rom. 5:6.
[ao]Rom. 5:6.
[ap]Rom. 5:8.
[aq]Rom. 5:10.
[ar]2 Cor. 5:21.

The obedience of Christ has a twofold efficacy, satisfactory and meritorious; the former by which we are freed from the punishments incurred by sin; the latter by which (through the remission of sin) a right to eternal life and salvation is acquired for us. For as sin has brought upon us two evils—the loss of life and exposure to death—so redemption must procure the two opposite benefits—deliverance from death and a right to life, escape from hell and an entrance into heaven.[30]

The benefits of Christ's righteousness are proclaimed in Romans 5:18–19: "Therefore, as one trespass led to condemnation for all men, so one act of righteousness leads to justification and life for all men. For as by the one man's disobedience the many were made sinners, so by the one man's obedience the many will be made righteous." John Calvin explains how Christ's obedience is the ground for our pardon: "To justify therefore, is nothing else than to acquit from the charge of guilt, as if innocence were proved. Hence, when God justifies us through the intercession of Christ, he does not acquit us on a proof of our own innocence, but by an imputation of righteousness, so that though not righteous in ourselves, we are deemed righteous in Christ."[31]

Not only are believers delivered from condemnation and exempted from eternal death because of *his* death, but they are also deemed worthy of reward and declared righteous because of Christ's sinless life. His purity is imputed to us and we are declared and judged righteous "in order that the righteous requirement of the law might be fulfilled in us."[as]

The work of Christ is a fulfillment of Isaiah 61:10: "I will greatly rejoice in the LORD; my soul shall exult in my God, for he has clothed me with the garments of salvation; he has covered me with the robe of righteousness." Jonathan Edwards writes: "Christ's perfect obedience shall be reckoned to our account so that we shall have the benefit of it, as though we had performed it ourselves: and so we suppose that a title to eternal life is given us as the reward of this righteousness."[32]

Jesus did not just come that our sins would be removed, but he also came that we might receive his righteousness, which was only possible after the debt for our sin had been paid: "For our sake he made him to be sin who knew no sin, so that in him we might become the righteous-

---

[as]Rom. 8:4.

ness of God."[at] The benefit of this is reconciliation and a new identity. In Colossians 1:21–22, we read an amazing promise: "And you, who once were alienated and hostile in mind, doing evil deeds, he has now reconciled in his body of flesh by his death, in order to present you holy and blameless and above reproach before him." Notice the words, "holy," "blameless," and "above reproach." These descriptive words are usually used in reference to Jesus Christ. But now, because of what Jesus Christ has done for us, paying the penalty of sins, we can now stand before God our Creator holy, blameless, and above reproach. By faith we are "in Christ" and as such we are seen as he is. Because of faith in Christ, you are the righteousness of God.

Jesus Gave Us Access to God

By his death and resurrection, Jesus becomes our way to God. His death is the sacrifice for us. He is the Lamb of God who takes away your sins, but he is also your priest. In the OT, the priest represented God to the people and the people back to God. But now Jesus is your High Priest. Being both God and man, he fulfills the role of priest perfectly. The temple was where God was present, but in the temple was a veil that separated sinful humans from the presence of the holy God. But in Jesus, humanity had the most personal presence of God possible. He was called Immanuel, meaning "God with us." Jesus called himself the Temple of God. And when Jesus died, the veil in the temple—the barrier between God and us—was torn in two from top to bottom. This means that God tore his own temple veil and makes himself accessible to us through the death of Jesus.

First Timothy 2:5 calls Jesus the only mediator between God and humanity. Hebrews refers to Jesus twice as the mediator of the new covenant.[au] In Jesus you have unbridled and unhindered access to God. You can now approach God without fear of judgment and with boldness.[av] God has made himself accessible. Jesus, the "great high priest," has enabled you to "draw near to the throne of grace" of the Father with "confidence."[aw] No longer do you have to hold your head in shame in prayer, but you can come to the Father with Christ-centered confidence.

[at]2 Cor. 5:21.
[au]Heb. 9:15; 12:24.
[av]Eph. 3:12.
[aw]Heb. 4:16.

Jesus Conquered Our Enemy

Much of the focus so far has been on the cross as God's gracious response to our own sinful and willful irresponsibility, choices, and actions. This is because we are perpetrators of evil—and this is what separates us from God. It is this aspect of sin that has been dealt with by the vicarious sacrifice theme of the atonement.

However, we are also victims of evil and have enemies who harm us. We are victims who have been sinned against in numerous ways. Because of sins done to us, we are also captive, held in bondage by powers in some sense external to us and greater than we are. Or we may be held in bondage to our own desires or fears, our self-centeredness or despair. Sometimes the Bible describes the human problem understood as suffering, being in bondage, slavery, or captivity, each and all of which separate us from God.

What we need in this regard is for God to fight on our behalf, against our enemy, for our freedom from bondage. This is what God did in the exodus for his people. The clearest and most powerful manifestation of God doing this for us is Christ's victory over death in the resurrection.[ax] In this victory over the principalities, powers, and death, the Son reclaims creation for the Father and freedom for you. "He disarmed the rulers and authorities and put them to open shame, by triumphing over them in him."[ay]

In answering the question, "How does Christ's resurrection benefit us?" the Heidelberg Catechism answers: "First, by his resurrection he has overcome death, so that he might make us share in the righteousness he won for us by his death. Second, by his power we too are already now resurrected to a new life. Third, Christ's resurrection is a guarantee of our glorious resurrection."

God accomplished redemption in Christ's victory over sin and death, but the effects of that victory have yet to be fully realized. So while the ultimate outcome has been assured,[az] the struggle between life and death, good and evil, continues. However, the *shalom*, freedom, and rest of redemption will one day be fully realized when Jesus returns.

Christ's victory gives us back our identity and restores our meaning. We recognize, and may truly know for the first time, that we have

---

[ax]Eph. 1:19–20.
[ay]Col. 2:15.
[az]Rom. 8:18–21; 1 Cor. 15:51–57; Revelation 21.

a future that ends in peace, as well as a past that can be healed and forgiven, and now live in the hope of the gospel. Christ opens up for us a new identity because he himself remained always true to his own identity, a share of which he offers to us.

In Christ's victory, fear and shame are banished, to be replaced by profound joy that we are no longer strangers to God and to one another, that we are no longer so utterly isolated and alone. Robert Sherman writes: "Liberation from the bondage of our past and yearning for a fulfilled future find their realization in Christ's reclaiming of the creation."[33]

Our Future Salvation

The blessings of Christ's work will be enjoyed by all of the redeemed into the ages of eternity. Paul writes:

> God, being rich in mercy, because of the great love with which he loved us, even when we were dead in our trespasses, made us alive together with Christ—by grace you have been saved—and raised us up with him and seated us with him in the heavenly places in Christ Jesus, *so that in the coming ages* he might show the immeasurable riches of his grace in kindness toward us in Christ Jesus.[ba]

One of the purposes of God's redemptive work for us in Christ was to demonstrate the riches of his grace for all eternity.[34]

For this reason, it is helpful to understand more fully the implications of the atonement for the age to come. According to Yarbrough:

> "Atonement" may be defined as God's work on sinners' behalf to reconcile them to himself. It is the divine activity that confronts and resolves the problem of human sin so that people may enjoy full fellowship with God both now and in the age to come. While in one sense the meaning of atonement is as broad and diverse as all of God's saving work throughout time and eternity, in another it is as particular and restricted as the crucifixion of Jesus. For in the final analysis Scripture presents his sacrificial death as the central component of God's reconciling mercy. This explains why Revelation 22:3, for example, shows not only God but also the Lamb—slain to atone for sin—occupying the throne of heaven in the age to come.[35]

[ba]Eph. 2:4–7, emphasis added.

The new heavens and the new earth described in Revelation 21:1–6 is a picture of perfection:

> Then I saw a new heaven and a new earth, for the first heaven and the first earth had passed away, and the sea was no more. And I saw the holy city, new Jerusalem, coming down out of heaven from God, prepared as a bride adorned for her husband. And I heard a loud voice from the throne saying, "Behold, the dwelling place of God is with man. He will dwell with them, and they will be his people, and God himself will be with them as their God. He will wipe away every tear from their eyes, and death shall be no more, neither shall there be mourning, nor crying, nor pain anymore, for the former things have passed away." And he who was seated on the throne said, "Behold, I am making all things new." Also he said, "Write this down, for these words are trustworthy and true." And he said to me, "It is done! I am the Alpha and the Omega, the beginning and the end. To the thirsty I will give from the spring of the water of life without payment."

Revelation 21 describes a world reborn, a new creation where everything we lost in the fall is regained. This vision of a new creation,[bb] a new heaven and a new earth after judgment, reminds us of God's promise to Noah to make all things new despite sin. The covenantal refrain repeated in Exodus is also fulfilled in the new creation—"They will be his people, and God himself will be with them."[bc] Immanuel, "God with us," is not just about the incarnation but is the eternal presence. The final home for believers will not be a disembodied heaven but rather a fully glorified and bodied existence in the new heaven and new earth. It won't just be Eden restored—but rather it will be a whole new world reborn, a place where the curse is completely and totally reversed! Death will be replaced by life.[bd] Night will be replaced by light.[be] The light of the world will be the light of heaven! Corruption will be replaced by purity.[bf] Disgrace will be replaced by grace.

God himself will dwell with his people, in his perfect place, and will bless his people with his presence. Forever. The chief reason why this place will be perfect is because believers will be in the presence of

---

[bb]Rev. 21:1.
[bc]Rev. 21:3.
[bd]Rev. 21:4.
[be]Rev. 21:23–25.
[bf]Rev. 21:27.

Almighty God. God will once again dwell with his people, and we will see him face-to-face![bg] Faith will give way to sight, and prayer to praise. Sin and violence will be ultimately and finally replaced by *shalom*.

Our eyes will be fixed upon the Lamb of God, slain for sinners, who occupies the throne of God. John calls Jesus "Lamb" twenty-eight times in the book of Revelation.[bh] This is a clear reference to the sacrifices of Passover and the Day of Atonement. This Lamb is also on a throne, symbolizing that he is victorious King. John tells us that Jesus conquered by suffering and dying on the cross. He shed his blood to cleanse his people of their sins.

Christopher J. H. Wright explains that the work of Jesus restores the peace that was vandalized in Genesis 3:

> And the river and tree of life, from which humanity had been barred in the earliest chapters of the Bible's grand narrative, will, in its final chapter, provide the healing of the nations which the narrative has longed for ever since the scattering of Babel (Rev. 22:2). The curse will be gone from the whole of creation (Rev. 22:3). The earth will be filled with the glory of God and all the nations of humanity will walk in His light (Rev. 21:24). Such is the glorious climax of the Bible's grand narrative.[36]

The Gospel Is *Hesed*

In the Bible, suffering is regarded as an intrusion into this created world. Creation was made good.[bi] When sin entered, suffering also entered in the form of conflict, pain, corruption, drudgery, and death.[bj] The work of Christ is to deliver us from suffering, corruption, and death,[bk] as well as from sin.[bl] In the new heaven and new earth, suffering has been finally abolished.[bm]

In the gospel of Jesus Christ, God demonstrates that he is for us and not against us. Everything we have as believers has been granted to us because of what Jesus has already done for us. According to D. A. Carson:

> Everything that is coming to us from God comes through Christ Jesus. Christ Jesus has won our pardon; He has reconciled us to God; He

---

[bg]Rev. 22:4.
[bh]Rev. 5:6, 8, 12ff.; 6:1, 16; 7:9ff., 14, 17; 8:1; 12:11; 13:8; 14:1, 4, 10; 15:3; 17:14; 19:7, 9; 21:9, 14, 22ff.; 22:1, 3.
[bi]Gen. 1:31.
[bj]Gen. 3:15–19.
[bk]Rom. 8:21; 1 Cor. 15:26.
[bl]Matt. 1:21.
[bm]Rev. 21:4; Isa. 65:17ff.

has canceled our sin; He has secured the gift of the Spirit for us; He has granted eternal life to us and promises us the life of the consummation; He has made us children of the new covenant; His righteousness has been accounted as ours; He has risen from the dead, and all of God's sovereignty is mediated through Him and directed to our good and to God's glory. This is the Son whom God sent to redeem us. In God's all-wise plan and all-powerful action, all these blessings have been won by His Son's odious death and triumphant resurrection. All the blessings God has for us are tied up with the work of Christ.[37]

And all of these blessings are freely yours in Jesus Christ. Now and forever. All by grace. Grace is available because Jesus went through the valley of the shadow of death and rose from death. The gospel engages our life with all its pain, shame, rejection, lostness, sin, and death. So now, to your pain, the gospel says, "You will be healed." To your shame, the gospel says, "You can now come to God in confidence." To your rejection, the gospel says, "You are accepted!" To your lostness, the gospel says, "You are found and I won't ever let you go." To your sin, the gospel says, "You are forgiven and God declares you pure and righteous." To your death, the gospel says, "You once were dead, but now you are alive."

Because of his finished work, anyone who trusts in Jesus Christ can have this comfort in life and in death:

> That I am not my own, but belong—body and soul, in life and in death—to my faithful Savior Jesus Christ. He has fully paid for all my sins with his precious blood, and has set me free from the tyranny of the devil. He also watches over me in such a way that not a hair can fall from my head without the will of my Father in heaven: in fact, all things must work together for my salvation. Because I belong to him, Christ, by his Holy Spirit, assures me of eternal life and makes me wholeheartedly willing and ready from now on to live for him.[38]

The gospel of Jesus Christ is the fulfillment of God's *hesed*—God's steadfast love that endures forever.

Concluding Prayer

"Wave upon Wave of Grace"

O God of grace, teach me to know that grace precedes, accompanies, and follows my salvation; that it sustains the redeemed soul, that not one link of its chain can ever break.

From Calvary's cross, wave upon wave of grace
reaches me,
deals with my sin,
washes me clean,
renews my heart,
strengthens my will,
draws out my affection,
kindles a flame in my soul,
rules throughout my inner man,
consecrates my every thought, word, work,
teaches me Your immeasurable love.
How great are my privileges in Christ Jesus.
Without him I stand far off, a stranger, an outcast;
in him I draw near and touch His kingly scepter.
Without him I dare not lift up my guilty eyes;
in him I gaze upon my Father-God and friend.
Without him I hide my lips in trembling shame;
in him I open my mouth in petition and praise.
Without him all is wrath and consuming fire;
in him is all love, and the repose of my soul.
Without him is gaping hell below me, and eternal anguish;
in him its gates are barred to me by His precious blood!
Without him darkness spreads its horrors before me;
in him an eternity of glory is my boundless horizon.
Without him all within me is terror and dismay,
in him every accusation is charmed into joy and peace.
Without him all things external call for my condemnation;
in him they minister to my comfort,
and are to be enjoyed with thanksgiving.
Praise be to you for grace,
and for the unspeakable gift of Jesus.[1]

Notes

Chapter 1: Disgrace and Grace

1. Paul F. M. Zahl, *Grace in Practice: A Theology of Everyday Life* (Grand Rapids, MI: Eerdmans, 2007), 64.

2. Marjorie Suchocki, *The Fall to Violence: Original Sin in Relational Theology* (New York: Continuum, 1994), 149. Jennifer Erin Beste argues that, according to Suchocki's view, "when a moral loss is involved, it must be that violator and violated are coresponsible for the resulting harms." Jennifer Erin Beste, *God and the Victim: Traumatic Intrusion on Grace and Freedom* (New York: Oxford University Press, 2007), 12.

3. Ellen Bass and Laura Davis, *Beginning to Heal: A First Book for Men and Women Who Were Sexually Abused as Children* (New York: HarperCollins, 2003), 5. Earlier in their book they write: "There's nothing as wonderful as starting to heal, waking up in the morning and knowing that nobody can hurt you *if you don't let them*" (2, emphasis ours). The message is that healing begins with and is maintained primarily by the victim.

4. This quote is attributed to Josh Billings, Henry Wheeler Shaw, and J. G. Holland.

5. The experience of many victims is that people offer them platitudes, suspicious questions, surface empathy, shallow theology, and simplistic notions of forgiveness and reconciliation.

6. A powerful prayer reflecting this truth is the prayer for the Third Sunday in Lent in *The Book of Common Prayer*: "Almighty God, you know that we have no power in ourselves to help ourselves: Keep us both outwardly in our bodies and inwardly in our souls, that we may be defended from all adversities which may happen to the body, and from all evil thoughts which may assault and hurt the soul; through Jesus Christ our Lord, who lives and reigns with you and the Holy Spirit, one God, for ever and ever. Amen." *The Book of Common Prayer* (New York: Oxford University Press, 1979), 218.

7. *Shalom* is the Hebrew word for "peace." For more on this see chapter 10.

8. This line is from the hymn, "Joy to the World":
    "No more let sins and sorrows grow,
    Nor thorns infest the ground;
    He comes to make his blessings flow
    Far as the curse is found,
    Far as the curse is found,
    Far as, far as the curse is found."
Isaac Watts, *Joy to the World! the Lord is come!* (1719). The blessings of Jesus' redemption flow as far as the curse is found, wherever that curse is found. It is not a gospel simply for a disembodied existence on the other side of death. This hymn reminds us that the gospel is good news to a world where every aspect of the cosmos and our existence in it is twisted away from the intention of the Creator's design by the powers of sin and death.

9. Martin Luther, *The Seven Penitential Psalms*, 1517, as quoted in *Day by Day We Magnify Thee: Daily Readings* (Minneapolis, MN: Fortress, 1982), 321.

10. Hilary Lipka, *Sexual Transgression in the Hebrew Bible* (Sheffield, England: Sheffield Phoenix, 2006), 200–23, 248–54.

11. Phyllis Trible, *Texts of Terror: Literary-Feminist Readings of Biblical Narratives* (Minneapolis, MN: Augsburg Fortress, 1984), 157–58. Throughout the entire course of events, Amnon depersonalizes her. Before and after the assault he refuses to listen to or even acknowledge what she says.

12. Ibid.

13. Mieke Bal, *Death and Dissymmetry: The Politics of Coherence in the Book of Judges*, Chicago Studies in the History of Judaism (Chicago: University Press, 1988), 48. Also see Fokkelieb van Dijk-Hemmes, "Tamar and the Limits of Patriarchy: Between Rape and Seduction (2 Samuel 13 and Genesis 38)," in *Anti-Covenant: Counter-Reading Women's Lives in the Hebrew Bible*, Bible and Literature Series, vol. 22 (Sheffield, England: Almond, 1989), 143.

14. G. Wanke, "*āpār*' dust," in *Theological Lexicon of the Old Testament*, ed. Ernst Jenni and Claus Westermann, trans. Mark E. Biddle (Peabody, MA: Hendrickson, 2001), 2:939–41; T. W. Cartledge, *1 & 2 Samuel* (Macon, GA; Smyth & Helwys, 2001), 538.

15. P. K. McCarter, *II Samuel* (New York: Doubleday, 1984), 326.

16. Mark Gray, "Amnon: A Chip Off the Old Block? Rhetorical Strategy in 2 Samuel 13.7–15: The Rape of Tamar and the Humiliation of the Poor," *Journal for the Study of the Old Testament* 77 (1998): 43–44.

17. This book is a resource for healing and hope, not a substitute for counseling, pastoral care, medical care, or family and community support. We focus exclusively on the emotional pain resulting from the assault. We have ministered to many victims who want and need a clear explanation of how the gospel applies to their experiences of sexual assault and its effects on their lives. We have also talked to many ministers who are looking for a solid, gospel-based book that would be helpful in serving victims. The term "victim" signifies the cruelty and unfairness of sexual assault and puts the responsibility for the assault where it belongs—on the assailant. In this book, we will use the term "victim," though "survivor" can also be appropriate to describe healing as a journey. Generally, the terms are used interchangeably by people who have experienced sexual assault and by the professionals who interact with them. However, there are distinctions. "Victim" is often associated with the early trauma following a sexual assault and emphasizes the fact that a crime has been committed. This term is used for emergency department responses. The terms "survivor" and "victim/survivor" emerged as part of the sexual assault victims' rights movement to describe individuals who have experienced a violent incident, but no longer want any association with the perpetrator or the stigma of being viewed as remaining under the perpetrator's influence and control. This term is used most often for the later periods of recovery and instead of "victim" in order to reclaim power.

18. *Hesed* is the Hebrew word for "God's steadfast, unfailing love for his people." For more on this see chapter 11.

Chapter 2: What Is Sexual Assault?

1. "Rape" is forced sexual intercourse, including vaginal, anal, or oral penetration. Penetration may be with a body part or an object. "Sexual assault" includes any unwanted sexual behavior or contact with a person without consent. Sexual assault may include force, threats, or intimidation. "Sexual abuse" usually refers to the sexual

assault of a child, which is defined as sexual contact with a minor by force, trickery, intimidation, or bribery where there is an imbalance in age, size, power, or knowledge.

2. According to the National Institute of Justice, sexual assault is defined as "contact or interaction between a victim and a perpetrator when the victim is being used for the sexual stimulation of that perpetrator or another person without the victim's consent." L. Taylor and N. Gaskin-Laniyan, "Sexual Assault in Abusive Relationships," *National Institute of Justice Journal* 256 (2007): 1–3. More simply, sexual assault has been defined as "any form of sexual contact without voluntary consent." C. Classen, O. Palesh, R. Aggarwal, "Sexual Revictimization: A Review of the Empirical Literature," *Trauma, Violence, & Abuse* 6, no. 2 (2005): 103–4. Other definitions attempt to outline the parameters of sexual assault by giving overwhelmingly vague and open definitions. As stated by the *Journal of Behavior Modification*, sexual assault is "a form of sexual harassment and can range from fondling someone without their consent to serious acts of physical violence." A. Deliramich, M. Gray, "Changes in Women's Sexual Behavior Following Sexual Assault," *Journal of Behavior Modification* 32, no. 5 (2008): 611–20. The legal definition of criminal sexual assault is any genital, oral, or anal penetration by a part of the accused's body or by an object, using force or without the victim's consent. Aggravated criminal sexual assault occurs when any of the following circumstances accompany the attack: use or display of a weapon; the life of the victim or someone else's life is endangered or threatened; the victim is over age sixty, physically handicapped, or profoundly mentally retarded; the perpetrator causes bodily harm to the victim; the attack occurs during the commission of another felony; or force is used, including either physical violence or threat of bodily harm. See American Medical Association, *Strategies for the Treatment and Prevention of Sexual Assault* (Chicago: American Medical Association, 1995).

3. Although both interpretations do have their respective merits, each has its shortcomings as well. Narrow definitions limit the scope of sexual assault in a way that mitigates a prevalent crime, as well as prevents appropriate amounts of state and federal funding from being allocated to the programs that help victims. In contrast, broad definitions interpret sexual assault in such a way that criticisms of this approach often blame it for overinflating statistics that grossly exaggerate the incidence of this crime.

4. K. C. Basile and L. E. Saltzman, "Sexual Violence Surveillance: Uniform Definitions and Recommended Data Elements," version 1.0 (Atlanta, GA: Centers for Disease Control and Prevention, National Center for Injury Prevention and Control, 2002), http://www.cdc.gov/violenceprevention/pdf/SV_Surveillance_Definitionsl-2009-a.pdf.

5. The definition of rape is straightforward in nature. As defined in the *American Journal of Psychiatry*, rape is "forced sexual intercourse that may be heterosexual or homosexual which involves insertion of an erect penis or an inanimate object into the female vagina or the male anus; in both sexes, rape may also include forced oral or anal penetration." C. Faravelli et al., "Psychopathology after Rape," *American Journal of Psychiatry* 61, no. 8 (2004): 1483–85. The definition of rape is then broken down into varying categories based on the relationship between the victim and the perpetrator. Acquaintance rape is rape in which the victim knows the offender but has had no dating relationship with him or her. Date rape is rape in which the victim knows the perpetrator through some level of social interaction. Statutory rape is rape in which intercourse may be a consensual event but the act between the two individuals violates the age-of-consent law. Spousal rape is rape in which the victim and perpetrator are married or participating in a *de facto* living situation (Alan Wertheimer, *Consent*

to Sexual Relations, Cambridge Studies in Philosophy and Law [Cambridge, England: Cambridge University Press, 2003], 74–77).

6. R. Hall, *Ask Any Woman: A London Inquiry into Rape and Sexual Assault* (London: Falling Wall, 1985); M. Koss, C. A. Gidycz, and N. Wisniewski, "The Scope of Rape: Incidence and Prevalence of Sexual Aggression and Victimization in a National Sample of Higher Education Students," *Journal of Consulting and Clinical Psychology* 55 (1987): 162–70; M. Koss, "Rape: Scope, Impact, Interventions, and Public Policy Responses," *American Psychologist* 48 (1993): 1062–69; D. G. Kilpatrick et al., "Criminal Victimization: Lifetime Prevalence, Reporting to Police, and Psychological Impact," *Crime and Delinquency* 33 (1987): 479–89; D. G. Kilpatrick and A. Seymour, "Rape in America: A Report to the Nation" (National Victims Center: Arlington, VA, and Crime Victims Research and Treatment Center: Charleston, SC, 1992); M. Koss and T. E. Dinero, "Discrimination Analysis of Risk Factors for Sexual Victimization among a National Sample of College Women," *Journal of Consulting and Clinical Psychology* 57 (1989): 242–50; P. Tjaden and N. Thoennes, "Prevalence, Incidence, and Consequences of Violence Against Women: Findings from the National Violence Against Women Survey" (Washington, DC: US Department of Justice, 1998); and S. B. Sorenson et al., "The Prevalence of Adult Sexual Assault: The Los Angeles Epidemiologic Catchment Area Project," *American Journal of Epidemiology* 126 (1987): 1154–64. An estimated 20–25 percent of college women in the United States experience attempted or completed rape during their college careers (B. S. Fisher, F. T. Cullen, M. G. Turner, "The Sexual Victimization of College Women," [Washington, DC: Department of Justice, National Institute of Justice, 2000]). On college campuses, 74 percent of victims knew their assailant and nine out of ten offenders included boyfriends, ex-boyfriends, classmates, friends, and acquaintances (Timothy Hart, *Violent Victimization of College Students* [US Department of Justice: Office of Justice Programs, Bureau of Justice Statistics Special Report: 2003] http://bjs.ojp.usdoj.gov/index.cfm?ty=pbdetail&iid=496).

7. One study suggests the rate of abused males may be far higher, between 20–30 percent. See J. Briere, *Child Abuse Trauma: Theory and Treatment of the Lasting Effects* (Newbury Park, London: Sage, 1992), 4. A 2005 study conducted by the US Centers for Disease Control and Prevention, on San Diego Kaiser Permanente HMO members, reported that 16 percent of males were sexually abused by the age of eighteen (S. R. Dube et al., "Long-Term Consequences of Childhood Sexual Abuse by Gender of Victim," *American Journal of Preventive Medicine* 28 [2005]: 430–38). A 2003 national study of US adults reported that 14.2 percent of men were sexually abused before the age of eighteen (J. Briere and D. M. Elliot, "Prevalence and Symptomatic Sequelae of Self-Reported Childhood Physical and Sexual Abuse in a General Population Sample of Men and Women," *Child Abuse & Neglect: The International Journal* 27 [2003]: 1205–22). A 1998 study reviewing research on male childhood sexual abuse concluded that the problem is "common, under-reported, under-recognized, and under-treated" (W. C. Holmes and G. B. Slap, "Sexual Abuse of Boys: Definition, Prevalence, Correlates, Sequelae, and Management," *Journal of the American Medical Association* 280 [1998]:1855–62). A 1996 study of male university students in the Boston area reported that 18 percent of men were sexually abused before the age of sixteen (D. Lisak, J. Hopper, and P. Song, "Factors in the Cycle of Violence: Gender Rigidity and Emotional Constriction," *Journal of Traumatic Stress* 9 [1999]: 721–43). A 1990 national study of US adults reported that 16 percent of men were sexually abused before the age of eighteen (D. G. Finkelhor et al., "Sexual Abuse in a National Survey of Adult Men and Women: Prevalence, Characteristics, and Risk Factors," *Child Abuse & Neglect: The International Journal* 14 [1990]: 19–28). Within the past few years, North American researchers have found that one out of six

boys is a victim of sexual abuse. See M. Dorais, *Don't Tell: The Sexual Abuse of Boys* (Montreal: McGill-Queens University Press, 2002), 16. G. R. Holmes, L. Offen, and G. Waller, "See No Evil, Hear No Evil, Speak No Evil: Why Do Relatively Few Male Victims of Childhood Sexual Abuse Receive Help for Abuse-Related Issues in Adulthood?" *Clinical Psychology Review* 17 (1997): 69–88. Only 16 percent of men with documented histories of sexual abuse considered themselves to have been sexually abused (C. S. Widom and S. Morris, "Accuracy of Adult Recollections of Childhood Victimization: Part 2. Childhood Sexual Abuse," *Psychological Assessment* 9 [1997]: 34–46).

8. US Department of Justice, *2007 National Crime Victimization Survey* (2007). According to the US Department of Justice's National Crime Victimization Survey, in 2007, there were 248,280 victims of rape, attempted rape, or sexual assault, and these figures do not include victims age twelve or younger. What this means is that every two minutes someone in the United States is sexually assaulted.

9. D. G. Finkelhor, "What's Wrong with Sex Between Adults and Children?" *American Journal of Orthopsychiatry* 49, no. 4 (1979): 692–97; A. W. Baker and S. P. Duncan, "Child Sexual Abuse: A Study of Prevalence in Great Britain," *Child Abuse & Neglect: The International Journal* 9 (1985): 457.

10. P. Tjaden and N. Thoennes, "Extent, Nature, and Consequences of Intimate Partner Violence: Findings From the National Violence Against Women Survey," (Washington, DC: US Department of Justice, 2000).

11. Callie Marie Rennison, *Criminal Victimization in the United States, 1999: Statistical Tables* (Washington, DC: US Department of Justice, Office of Justice Programs, 2001); Aaronette White, "I Am Because We Are: Combined Race and Gender Political Consciousness among African American Women and Men Anti-Rape Activists," *Women's Studies International Forum* 24, no. 1 (2001): 12–13; and Aaronette White, "Talking Feminist, Talking Black: Micromobilization Process in a Collective Protest Against Rape," *Gender & Society* 13, no. 1 (1999): 97.

12. White, "I Am Because We Are," 12–13.

13. Shannon M. Catalano, "Criminal Victimization, 2005," (Washington, DC: Bureau of Justice Statistics, 2006).

14. Some studies show that sexual abuse may be as high as 54 percent for girls and 16 percent for boys (Herbert W. Helm Jr., Jonathan R. Cook, and John M. Berecz, "The Implications of Conjunctive and Disjunctive Forgiveness for Sexual Abuse," *Pastoral Psychology* 54 [2005]: 23–34). These statistics are consistent with an earlier study, D. G. Finkelhor, *Sexually Victimized Children* (New York: Free Press, 1979). One study reports that 93 percent of child sexual assault victims know their assailant (US Bureau of Justice Statistics, *2000 Sexual Assault of Young Children as Reported to Law Enforcement*, 2000).

15. R. K. Bergen, *Wife Rape: Understanding the Response of Survivors and Service Providers* (Thousand Oaks, CA: Sage, 1996); D. G. Finkelhor and K. Yllo, *License to Rape: Sexual Abuse of Wives* (New York: Holt, Rinehart, and Winston, 1985); D. E. H. Russell, *Rape in Marriage* (Indianapolis, IN: Indiana University Press, 1990); P. Mahoney and L. Williams, "Sexual Assault in Marriage: Prevalence, Consequences and Treatment for Wife Rape," in *Partner Violence: A Comprehensive Review of 20 Years of Research*, eds. J. L. Jasinski and L. M. Williams (Thousand Oaks, CA: Sage, 1998).

16. J. Briere and M. Runtz, "University Males' Sexual Interest in Children: Predicting Potential Indices of 'Pedophilia' in a Nonforensic Sample," *Child Abuse & Neglect: The International Journal* 13 (1989): 65–75; Finkelhor et al., "Sexual Abuse in a National Survey of Adult Men and Women," 19–28; D. E. H. Russell, "The Incidence and Preva-

lence of Intrafamilial and Extrafamilial Sexual Abuse of Female Children," *Child Abuse & Neglect: The International Journal* 7 (1983): 133–46.

17. Jean Renvoize, *Innocence Destroyed: A Study of Child Sexual Abuse* (New York: Routledge, 1993).

18. Finkelhor et al., "Sexual Abuse in a National Survey of Adult Men and Women," 19–28; John C. Gonsiorek, Walter Bera, and Don LeTourneau, *Male Sexual Abuse: A Trilogy of Intervention Strategies* (Newbury Park, CA: Sage, 1994).

19. H. Johnson and V. Pottie Bunge, "Prevalence and Consequences of Spousal Assault in Canada," *Canadian Journal of Criminology* 43, no. 1 (2001): 27–45; R. Kimerling et al., "Gender Differences in Victim and Crime Characteristics of Sexual Assault," *Journal of Interpersonal Violence* 17 (2002): 526–32; and Tjaden and Thoennes, "Prevalence, Incidence, and Consequences of Violence Against Women," 1998.

20. P. A. Frazier, "A Comparative Study of Male and Female Rape Victims Seen at Hospital-Based Rape Crisis Programs," *Journal of Interpersonal Violence* 8 (1993): 65–79; and A. Kaufman et al., "Male Rape Victims: Noninstitutionalized Assault," *American Journal of Psychiatry* 137 (1980): 221–3.

21. US Department of Justice, *2004 National Crime Victimization Survey* (2004).

22. US Bureau of Justice Statistics, *2000 Sexual Assault of Young Children as Reported to Law Enforcement* (2000).

23. D. G. Finkelhor, "Epidemiological Factors in the Clinical Identification of Child Sexual Abuse," *Child Abuse & Neglect: The International Journal* 17 (1993): 67–70.

24. A. H. Maker, M. Kemmelmeier, and C. Peterson, "Child Sexual Abuse, Peer Sexual Abuse, and Sexual Assault in Adulthood: A Multi-risk Model of Revictimization," *Journal of Traumatic Stress* 14 (2001): 351–68.

25. Diana M. Elliot, Doris S. Mok, and J. Briere, "Adult Sexual Assault: Prevalence, Symptomatology, and Sex Differences in General Population," *Journal of Traumatic Stress* 17, no. 3 (2004): 203.

26. Ibid., 203–11.

27. N. N. Sarkar and Rina Sarkar. "Sexual Assault on Woman: Its Impact on Her Life and Living in Society," *Sexual and Relationship Therapy* 20 (2005): 407–19.

28. Elliot, Mok, and Briere, "Adult Sexual Assault," 203–11.

29. A. Coxell et al., "Lifetime Prevalence, Characteristics, and Associated Problems of Non-Consensual Sex in Men: Cross Sectional Survey," *British Medical Journal* 318 (1999): 846–50; and S. Desai, I. Arias, and M. P. Thompson, "Childhood Victimization and Subsequent Adult Revictimization Assessed in a Nationally Representative Sample of Women and Men," *Violence and Victims* 17 (2002): 639–53.

30. The National Statistics of Crime and Safety Survey 2002 found that 93 percent of perpetrators were male. The Bureau of Justice found that 99 percent of perpetrators are male.

31. Callie Marie Rennison, *National Crime Victimization Survey: Criminal Victimization 2001* (Washington, DC: US Department of Justice, Office of Justice Programs, 2002), 8.

32. Of female sexual assault victims, 73 percent were assaulted by an acquaintance, and 26 percent were assaulted by a stranger. Thirty-eight percent of women assaulted by a known offender were friends or acquaintances of the rapist, and 28 percent were intimate partners (Catalano, "Criminal Victimization."). Offenders can

be acquaintances, bosses, coaches, therapists, medical personnel, coworkers, dating partners, friends, spouses, family members, or strangers.

33. Scott Lindquist, *The Date Rape Prevention Book: The Essential Guide for Girls and Women* (Naperville, IL: Sourcebooks, 2000), 52; *Federal Bureau of Investigation, Crime in the United States 2000* (Washington, DC: Government Printing Office, 2001), Table 44; and Helen Benedict, *Recovery: How to Survive Sexual Assault for Women, Men, Teenagers, Their Friends and Families* (New York: Columbia University Press, 1994), 9.

34. Rennison, *National Crime Victimization Survey*, 8.

35. Gene Abel et al., "Self-Reported Sex Crimes of Nonincarcerated Paraphiliacs," *Journal of Interpersonal Violence* 2, no. 1 (1987): 3–25.

36. White, "Talking Feminist, Talking Black," 97.

37. Federal Bureau of Investigation, *Uniform Crime Report* (1973), 15.

38. Menachem Amir, *Patterns in Forcible Rape* (Chicago: University of Chicago Press, 1971), 27–28.

39. Catalano, "Criminal Victimization."

40. Holmes, Offen, and Waller, "See No Evil, Hear No Evil, Speak No Evil," 69–88. Only 16 percent of men with documented histories of sexual abuse considered themselves to have been sexually abused (Widom and Morris, "Adult Recollections of Childhood Victimization," 34–46).

41. M. Dorais, *Don't Tell: The Sexual Abuse of Boys* (Montreal: McGill-Queens University Press, 2002), 17.

Chapter 3: What Are the Effects of Sexual Assault?

1. "Because the person in pain is ordinarily so bereft of the resources of speech, it is not surprising that the language for pain should sometimes be brought into being by those who are not themselves in pain but who speak on behalf of those who are. Though there are very great impediments to expressing another's sentient distress, so are there also very great reasons why one might want to do so, and thus there come to be avenues by which this most radically private of experiences begins to enter the realm of public discourse." Susan Sontag, *Regarding the Pain of Others* (New York: Farrar, Straus and Giroux, 2002), 6.

2. Jennifer Erin Beste, *God and the Victim: Traumatic Intrusions on Grace and Freedom* (New York: Oxford University Press, 2007), 38. This is due to the fact that victims of human-induced trauma experience firsthand the degree of cruelty that persons are capable of inflicting on one another. Thus, they suffer from intensified forms of shattered trust and betrayal.

3. D. G. Kilpatrick et al., "Victim and Crime Factors Associated with the Development of Crime-Related Post-Traumatic Stress Disorder," *Behavior Therapy* 20 (1989): 199–214.

4. D. G. Kilpatrick, L. J. Veronen, and P. A. Resick, "The Aftermath of Rape: Recent Empirical Findings," *American Journal of Orthopsychiatry* 49 (1979): 658–69; D. G. Kilpatrick, P. A. Resick, and L. J. Veronen, "Longitudinal Effects of a Rape Experience," *Journal of Social Issues* 37 (1981): 105–22; and P. A. Resick, "The Psychological Impact of Rape," *Journal of Interpersonal Violence* 8 (1993): 223–55.

5. E. Frank, S. M. Turner, and B. Duffy, "Depressive Symptoms in Rape Victims," *Journal of Affective Disorders* 1 (1979): 269–77; E. Frank and B. D. Stewart, "Depressive Symptoms in Rape Victims: A Revisit," *Journal of Affective Disorders* 7 (1984): 77–82;

B. M. Atkeson et al., "Victims of Rape: Repeated Assessment of Depressive Symptoms," *Journal of Consulting and Clinical Psychology* 50 (1982): 96–102.

6. Studies have found depressive symptoms to persist for longer periods of time. See D. G. Kilpatrick et al., "Criminal Victimization: Lifetime Prevalence, Reporting to Police, and Psychological Impact," *Crime and Delinquency* 33 (1987): 479–89; and T. Mackey et al., "Factors Associated with Long-term Depressive Symptoms of Sexual Assault Victims," *Archives of Psychiatric Nursing* 6 (1992): 10–25. Compared to nonvictims, victims have reported higher levels of depression one year and one decade postassault. See D. G. Kilpatrick and L. J. Vernon, "Treatment of Fear and Anxiety in Victims of Rape," Final Report, grant #MH29602 (Washington, DC: National Institute of Mental Health, 1984); and Kilpatrick, et al., "Criminal Victimization," 479–89.

7. Such cycling—between being alert for danger and feeling emotionally shutdown—can result in emotional instability, which undermines or distorts the victim's self-perception, relationships, and ability to function.

8. These may include the age and developmental maturity of the victim; the social support network available to the victim; the victim's relationship to the offender; the response to the attack by police, medical personnel, and victim advocates; the response to the attack by the victim's loved ones; the frequency, severity, and duration of the assault(s); the setting of the attack; the level of violence and injury inflicted; the response by the criminal justice system; community attitudes and values; and the meaning attributed to the traumatic event by the sexual assault survivor. See M. Koss and Mary Harvey, *The Rape Victim: Clinical and Community Interventions* (Newbury Park, CA: Sage Library of Social Research, 1991), 42–88.

9. Kilpatrick, et al., "Victim and Crime Factors," 199–214.

10. Hyperarousal disrupts the body's regulation of arousal and stress adaptation. During a traumatic event a person's ability to defend one's self is overwhelmed and ineffective. As a result, the self-defense system becomes disorganized and confused, and the person begins to experience a persistent state of hyperarousal. Such persistent physiological and psychological states or arousal can cause permanent changes on cognitive, affective, and neurobiological levels. See Elizabeth Waites, *Trauma and Survival: Post-Traumatic and Dissociative Disorders in Women* (New York: Norton, 1993), 100.

11. The study used the Traumatic Symptom Inventory (TSI) to look at trauma symptoms. The Traumatic Events Survey evaluates a wide range of childhood and adult traumas. It has been used in numerous published trauma studies and appears to be a valid measure of exposure to potentially traumatic events. TSI measures anxious arousal, depression, anger/irritability, intrusive experiences, defensive avoidance, dissociation, sexual concerns, dysfunctional sexual behavior, impaired self-reference, and tension reduction behavior.

12. D. M. Elliot, Doris S. Mok, and J. Briere, "Adult Sexual Assault: Prevalence, Symptomatology, and Sex Differences in General Population," *Journal of Traumatic Stress* 17, no. 3 (2004): 209.

13. Doni Whitsett, "The Psychobiology of Trauma and Child Maltreatment," *Cultic Studies Review* 5, no. 3 (2006): 367.

14. Beste, *God and the Victim*, 5.

15. Most sexual assault victims experience some kind of post-traumatic distress. The term "post-traumatic stress" does not denote an illness or abnormal reaction, but rather describes common and normal reactions that might occur for both women and men following a sexual assault. A victim of sexual assault may

develop PTSD. PTSD is primarily characterized by chronic anxiety, depression, and flashbacks, which develop after experiencing significant trauma such as combat, natural disaster, or violent crime victimization.

PTSD is diagnosed by a mental health professional when the biological, psychological, and social effects of trauma are severe enough to have impaired a survivor's social and occupational functioning (Jon Allen, *Coping with Trauma: A Guide to Self-Understanding* [Washington, DC: American Psychiatric, 1995]). Many sexual assault victims suffer from PTSD that may make the victim feel very disoriented. The National Center for Post-traumatic Stress Disorder defines PTSD as "an anxiety disorder that can occur after [an individual has] been through a traumatic event" (http: www.ptsd.va.gov/public/pages/what-is-ptsd.asp). PTSD is different than other mental health disorders in that it results from a specific life experience. We can understand a traumatic experience as one that involves the potential for death or serious injury, resulting in intense fear, helplessness, or horror. PTSD is characterized by a set of symptoms including: reexperiencing, avoidance, numbing, and arousal. Reexperiencing can take the form of nightmares or thoughts, acting as a mental replay of the trauma. Avoidance symptoms have to do with the isolation of oneself from activities, places, and people who remind the survivor of the trauma. Numbing symptoms describe a loss of emotion, especially positive emotion. Arousal symptoms involve excessive physiological activation and include a heightened sense of being on guard as well as difficulty with sleep and concentration. To be formally diagnosed, the symptoms of PTSD must persist for over one month, cause significant distress, and greatly affect the individual's ability to perform and interact with others. See Meredith Klump, "Posttraumatic Stress Disorder and Sexual Assault in Women," *Journal of College Student Psychotherapy* 21, no. 2 (2006).

16. Bessel van der Kolk and Alexander McFarlane, "Black Hole of Trauma," in *Traumatic Stress: The Effects of Overwhelming Experience on Mind, Body, and Society*, eds. Bessel van der Kolk, Alexander McFarlane, and Lars Weisaeth (New York: Guilford, 1996), 6–7. They also explain that, for some victims, being preoccupied with the traumatic event gradually allows them to integrate it into their life story and to view it as a painful past experience (5).

17. National Center for Victims of Crime and Crime Victims Research and Treatment Center, *Rape in America: A Report to the Nation* (Arlington, VA: National Center for Victims of Crime, 1992).

18. Susan Brownmiller, *Against Our Will: Men, Women, and Rape* (New York: Bantam, 1975) and M. R. Burt, "Cultural Myths and Supports for Rape," *Journal of Personality and Social Psychology* 33 (1980): 217–30.

19. Negative reactions to sexual assault victims, such as attributing blame or responsibility to the victim, generally have been found to be greater for assaults by acquaintances and especially dates, sexually active victims, less "respectable" victims, nonresisting victims; assaults in which victims used alcohol prior to the assault; and assaults in which victims engaged in nonstereotypical gender-role behavior prior to attack.

20. Sarah E. Ullman, "Social Reactions, Coping Strategies, and Self-Blame Attributions in Adjustment to Sexual Assault," *Psychology of Women Quarterly* 20 (1996): 505–26.

21. Patricia A. Frazier, Heather Mortenson, and Jason Steward, "Coping Strategies as Mediators of the Relations among Perceived Control and Distress in Sexual Assault Survivors," *Journal of Counseling Psychology* 52 (2005): 267–78; Patricia A. Frazier,

"Perceived Control and Distress Following Sexual Assault: A Longitudinal Test of a New Model," *Journal of Personality and Social Psychology* 84, no. 6 (2003): 1257–69; C. M. Arata, "Coping with Rape: The Roles of Prior Sexual Abuse and Attribution of Blame," *Journal of Interpersonal Violence* 14 (1999): 62–78; Patricia A. Frazier, "Victim Attribution and Post-Rape Trauma," *Journal of Personality and Social Psychology* 59 (1990): 298–304; Patricia A. Frazier, "The Role of Attribution and Perceived Control in Recovery from Rape," *Journal of Personal and Interpersonal Loss* 5 (2000): 203–25; Patricia A. Frazier and L. Schauben, "Causal Attributions and Recovery from Rape and Other Stressful Life Events," *Journal of Social and Clinical Psychology* 13 (1994): 1–14; B. Meyer and S. Taylor, "Adjustments to Rape," *Journal of Personality and Social Psychology* 50 (1986): 1226–34; and M. Koss, A. Figueredo, and R. Prince, "Cognitive Mediation of Rape's Mental, Physical, and Social Health Impact: Test of Four Models in Cross-Sectional Data," *Journal of Consulting and Clinical Psychology* 70 (2002): 926–41.

22. N. N. Sarkar and Rina Sarkar, "Sexual Assault on Woman: Its Impact on Her Life and Living in Society," *Sexual and Relationship Therapy* 20 (2005): 407–19.

23. J. Briere et al., "Lifetime Victimization History, Demographics, and Clinical Status in Female Psychiatric Emergency Room Patients," *Journal of Nervous and Mental Disease* 185 (1997): 95–101; M. A. Burnam et al., "Sexual Assault and Mental Disorders in a Community Population," *Journal of Consulting and Clinical Psychology* 56 (1988): 843–50; R. F. Hanson et al., "Violent Crime and Mental Health," in J. R. Freedy and S. E. Hobfoll, eds., *Traumatic Stress: From Theory to Practice* (New York: Plenum, 1995), 129–61; Kilpatrick et al., "Criminal Victimization," 479–89; and P. A. Resick, "Reactions of Female and Male Victims of Rape or Robbery," Final Report, grant #MH 37296, (Washington, DC: National Institute of Mental Health, 1988).

24. A. Kaufman et al., "Male Rape Victims: Noninstitutionalized Assault," *American Journal of Psychiatry* 137 (1980): 221–23.

25. Patricia A. Frazier, "A Comparative Study of Male and Female Rape Victims Seen at Hospital-Based Rape Crisis Program," *Journal of Interpersonal Violence* 8 (1993): 65–79.

26. K. B. Hoyenga and K. T. Hoyenga, *The Question of Sex Differences: Psychological, Cultural and Biological Issues* (Boston: Little, Brown, 1979); and F. H. Norris, "Epidemiology of Trauma: Frequency and Impact of Different Potentially Traumatic Events on Different Demographic Groups," *Journal of Consulting and Clinical Psychology* 60 (1992): 409–18.

27. M. F. Meyers, "Men Sexually Assaulted as Adults and Sexually Abused as Boys," *Archives of Sexual Behavior* 18 (1989): 203–15.

28. Elliot, Mok, and Briere, "Adult Sexual Assault," 210.

29. Ibid., 209.

30. Ibid.

31. Ann J. Cahill, *Rethinking Rape* (Ithaca, NY: Cornell University Press, 2001), 169–75, 192–94; Ann Wolbert Burgess and Lynda Lytle Holmstrom, "Rape Trauma Syndrome," in *Forcible Rape: The Crime, the Victim, and the Offender* (New York: Columbia University Press, 1977), 320–25; Ann Wolbert Burgess, "Rape Trauma Syndrome," in *Rape and Society: Readings on the Problem of Sexual Assault*, eds. Patricia Searles and Ronald J. Berger (Boulder, CO: Westview, 1995), 240–43; Liz Kelly, *Surviving Sexual Violence* (Minneapolis, MN: University of Minnesota Press, 1988), 39, 187–214; David Archard, *Sexual Consent* (Boulder, CO: Westview, 1998), 20–41, 44–53; and Brownmiller, *Against Our Will*, 18, 376.

32. B. O. Rothbaum et al., "A Prospective Examination of Post-Traumatic Stress Disorder in Rape Victims," *Journal of Traumatic Stress* 5, no. 3 (1992): 455–75; G. Steketee and E. B. Foa, "Rape Victims: Post-Traumatic Stress Responses and Their Treatment: A Review of the Literature," *Journal of Anxiety Disorders* 1 no. 1 (1987): 69–86; H. S. Resnick et al., "Prevalence of Civilian Trauma and Posttraumatic Stress Disorder in a Representative National Sample of Women," *Journal of Consulting and Clinical Psychology* 61, no. 6 (1993): 984–91; and R. Graziano, "Treating Women Incest Survivors: A Bridge Between 'Cumulative Trauma' and 'Post-Traumatic Stress,'" *Social Work in Health Care* 17, no. 1 (1992): 69–85.

33. W. Proudfoot, "Religious Experience, Emotion, and Belief," *Harvard Theological Review* 70 no. 3/4 (1977): 348.

34. Matthew A. Elliott, *Faithful Feelings: Rethinking Emotion in the New Testament* (Grand Rapids, MI: Kregel, 2006), 31.

35. W. Lyons, *Emotion* (Cambridge: Cambridge University Press, 1980), 58–59.

36. Elliott, *Faithful Feelings*, 42.

37. Paul Holmer, *Making Christian Sense* (Louisville, KY: Westminster, 1984), 24.

38. Don E. Saliers, *Soul in Paraphrase: Prayer and Religious Affections* (Nitro, WV: OSL, 1991), 11.

39. Joanne V. Wood, W. Q. Elaine Perunovic, and John W. Less, "Positive Self-Statements: Power for Some, Peril for Others," *Psychological Science* 20, no. 7 (2009): 860.

40. M. P. Zanna, "Message Receptivity: A New Look at the Old Problem of Open-Versus Closed-Mindedness," in *Advertising Exposure, Memory and Choice*, ed. A. Mitchell (Hillsdale, NJ: Erlbaum, 1993), 141–62.

41. Wood, Perunovic, and Less, "Positive Self-Statements," 865.

42. Ibid., 861, 865.

43. Martin Luther, "Thesis 28 of the Heidelberg Disputation." http://www.ccel.org/creeds/heidelberg-cat.html.

Chapter 4: Denial

1. In *The Bluest Eyes*, a novel about a young woman's rape, Toni Morrison describes how disgrace is extended: "We tried to see her without looking at her and never, never went near. Not because she was absurd, or repulsive, or because we were frightened, but because we had failed her." Toni Morrison, *The Bluest Eyes* (New York: Pocket, 1970), 158.

2. John Calvin, *Commentary on the Book of Psalms*, Calvin's Commentaries (Edinburgh, Scotland: Calvin Translation Society, 1845), 1:37.

3. See chapter 10 for more on being an "image of God."

4. For further study of the exodus, see chapter 11.

5. Elaine Scarry, *The Body in Pain: The Making and Unmaking* (New York: Oxford University Press, 1987), 213.

6. Steve Jeffery, Michael Ovey, and Andrew Sach, *Pierced for Our Transgressions: Rediscovering the Glory of Penal Substitution* (Wheaton, IL: Crossway, 2007), 151.

7. John Calvin, *Commentaries on the Epistle of Paul the Apostle to the Hebrews*, trans. John Owen (Edinburgh, Scotland: Calvin Translation Society, 1853), 74–76. Calvin is commenting on Hebrews 2:17.

8. Walter Brueggemann, *Theology of the Old Testament: Testimony, Dispute, Advocacy* (Minneapolis, MN: Fortress, 1997), 254.

9. Geerhardus Vos, *Grace and Glory: Sermons Preached in Chapel at Princeton Theological Seminary* (Grand Rapids, MI: Reformed, 1922), 94–95.

10. Miroslav Volf, *End of Memory: Remembering Rightly in a Violent World* (Grand Rapids, MI: Eerdmans, 2006), 75.

11. Brueggemann, *Theology of the Old Testament*, 29.

Chapter 5: Distorted Self-Image

1. Judith Lewis Herman, "Complex PTSD: A Syndrome in Survivors of Prolonged and Repeated Trauma," in *Psychotraumatology: Key Papers and Core Concepts in Post-Traumatic Stress*, ed. George S. Everyl, Jr. and Jeffrey M. Lating (New York: Plenum, 1995), 94–95.

2. Frances Driscoll, "All Of This Happens In A Warm Coastal Climate," in *The Rape Poems* (Port Angeles, WA: Pleasure Boat, 1997), 60.

3. Joanne V. Wood, W. Q. Elaine Perunovic, and John W. Less, "Positive Self-Statements: Power for Some, Peril for Others," *Psychological Science* 20, no. 7 (2009): 860.

4. M. P. Zanna, "Message Receptivity: A New Look at the Old Problem of Open-Versus Closed-Mindedness," in *Advertising Exposure, Memory and Choice,* ed. A. Mitchell (Hillsdale, NJ: Erlbaum, 1993), 141–62.

5. Wood, Perunovic, and Less, "Positive Self-Statements," 860.

6. Ibid., 865.

7. Ibid., 861, 865.

8. Lewis B. Smedes, *Shame and Grace* (San Francisco: HarperCollins, 1993), 80.

9. Voltaire, *Toleration and Other Essays*, trans. Joseph McCabe (New York: G. P. Putnam's Sons, 1912), 259, 262 (excerpts from "Poem on the Lisbon Disaster; Or an Examination of the Axiom, 'All is Well,'" 255–63).

10. The Puritan theologian Thomas Brooks wrote: "Jesus Christ is mine. I can with the greatest confidence and boldness affirm it. He is my Head, my Husband, my Lord, my Redeemer, my Justifier, my Savior. And I am His. I am as sure that I am His, as I am sure that I live. I am His by purchase and I am His by conquest; I am His by donation and I am His by election; I am His by covenant and I am His by marriage; I am wholly His; I am peculiarly His; I am universally His; I am eternally His." Thomas Brooks, *Heaven on Earth*, in *The Complete Works of Thomas Brooks*, ed. Alexander B. Grosart (Edinburgh: James Nichol, 1866) 2:320.

11. See chapter 11 for further explanation of this.

12. J. I. Packer, *Knowing God* (Downers Grove, IL: InterVarsity, 1973), 206. The concept of divine sonship through a believer's adoption in Christ must certainly be applied and expounded in dealing with those suffering from the ongoing consequences of sin, guilt, and shame. Divine sonship through adoption is one of the glorious benefits of the gospel. Consider how Jonathan Edwards applied the wonder of divine sonship to his hearers: "This God, to whom there is none in heaven to be compared, nor any among the sons of the mighty to be likened; this God who is from everlasting to everlasting, an infinitely powerful, wise, holy, and lovely being, who is the Alpha and Omega, the beginning and the end, is your God. He is reconciled to you and is become your friend. There is a friendship between you and the Almighty; you are become acquainted with Him, and He has made known Himself to you, and communicates Him-

self to you, converses with you as a friend, dwells with you, and in you, by His Holy Spirit. Yea, He has taken you into a nearer relation to Him: He is become your Father, and owns you for His child, and doth by you, and will do by you, as a child; He cares for you, will see that you are provided for, will see that you never shall want anything that will be useful to you. He has made you one of His heirs, and a co-heir with His Son, and will bestow an inheritance upon you, as it is bestowed upon a child of the King of Kings. You are now in some measure sanctified, and have the image of God upon your souls, but hereafter, when God shall receive you, His dear child, into His arms, and shall admit you to the perfect enjoyment of Him as your portion, you will be entirely transformed into His likeness, for you shall see Him as He is. The consideration of having such a glorious God for your God, your friend, your Father, and your portion, and that you shall eternally enjoy Him as such, is enough to make you despise all worldly afflictions and adversities, and even death itself, and to trample them under your feet." Jonathan Edwards, "God's Excellencies" in *The Works of Jonathan Edwards*, vol. 10, *Sermons and Discourses 1720–1723*, ed. Wilson H. Kimnach (New Haven, CT: Yale University Press, 1992), 435. Emphasis added.

13. J. I. Packer writes: "If you want to judge how well a person understands Christianity, find out how much he makes of the thought of being God's child, and having God as his Father. If this is not the thought that prompts and controls his worship and prayers and his whole outlook on life, it means that he does not understand Christianity very well at all. . . . Our understanding of Christianity cannot be better than our grasp of adoption." Packer, *Knowing God*, 201–2.

14. John Owen, *Communion with God*, ed. R. K. Law (Carlisle, PA: Banner of Truth, 1991), 109.

15. See chapter 12. "All those that are justified, God vouchsafes, in and for His only Son Jesus Christ, to make partakers of the grace of adoption, by which they are taken into the number, and enjoy the liberties and privileges of the children of God, have His name put upon them, receive the spirit of adoption, have access to the throne of grace with boldness, are enabled to cry, Abba, Father, are pitied, protected, provided for, and chastened by Him as by a Father: yet never cast off, but sealed to the day of redemption, and inherit the promises, as heirs of everlasting salvation." G. I. Williamson, *Westminster Confession of Faith for Study Classes* (Philadelphia: Presbyterian and Reformed, 1964), 103.

16. John Calvin, *Institutes of the Christian Religion*, ed. J. T. McNeil, trans. Ford Lewis Battles (Philadelphia: Westminster, 1960), 3.7.8.

17. Francis Turretin, *Institutes of Elenctic Theology*, ed. James T. Dennison Jr., trans. George Musgrave Giger (Phillipsburg: P&R, 1992), 2:648.

18. Martin Luther, "On the Freedom of the Christian," in *Luther's Works*, vol. 31, *Career of the Reformer*, ed. Harold J. Grimm and Helmut T. Lehmann (Minneapolis, MN: Fortress, 1957), 371.

19. Dietrich Bonhoeffer, "Who am I?" in *Letters and Papers from Prison* (1953; repr., New York: Touchstone, 1997), 347–48.

Chapter 6: Shame

1. June Price Tangney and Ronda L. Dearing have defined shame as: "an acutely painful emotion that is typically accompanied by a sense of shrinking or of 'being small' and by a sense of worthlessness and powerlessness. . . . [Shame leads to] a split in self-functioning in which the self is both agent and object of observation and

disapproval. An observing self witnesses and denigrates the focal self as unworthy and reprehensible." June Price Tangney and Ronda L. Dearing, *Shame and Guilt* (New York: Guilford, 2002), 18.

2. Tangney and Dearing, *Shame and Guilt*, 18.

3. Dan B. Allender and Tremper Longman III, *The Cry of the Soul: How Our Emotions Reveal Our Deepest Questions About God* (Colorado Springs: NavPress, 1994), 193.

4. Johanna Stiebert writes: "Shame is a complex phenomenon straddling psychological, cultural, social, and ethical aspects of human experience." Johanna Stiebert, *The Construction of Shame in the Hebrew Bible: The Prophetic Contribution,* Journal for the Study of the Old Testament: Supplement Series 346 (Sheffield, England: Sheffield Academic, 2002): 3.

5. "Shame is an inner sense of being completely diminished or insufficient as a person. . . . A moment of shame may be humiliation so painful or an indignity so profound that one feels one has been robbed of her or his dignity or exposed as basically inadequate, bad, or worthy of rejection. A pervasive sense of shame is the ongoing premise that one is fundamentally bad, inadequate, defective, unworthy, or not fully valid as a human being." Merle A. Fossum and Marilyn J. Mason, *Facing Shame: Families in Recovery* (New York: W. W. Norton, 1989), 5.

6. Stiebert, *The Construction of Shame,* 3; and K. C. Hanson, "How Honorable! How Shameful! A Cultural Analysis of Matthew's Makarisms and Reproaches," *Semeia* 68 (1996): 81–112. Also see Bruce J. Malina, *The New Testament World: Insights from Cultural Anthropology* (Atlanta, GA: Westminster, 2001).

7. Allender and Longman, *Cry of the Soul*, 197.

8. G. J. Wenham, *Leviticus*, The International Commentary on the Old Testament (Grand Rapids, MI: Eerdmans, 1979). For references to Wenham's commentary in this chapter, see "Unclean Animals," pp. 161–84. G. J. Wenham says that unclean and its cognates occur 132 times in the Old Testament. Over 50 percent of these are in Leviticus.

9. Stephen I. Wright, "Luke" in *Dictionary for Theological Interpretation of the New Testament,* ed. Kevin J. Vanhoozer (Grand Rapids, MI: Baker, 2008), 54.

10. C. Norman Kraus, *Jesus Christ Our Lord: Christology from a Disciple's Perspective* (Scottsdale, AZ: Herald, 1990), 217.

11. Darrell L. Bock, "Luke-Acts," in *New Dictionary of Biblical Theology,* eds. T. Desmond Alexander and Brian S. Rosner (Downers Grove, IL: InterVarsity, 2001).

12. William L. Lane, *Hebrews 9–13*, Word Biblical Commentary, vol. 47B (Nashville: Word, 1991), 523.

13. Wenham, *Leviticus*, 233–35.

14. Martin Hengel, *Crucifixion in the Ancient World and the Folly of the Message of the Cross*, trans. John Bowden (Philadelphia: Augsburg, 1977), 88–89.

15. Mike Wilkerson, *Redemption: Freed by Jesus from the Idols We Worship and the Wounds We Carry* (Wheaton, IL: Crossway, 2011), chapter 4.

16. David A. DeSilva, "Despising Shame: A Cultural-Anthropological Investigation of the Epistle to the Hebrews," *Journal of Biblical Literature* 113/3 (1994): 439–61.

17. F. F. Bruce, *The Epistle to the Hebrews*, New International Commentary of the New Testament (Grand Rapids, MI: Eerdmans, 1996), 338.

18. Martin Luther, *Commentary on St. Paul's Epistle to the Galatians*, trans. Theodore Conrad Graebner (Grand Rapids, MI: Zondervan, 1939), 11–12.

19. Allender and Longman, *Cry of the Soul*, 219.

20. John Calvin, "Preface to Olivetan's New Testament," in *Calvin: Commentaries* vol. 23, Library of Christian Classics, ed. Joseph Haroutunian (Louisville, KY: Westminster, 1958), 69–70.

21. Allender and Longman, *Cry of the Soul*, 211–12.

Chapter 7: Guilt

1. R. C. Sproul, *The Holiness of God* (Wheaton, IL: Tyndale, 1985), 115–16.

2. Phillip Yancey, *What's So Amazing About Grace?* (Grand Rapids, MI: Zondervan, 1997), 31.

3. J. Gresham Machen, "What the Bible Teaches about Jesus," in *Selected Shorter Writings*, ed. D. G. Hart (Phillipsburg, NJ: Presbyterian and Reformed, 2004), 31–32.

4. Martin Luther, *Werke* (Weimar, 1883), 5:608.

5. Ed Welch, *When People Are Big and God Is Small: Overcoming Peer Pressure, Codependency, and the Fear of Man* (Phillipsburg, NJ: P&R, 1997), 34.

6. John Calvin, *Commentaries on the Epistle of Paul the Apostle to the Hebrews*, trans. John Owen (Edinburgh, Scotland: Calvin Translation Society, 1853), 74–76. Calvin is commenting on Hebrews 2:17.

7. Dietrich Bonhoeffer, *The Cost of Discipleship* (New York: Touchstone, 1995), 45.

8. *The Book of Common Prayer* (New York: Oxford University Press, 1979), 331.

9. Ibid., 360.

10. *The Hymnal 1982* (Harrisburg, PA: Church Publishing, 1985), S241.

11. The Heidelberg Catechism, Question and Answer 60. http://www.ccel.org/creeds/heidelberg-cat.html.

12. A good example of this is found in the following quote: "The Lord Jesus Christ did not come into the world to meet with His friends. He came to die for His enemies. . . . We were objects of wrath, rightly facing the unmitigated, everlasting fury of an incensed God, but now in Christ we have found mercy. We have been brought from death to life, from corruption to glory. We were slaves to sin, the world and the devil, but are now adopted children of our heavenly Father. We were stained with the filth of a wicked life and tormented by the pain of a guilty conscience, but are now pardoned and forgiven, standing blameless before Him as a pure bride, clothed in the clean, white robes of Christ's righteousness." Steve Jeffery, Michael Ovey, and Andrew Sach, *Pierced for Our Transgressions: Rediscovering the Glory of Penal Substitution* (Wheaton, IL: Crossway, 2007), 152.

13. Ibid., 152–53.

14. Søren Kierkegaard, *A Kierkegaard Anthology*, ed. Robert Bretall (Princeton: Princeton University Press, 1973), 165.

15. J. C. Ryle, *Startling Questions* (New York: Robert Carter & Brothers, 1853), 287–88.

Chapter 8: Anger

1. Lynn Heitritter and Jeanette Vought, *Helping Victims of Sexual Abuse A Sensitive Biblical Guide for Counselors, Victims, and Families* (Minneapolis, MN: Bethany House, 2006), 173.

2. Dan B. Allender and Tremper Longman III, *The Cry of the Soul: How Our Emotions Reveal Our Deepest Questions about God* (Colorado Springs: NavPress, 1999), 35.

3. David Powlison, "Anger Part 1: Understanding Anger," *The Journal of Biblical Counseling* 14, no. 1 (1995): 40.

4. B. B. Warfield, "The Emotional Life of Our Lord," in *The Person and Work of Christ* (Philadelphia: Presbyterian & Reformed, 1950), 107.

5. B. Baloian, *Anger in the Old Testament* (New York: Peter Lang, 1992), 73.

6. Stanley Grenz, *Theology for the Community of God* (Grand Rapids, MI: Eerdmans, 2000), 642.

7. Warfield, "The Emotional Life of Our Lord," 122.

8. John R. W. Stott, *The Cross of Christ* (Downers Grove, IL: InterVarsity, 1986), 173.

9. Powlison, "Anger Part 1: Understanding Anger," 42.

10. Ibid.

11. Allender and Longman, *Cry of the Soul*, 61.

12. Quoted in Powlison, "Anger Part 1: Understanding Anger," 51.

13. Allender and Longman, *Cry of the Soul*, 46.

14. Ibid., 62.

15. Donald W. Shriver Jr., *An Ethics for Enemies: Forgiveness in Politics* (New York: Oxford University Press, 1995), 19.

16. Hannah Arendt, *The Human Condition: A Study of the Central Dilemma Facing Modern Man* (Garden City, NY: Doubleday, 1959), 216.

17. Lewis B. Smedes, *Forgive and Forget: Healing the Hurts We Don't Deserve* (San Francisco: Harper & Row, 1984), 124.

18. Miroslav Volf, *Free of Charge: Giving and Forgiving in a Culture Stripped of Grace* (Grand Rapids, MI: Zondervan, 2006), 189.

19. Robert Kenneth Cheong, "Towards an Explicitly Theocentric Model of Forgiveness Based on God's Two-Fold Commandment of Love," (PhD diss., Southern Baptist Theological Seminary, 2005), 121.

20. Thomas Watson, *The Lord's Prayer* (1692; repr., Carlisle, PA: Banner of Truth, 1999), 239.

21. Volf, *Free of Charge*, 129–30.

22. Ibid., 153.

23. Ibid., 153, 183.

24. Ibid., 183. Also, "forgiveness does not *cause* repentance, but it does help make repentance possible" (186).

25. Miroslav Volf, *Exclusion and Embrace: A Theological Exploration of Identity, Otherness, and Reconciliation* (Nashville, TN: Abingdon, 1996), 120.

26. Dan B. Allender, *When Trust Is Lost: Healing for Victims of Sexual Abuse* (Grand Rapids, MI: RBC Ministries, 1992), 27.

27. Volf, *Exclusion and Embrace*, 123.

28. Dan B. Allender, "Forgive and Forget and Other Myths of Forgiveness," in *God and the Victim: Theological Reflections on Evil, Victimization, Justice, and Forgiveness*, ed. Lisa Barnes Lampman (Grand Rapids, MI: Eerdmans, 1999), 201.

29. Ibid., 206.

30. Volf, *Free of Charge*, 168.

31. The general claim is that forgiveness is hazardous and may cause further injury to the survivor: E. Bass and L. Davis, *The Courage to Heal: A Guide for Women Survivors of Child Sexual Abuse* (New York: Harper & Row, 1988); C. Courtois, *Healing the Incest Wound: Adult Survivors in Therapy* (New York: W. W. Norton, 1988); C. Courtois, "Theory, Sequencing, and Strategy in Treating Adult Survivors," *Treating Victims of Child Sexual Abuse* 51 (1991): 47–60. Others simply ignore the concept of forgiveness altogether: M. Lew, *Victims No Longer: Men Recovering from Incest and Other Sexual Child Abuse* (New York: HarperCollins, 1990).

32. S. Freedman and R. Enright, "Forgiveness as an Intervention Goal with Incest Survivors," *Journal of Consultation and Clinical Psychology* 64, no. 5 (1996): 983–92; V. Holeman and R. Myers, "Effects of Forgiveness of Perpetrators on Marital Adjustment for Survivors of Sexual Abuse," *The Family Journal* 6, no. 3 (1998): 182–88; H. Wilson, "Forgiveness and Survivors of Sexual Abuse: Relationships among Forgiveness of the Perpetrator, Spiritual Well-being, Depression and Anxiety" (PhD diss., Boston University, 1994); V. Holeman, "The Relationship between Forgiveness of a Perpetrator and Current Marital Adjustment for Female Survivors of Childhood Sexual Abuse" (PhD diss., Kent State University, 1994).

33. Walter Brueggemann, *The Message of the Psalms: A Theological Commentary* (Minneapolis, MN: Augsburg, 1984), 77.

Chapter 9: Despair

1. Paul F. M. Zahl, *Who Will Deliver Us? The Present Power of the Death of Christ* (Eugene, OR: Wipf and Stock, 1983), 12–13.

2. Eric L. Johnson, *Foundations for Soul Care: A Christian Psychology Proposal* (Downers Grove, IL: IVP Academic, 2007), 430.

3. William Styron, *Darkness Visible: A Memoir of Madness* (New York: Vintage, 1990), 50.

4. Dan B. Allender and Tremper Longman III, *The Cry of the Soul: How Our Emotions Reveal Our Deepest Questions about God*, (Colorado Springs: NavPress, 1999), 135.

5. Sam Storms, *One Thing: Developing a Passion for the Beauty of God* (Ross-shire, Scotland: Christian Focus, 2004), 178–79.

6. Mike Wilkerson, "Bricks without Straw: How Long, Oh Lord?" in *Redemption: Freed by Jesus from the Idols We Worship and the Wounds We Carry* (Wheaton, IL: Crossway, 2011).

7. John Chrysostom, "Homily on Ephesians I. I. 8" in *Galatians, Ephesians, Philippians, Ancient Christian Commentary on Scripture,* ed. Mark J. Edwards (Downers Grove, IL: InterVarsity, 1999), 8:114.

8. Magda B. Arnold, *Emotion and Personality*, vol. 1, *Psychological Aspects* (New York: Columbia University Press, 1960), 196.

9. Gabriel Marcel, "Sketch of a Phenomenology and Metaphysics of Hope," in *Homo Viator: Introduction to the Metaphysics of Hope*, trans. Emma Craufurd and Paul Seaton (Chicago: Regnery, 1951), 29–67.

Chapter 10: Sin, Violence, and Sexual Assault

1. In the original language of Genesis this expression meant that God made humans "into" his image, much like one would say a potter makes a lump of clay "into" a vase. That is to say, humanity is not *in* the image of God; we actually *are* the image of God.

2. Richard Pratt explains that the title "image of God" is both a title of humility and dignity. Humans are only finite, physical representations of their Creator. We are images of God, but that is all that we are—images. "The Bible insists that we are not gods; we are merely *images* of God. We are not equal with our Maker; we don't have a spark of divinity within us. We are nothing more than creatures that reflect our Creator." Richard L. Pratt Jr., *Designed for Dignity: What God Has Made It Possible for You to Be* (Phillipsburg: P&R, 1993), 4. While this points to humility, "image of God" also reflects our dignity: "We are images, but we are images *of God* (Gen. 1:27). God did not make Adam and Eve to resemble rocks, trees, or animals. Nothing so common was in his design for us. Instead, God carefully shaped the first man and woman so that they were in *his* likeness. He determined to make us creatures of incomparable dignity" (Pratt, *Designed for Dignity*, 8–9).

3. Francis Schaeffer writes: "So fallen man has dominion over nature, but he uses it wrongly. The Christian is called upon to exhibit this dominion, but exhibit it rightly: treating the thing as having value itself, exercising dominion without being destructive. The church should always have taught and done this, but she has generally failed to do so, and we need to confess our failure. . . . By and large we must say that for a long, long time Christian teachers, including the best orthodox theologians, have shown a real poverty here." Francis Schaeffer and Udo Middelmann, *Pollution and the Death of Man* (Wheaton, IL: Crossway, 1992), 72.

4. Pratt, *Designed for Dignity*, 22.

5. Ibid., 23.

6. Cornelius Plantinga Jr., *Not the Way It's Supposed to Be: A Breviary of Sin* (Grand Rapids, MI: Eerdmans, 1995), 10.

7. Plantinga, *Not the Way It's Supposed to Be*, 10; Francis Brown, Samuel Rolles Driver, and Charles Augustus Briggs, *Enhanced Brown-Driver-Briggs Hebrew and English Lexicon*, electronic ed. (Oak Harbor, WA: Logos Research Systems, 2000), 1022.

8. Richard Pratt describes the effects of sin: "The rest of Scripture teaches that sin has affected every dimension of human character. We are totally depraved. To be sure, none of us are as bad as we could be. God restrains sin and enables us to avoid absolute ruin. When left to our own devices, however, we are utterly corrupted in all our faculties. Our thinking processes are so darkened that we twist and pervert the truth (1 Cor. 2:14; John 1:5; Rom. 8:7; Eph. 4:18; Titus 1:15). Our wills have been rendered unable to choose for spiritual good (John 8:34; 2 Tim. 3:2–4). Our affections have been marred and misdirected so that we love the world and its evil pleasures (John 5:42; Heb. 3:12; 1 John 2:15–17). For these reasons, we are under the judgment of God (John 3:18–19) and unable to do anything to redeem ourselves (John 6:44; 3:5; Rom. 7:18, 23). The sin of Adam and Eve has had devastating effects on human character." Pratt, *Designed for Dignity*, 51.

9. Paul David Tripp, *A Quest for More: Living for Something Bigger Than You* (Greensboro, NC: New Growth, 2008), 40.

10. "The Bible presents sin by way of major concepts, principally lawlessness and faithlessness, expressed in an array of images: sin is the missing of a target, a wandering from the path, a straying from the fold. Sin is a hard heart and a stiff neck. Sin is blindness and deafness. It is both the overstepping of a line and the failure to reach it—both transgression and shortcoming. Sin is a beast crouching at the door. In sin, people attack or evade or neglect their divine calling. These and other images suggest deviance: even when it is familiar, sin is never normal. Sin is disruption of

created harmony and then resistance to divine restoration of that harmony. Above all, sin disrupts and resists the vital human relation to God." Plantinga, *Not the Way It's Supposed to Be*, 5.

11. Ibid., 14.

12. Ibid., 30.

13. Ibid., 14.

14. Ibid., 13.

15. G. K. Beale, *We Become What We Worship: A Biblical Theology of Idolatry* (Downers Grove, IL: InterVarsity, 2008), 16.

16. Sigmund Freud serves unexpectedly as a theologian of original sin. In *A Short Account of Psychoanalysis* he writes that the "impulses . . . subjected to repression are those of selfishness and cruelty, which can be summed up in general as evil, but above all sexual wishful impulses, often of the crudest and most forbidden kind." Sigmund Freud, *A Short Account of Psychoanalysis*, Standard Edition 19, ed. and trans. James Strachey (London: Hogarth, 1953–74), 197. In *Civilization and Its Discontents*, Freud writes: "Men are not gentle, friendly creatures wishing for love, who simply defend themselves if they are attacked, but that a powerful measure of desire for aggression has to be reckoned as part of their instinctual endowment. The result is that their neighbor is to them not only a possible helper or sexual object, but also a temptation to them to gratify their aggressiveness on him, to exploit his capacity for work without recompense, to use him sexually without his consent, to seize his possessions, to humiliate him, to cause him pain, to torture and to kill him. *Homo homini lupus*; who has the courage to dispute it in the face of all the evidence in his own life and in history?" Sigmund Freud, *Civilization and Its Discontents*, trans. Joan Riviere (London: Hogarth, 1963), 58. Freud refers to Thomas Hobbes' famous *"Homo Homini Lupus Est,"* which is Latin for "man is a wolf to [his fellow] man."

17. D. G. Reid, "Violence," in *New Dictionary of Biblical Theology*, electronic ed., ed. T. Desmond Alexander and Brian S. Rosner (Downers Grove, IL: InterVarsity, 2001).

18. Plantinga, *Not the Way It's Supposed to Be*, 16.

19. "Stories of Violence" in *Dictionary of Biblical Imagery*, ed. Leland Ryken, Jim Wilhoit, and Tremper Longman III (Downers Grove, IL: InterVarsity, 1998), 916.

20. Plantinga, *Not the Way It's Supposed to Be*, 16.

21. Ibid., 30.

22. "Rape, Sexual Violence," in *Dictionary of Biblical Imagery*, 695.

23. Ibid., 581.

24. Susan Brownmiller, "War," in *Against Our Will: Men, Women, and Rape* (New York: Random House, 1975), 31–113.

25. Peggy Reeves Sanday, "The Socio-Cultural Context of Rape: A Cross-Cultural Study," *Journal of Social Issues* 37 (1981): 5–27.

26. Alexander McFarlane and Bessel van der Kolk, "Trauma and Its Challenge to Society," in *Traumatic Stress*, ed. Bessel van der Kolk, Alexander McFarlane, and Lars Weisaeth (New York: Guilford, 1996), 27, 35.

27. Simone Weil, *Waiting for God* (New York: Putnam, 1951), 119.

28. Marie Fortune, *Sexual Violence: The Unmentionable Sin* (New York: Pilgrim, 1984), 86–87.

29. Ann J. Cahill, *Rethinking Rape* (Ithaca, NY: Cornell University Press, 2001), 192–93.

30. For the effects on the sense of self, see Cahill, *Rethinking Rape*, 193–94; Ann Wolbert Burgess, "Rape Trauma Syndrome," in *Rape and Society: Readings on the Problem of Sexual Assault*, ed. Patricia Searles and Ronald J. Berger (Boulder, CO: Westview, 1995), 239–45; Liz Kelly, *Surviving Sexual Violence* (Minneapolis, MN: University of Minnesota Press, 1988), 39; and Joselyn Catty, *Writing Rape, Writing Women in Early Modern England: Unbridled Speech* (New York: St. Martin's, 1999), 4.

31. Burgess, "Rape Trauma Syndrome," 240–43; Kelly, *Surviving Sexual Violence*, 187–214; Catty, *Writing Rape, Writing Women in Early Modern England*, 4; Brownmiller, *Against Our Will*, 18, 376; Cahill, *Rethinking Rape*, 169–75, 192–94; Ann Wolbert Burgess and Lynda Lytle Holmstrom, "Rape Trauma Syndrome," in *Forcible Rape: The Crime, the Victim, and the Offender* (New York: Columbia University Press, 1977), 315–28; David Archard, *Sexual Consent* (Boulder, CO: Westview, 1998), 20–41, 44–53; and Patricia A. Harney and Charlene L. Muehlenhard, "Rape," in *Sexual Coercion: A Sourcebook on Its Nature, Causes and Prevention*, ed. Elizabeth Grauerholz and Mary A. Koralewski (Lexington, KY: Lexington, 1991), 3–6, 12–15.

32. Weil, *Waiting for God*, 122–23.

33. See Mary Douglas, *Purity and Danger: An Analysis of the Concepts of Pollution and Taboo* (London: Routledge and Kegan Paul, 1966), 5.

34. Hilary Lipka, *Sexual Trangression in the Hebrew Bible* (Sheffield, England: Sheffield Phoenix, 2000), 90–92.

35. Lipka, *Sexual Trangressions*, 242. Commenting on these laws, Reid writes: "The law given at Sinai and expounded in Deuteronomy restrains the violence of murder or rape, but it also sanctions the violence of punishment for sins, the violence of Yahweh's wars and the substitutionary violence of animal sacrifice. The law, however, cannot put an end to Israel's complicity in human violence. Murder and sexual violence, for example, do not cease in Israel but multiply. At times the text of the OT surges with violence, even including unspeakable violence within Israel (2 Kgs. 6:28–29; Ezek. 5:10; Lam. 2:20; Judg. 19:22–30)." D. G. Reid, "Violence," in *New Dictionary of Biblical Theology*, electronic ed., ed. T. Desmond Alexander and Brian S. Rosner (Downers Grove, IL: InterVarsity, 2001), 832.

36. Moshe Greenberg, "Some Postulates of Biblical Criminal Law," in *Yehezkel Kaufmann Jubilee Volume: Studies in Bible and Jewish Religion Dedicated to Yehezkel Kaufmann on the Occasion of His Seventieth Birthday*, ed. Menahem Haran (Jerusalem: Magnes, 1960), 36–41.

37. Dan B. Allender, "The Mark of Evil," in *God and the Victim: Theological Reflections on Evil, Victimization, Justice, and Forgiveness*, ed. Lisa Barnes Lampman (Grand Rapids, MI: Eerdmans, 1999), 52.

Chapter 11: Grace in the Old Testament

1. As sexual voyeurism, Ham's action falls under the category of noncontact sexual abuse, which includes exhibitionism, voyeurism, coercion to view or participate in child pornography, obscene sexual language, obscene sexual phone calls, and other intrusive behavior such as not allowing a child to undress or use the bathroom in privacy. Andrea Parrot, "Incest," in *Human Sexuality: An Encyclopedia*, ed. V. L. Bullough and B. Bullough (New York: Garland, 1994), 298.

2. E. J. Young, *Genesis 3* (Edinburgh, Scotland: Banner of Truth, 1966), 149.

3. Often in the Bible, "nakedness" represents unrighteousness. It symbolizes the ideas of judgment and humiliation in the biblical world. The Bible pictures the sinner as clothed in "filthy rags" or "naked and ashamed." The prophets described the sinful state of the nation of Israel as "nakedness" before God and the world (Isa. 47:3; Lam. 1:8; Ezek. 16:36). "'Remove the filthy garments from him.'" And to him he said, "'Behold, I have taken your iniquity away from you, and I will clothe you with pure vestments'" (Zech. 3:4). "I will greatly rejoice in the LORD; my soul shall exult in my God, for he has clothed me with the garments of salvation; he has covered me with the robe of righteousness" (Isa. 61:10). Adam and Eve were ashamed because of their unrighteousness. They were not able to stand naked in God's holy and righteous presence. Their consciences were deformed, their joy was turned to shame, and their relationship with God was corrupted. This happened because sin stripped them of the right standing with which they were created. By his grace, God created them in right standing. God responded to their calamity with an immediate act of mercy. He covered their shame. With animal skins God made temporary coverings of "righteousness" for them: "Unto Adam also and to his wife did the LORD God make coats of skins, and clothed them" (Gen. 3:21 KJV). God did not accept the fig leaves. He would only accept a cover that he alone had put on them. R. C. Sproul writes, "It may be said that the first act of God's redemptive grace occurred when he condescended to clothe his embarrassed fallen creatures." R. C. Sproul, *Faith Alone: The Evangelical Doctrine of Justification* (Grand Rapids, MI: Baker, 1999), 102. God in grace clothed these unrighteous first sinners with the skins of a sacrifice, made with his own hands, so that they could come to him and be saved.

4. Cornelius Plantinga Jr., *Not the Way It's Supposed to Be: A Breviary of Sin* (Grand Rapids, MI: Eerdmans, 1995), 199.

5. "Whole" in *Dictionary of Biblical Imagery*, ed. Leland Ryken, Jim Wilhoit, and Tremper Longman III (Downers Grove, IL: InterVarsity, 1998), 944.

6. Stephen G. Dempster, *Dominion and Dynasty: A Theology of the Hebrew Bible,* New Studies in Biblical Theology vol. 15 (Downers Grove, IL: InterVarsity, 2003), 72.

7. Paul R. Williamson, *Sealed with an Oath: Covenant in God's Unfolding Purpose,* New Studies in Biblical Theology vol. 23 (Downers Grove, IL: InterVarsity, 2007), 60–61.

8. Ibid., 76.

9. Mark Driscoll and Gerry Breshears, *Doctrine: What Christians Should Believe* (Wheaton, IL: Crossway, 2010), 180.

10. *Hesed* is the OT word for God's compassionate love. It is used 254 times. The NT word is *charis* (charity) and it is used over 150 times. *Hesed* refers to compassionate acts performed either spontaneously or in response to an appeal by one in dire straits. *Hesed* is not grounded in obligation or contract. The acts arise out of affection and goodness. *Charis* is about favor and friendship, as well as gifts from benefactors. Acts of *hesed* pertain to covenantal relations, but God enters into covenant with human beings freely; the establishment of the covenant is itself an act of *hesed* on God's part. *Charis* connotes spontaneous kindness and acts of generosity grounded in dispositions of compassion toward those in need.

11. Stephen G. Dempster, "Exodus and Biblical Theology: On Moving into the Neighborhood with a New Name," *Southern Baptist Journal of Theology* 12/3 (2008): 4. The importance of the exodus in the theology of the Hebrew Bible is breathtaking: "There are over 120 explicit OT references to the Exodus in law, narrative, prophecy and psalm, and it is difficult to exaggerate its importance. Foundational to Israel's self-perception

(Deut. 6:20–25)—they are here first designated a people (Exod. 1:9)—it is recalled in liturgy (*e.g.* Ps. 78, 105; Exod. 12:26–27), prayer (*e.g.* 2 Sam. 7:23; Jer. 32:16–21; Dan 9:4–19), and sermon (*e.g.* Josh. 24; Judg. 2:11–13; 1 Sam. 12:6–8; 1 Kings 8). As the pre-eminent saving event in their history (Deut. 4:32–40), the Exodus profoundly shaped Israel's social structures, calendars, remembrance of the ancient past, and hopes of future restoration." Rikki E. Watts, "Exodus," in *New Dictionary of Biblical Theology,* ed. T. Desmond Alexander and Brian S. Rosner (Downers Grove, IL: InterVarsity, 2001), 478–87.

12. Dempster, "Exodus and Biblical Theology," 4–5.

13. Peter Enns, "Exodus, Book of" in *New Dictionary of Biblical Theology*.

14. Dempster, "Exodus and Biblical Theology," 9.

15. D. G. Reid, "Violence," in *New Dictionary of Biblical Theology*.

16. Christopher J. H. Wright, *The Mission of God: Unlocking the Bible's Grand Narrative* (Downers Grove, IL: InterVarsity, 2006), 272.

17. John Goldingay, *Old Testament Theology* vol. 1 *Israel's Gospel* (Downers Grove, IL: InterVarsity, 2003), 302.

18. Wright, *The Mission of God*, 271.

19. The Passover is a sacrifice (Ex. 12:27; 34:25). It is described as "the LORD's offering" (Num. 9:7, 13), and the verb "to sacrifice" is used in reference to it (Deut. 16:2, 4, 5, 6).

20. Dempster, "Dominion and Dynasty," 99.

21. Leon Morris, *The Atonement: Its Meaning and Significance* (Downers Grove, IL: InterVarsity, 1983), 89.

22. Steve Jeffery, Michael Ovey, and Andrew Sach, *Pierced for Our Transgressions: Rediscovering the Glory of Penal Substitution* (Wheaton, IL: Crossway, 2007), 34.

23. Dempster, "Exodus and Biblical Theology," 12.

24. Morris, *The Atonement*, 68.

25. Jeffery, Ovey, and Sach, *Pierced for Our Transgressions*, 42.

26. D. A. Carson, R. T. France, and J. A. Motyer, *New Bible Commentary: 21st Century Edition*, ed. Gordon J. Wenham (Downers Grove, IL: IVP Academic, 1994).

27. David Peterson, "Atonement in The Old Testament," *Where Wrath and Mercy Meet: Proclaiming the Atonement Today* (Carlisle, UK: Paternoster, 2001), 11.

28. Jeffery, Ovey, and Sach, *Pierced for Our Transgressions*, 49.

29. Stanley Grenz, David Guretzki, and Cherith Fee Nordling, *Pocket Dictionary of Theological Terms* (Downers Grove, IL: InterVarsity, 1999), 96.

30. Ibid., 50.

31. Leland Ryken et al., eds., *Dictionary of Biblical Imagery* (Downers Grove, IL: InterVarsity, 2000), 55.

32. Paul R. Williamson, *Sealed with an Oath: Covenant in God's Unfolding Purpose,* New Studies in Biblical Theology vol. 23 (Downers Grove, IL: InterVarsity, 2007), 111.

33. According to Dumbrell, in the pre-Christian Targums, the Aramaic translation of Isaiah 53, "the Servant is defined as the messiah." William J. Dumbrell, *Search for Order: Biblical Eschatology in Focus* (Eugene, OR: Wipf and Stock, 2001), 120.

34. Jeffery, Ovey, and Sach, *Pierced for Our Transgressions*, 54.

35. Graham A. Cole, *God the Peacemaker: How Atonement Brings Shalom,* New Studies in Biblical Theology (Downers Grove, IL: InterVarsity Press, 2009), 100–101.

36. Reid, "Violence," 834.

37. Jeffery, Ovey, and Sach, *Pierced for Our Transgressions*, 57.

38. Emphasis added.

39. Alan J. Groves, "Atonement in Isaiah 53," in *The Glory of the Atonement: Biblical, Theological, and Practical Perspectives,* eds. C. E. Hill and F. A. James III (Downers Grove, IL: InterVarsity, 2004), 81.

40. Jeffery, Ovey, and Sach, *Pierced for Our Transgressions*, 61.

41. Plantinga, *Not the Way It's Supposed to Be*, 9–10.

42. Other similar passages include Micah 5:2–5 and Eph. 2:14. While some scholars would disagree, we would also include Psalm 72:7 in this list of passages. It, too, connects the reign of the future messianic king with the coming of *shalom*: "In his days may the righteous flourish, and peace (Heb. *shalom*) abound, till the moon be no more!" John H. Sailhamer, *The Meaning of the Pentateuch: Revelation, Composition, and Interpretation* (Downers Grove, IL: InterVarsity, 2009), 499–503.

43. See "Index of Allusions and Verbal Parallels," in *The Greek New Testament*, 4th ed., eds. B. Aland et al. (Stuttgart, Germany: Deutsche Bibelgesellschaft, 2001), 891–901.

44. "Stories of Violence" in *Dictionary of Biblical Imagery*, 916.

Chapter 12: Grace in the New Testament

1. D. G. Reid, "Violence," in *New Dictionary of Biblical Theology*, eds. T. Desmond Alexander and Brian S. Rosner, electronic ed. (Downers Grove, IL: InterVarsity, 2001), 832.

2. Reid, "Violence," 834.

3. 1 Corinthians 15:1–4: "Now I would remind you, brothers, of the gospel I preached to you, which you received, in which you stand, and by which you are being saved, if you hold fast to the word I preached to you—unless you believed in vain. For I delivered to you as of *first importance* what I also received: that Christ died for our sins in accordance with the Scriptures, that he was buried, that he was raised on the third day in accordance with the Scriptures" (my emphasis).

4. The four Gospels (Matthew, Mark, Luke, and John) were written to "bring together the words and deeds of the historical Jesus in a way that demonstrates the significance of his life, death, and resurrection." John H. Sailhamer, *The Life of Christ* (Grand Rapids, MI: Zondervan, 1995) 10.

5. Tim Keller, "The Gospel in All Its Forms," *Christianity Today* (May 2008).

6. "The Fourth Gospel's primary focus is the mission of Jesus: He is the one who comes into the world, accomplishes his work and returns to the Father; he is the one who descended from heaven and ascends again; he is the Sent One, who, in complete dependence and perfect obedience to his sender, fulfills the purpose for which the Father sent him." Andreas J. Köstenberger and Peter T. O'Brien, *Salvation to the Ends of the Earth: A Biblical Theology of Mission* (Downers Grove, IL: InterVarsity, 2001), 203.

7. There are seven so-called "I Am" sayings in John's Gospel: the bread of life (6:35, 48, 51); the light of the world (8:12; 9:5); the gate (10:7, 9); the good shepherd (10:11, 14); the resurrection and the life (11:25); the way and the truth and the life (14:6); and the true vine (15:1).

8. Rev. Samuel Billy Kyles, interviewed by Liane Hansen, *Weekend Edition Sunday*, NPR, January 17, 2010, http//www.npr.org/templates/story/story.php?StoryId-122670935.

9. David Powlison, "God's Grace in Your Sufferings," in *Suffering and the Sovereignty of God*, eds. John Piper and Justin Taylor (Wheaton, IL: Crossway, 2006), 172.

10. Matthew describes Jesus as the one who was born of a virgin and who was conceived by the third person of the Trinity, the omnipotent Holy Spirit (Matt. 1:20). At his baptism, we read that Jesus is God's beloved Son, in whom he is well pleased (3:17). Jesus is the one on whom the Holy Spirit descended like a dove (3:16). Jesus is the one who defeated Satan in the desert and who afterward was ministered to by myriads of angels (4:1–11). Jesus is the one who cleansed lepers, gave sight to the blind, healed the deaf, and cast out demons by simply speaking (8:1–4; 9:27–31; 8:28–34). Jesus is the one who taught the Scriptures with authority and who fulfilled prophecies (7:28–29). Jesus is the one whose wisdom was far greater than that of Solomon (12:42). Jesus is the one who said, "Heaven and earth will pass away, but my words will not pass away" (24:35). Jesus is the one who fed over five thousand people with five loaves and two fish (14:13–21). Jesus is the one who was transfigured in such a way that his face shone like the brightness of the noonday sun (17:1–13). Jesus is the one who predicted his death and resurrection in detail before they actually happened (17:22–23). Jesus is the one who is King of the Jews and who rode into Jerusalem on a donkey (21:1–11). Jesus is the one who pleaded with his Father in the garden of Gethsemane saying: "Let this cup pass from me. . . . Not as I will, but as you will" (26:39). Jesus is the one who kept silent before his accusers (27:14). Jesus is the one who was betrayed, forsaken, arrested, mocked, beaten, slapped, flogged, spat upon, stripped naked, crowned with thorns, and crucified on a cross outside Jerusalem (26–27). Jesus is the one who purchased the new covenant with his blood, which was poured out for the forgiveness of sins (26:28). Jesus is the one who fully drank the cup of God's wrath (27:45–54). Jesus is the one who died, who was buried, and who rose again on the third day (27:45–28:10). Jesus is the one who was given all authority in heaven and on earth (28:18). Jesus is the one who appeared to his disciples and commanded them to make disciples of all nations (28:19–20).

11. Sailhamer, *The Life of Christ*, 22.

12. Mark Driscoll and Gerry Breshears, *Death by Love: Letters from the Cross* (Wheaton, IL: Crossway, 2008), 17.

13. R. W. Yarbrough, "Atonement," in *New Dictionary of Biblical Theology*, 388.

14. For an extended exegetical, theological, and historical defense of penal substitutionary atonement see Steve Jeffery, Michael Ovey, and Andrew Sach, *Pierced for Our Transgressions: Rediscovering the Glory of Penal Substitution* (Wheaton, IL: Crossway, 2007).

15. Jeffery, Ovey, and Sach, *Pierced for Our Transgressions*, 23.

16. Ibid., 67.

17. For a fuller exposition of this idea see Graham A. Cole, *God the Peacemaker: How Atonement Brings Shalom,* New Studies in Biblical Theology (Downers Grove, IL: InterVarsity, 2009), 169–73.

18. "Jesus goes down to 'Egypt' and suffers oppression, completely submitting to the penalty of sin and death and, thus, paving the way for the Exodus of all peoples into the glorious liberty of the children of God! This firstborn son's blood is not spared but becomes the blood of the covenant sprinkled on the nations not as self-curse, but as a balm of cleansing, renewal, and forgiveness, binding them to him forever." Stephen G. Dempster, "Exodus and Biblical Theology: On Moving into the Neighborhood with a New Name," *Southern Baptist Journal of Theology* 12/3 (2008): 19–20.

19. "In the developing New Testament, Exodus language is pervasive. Herod's brutal murder of the infants in the district of Bethlehem echoes the slaughter of the Israelite newborns in Egypt (Matt. 2:16–18). Jesus' descent into Egypt and exodus from it as a child mirrors early Israel's experience (Matt. 2:13–15). His depiction as a new Moses giving his new commandments from the Mount is in both continuity and contrast with the old Moses at Sinai (Matthew 5–7). His feeding of the crowds in the wilderness with bread shows that he is the ultimate manna come down from heaven (John 6:35). His last supper recalls the original Passover, and his words of institution regarding the blood of the covenant deliberately recall Moses' words to the Israelites when sealing the Sinai covenant (Matt. 26:28, cf. Ex. 24:8). His entire life and ministry is viewed as the antitype of the tabernacle built at Sinai: The Word became flesh and moved into the neighborhood and we beheld his glory—not the old glory of the cloud filling the tent—but 'the glory of the One and Only, who came from the Father, full of grace and truth' (John 1:14 NIV; cf. Ex. 34:5). Those who dwell in the midst of this tabernacle, leave with a face set on fire by the divine presence, just like Moses (2 Cor. 3; cf. Ex. 34:29–35)." See Dempster, "Exodus and Biblical Theology," 5–6.

20. John Murray, *Redemption Accomplished and Applied* (Grand Rapids, MI: Eerdmans, 1984), 42–43.

21. N. T. Wright, *Following Jesus: Biblical Reflections on Discipleship* (Grand Rapids, MI: Eerdmans, 1994), 17. See also N. T. Wright, *Colossians and Philemon,* Tyndale New Testament Commentaries (Downers Grove, IL: InterVarsity, 1986), 60–63.

22. Jerry Bridges, *The Gospel for Real Life: Turn to the Liberating Power of the Cross . . . Every Day* (Colorado Springs: Navpress, 2002), 74.

23. J. I. Packer and Mark Dever, *In My Place Condemned He Stood: Celebrating the Glory of the Atonement* (Wheaton, IL: Crossway, 2007), 47.

24. Ibid.

25. Bridges, *The Gospel for Real Life,* 75.

26. Jeffery, Ovey, and Sach, *Pierced for Our Transgressions,* 151–2.

27. Packer and Dever, *In My Place Condemned He Stood,* 35.

28. John Murray, *The Atonement* (Philadelphia: P&R, 1962), 15.

29. Charles Spurgeon, "'Love and I'—A Mystery" (Sermon, Metropolitan Tabernacle, Newington, UK, July 2, 1882), http://www.ccel-org/ccel/spurgeon/sermons28.titlepage.html.

30. Francis Turretin, *Institutes of Elenctic Theology,* (Phillipsburg, NJ: P&R, 1993), 2:447.

31. John Calvin, *Institutes of the Christian Religion,* ed. J. T. McNeil, trans. Ford Lewis Battles (Philadelphia: Westminster, 1960), 3.9.3.

32. Quoted in Charles Hodge, *Systematic Theology,* (Edinburgh, Scotland: Hendrickson, 1999), 3:148.

33. Robert Sherman, *King, Priest, and Prophet: A Trinitarian Theology of Atonement* (New York: T&T Clark, 2004), 166.

34. "A leading ingredient in the Bible's eschatological images of the future age is the restored wholeness that glorified saints will finally enjoy in perpetuity. The book of Revelation contains all the important biblical motifs (which can be found scattered through OT apocalyptic visions as well). One is the union of people with God and Christ, pictured as a marriage (Rev 19:7; 21:2, 9) and as an existence in which the redeemed 'follow the Lamb wherever he goes' (Rev 14:4 RSV). To be whole is to be one

with the God whose 'dwelling . . . is among mortals' (Rev 21:3 NRSV). Social wholeness is also present, imaged in the single city where all the redeemed will reside through all eternity (cf. Jesus' homey image of heaven as a stately house with many rooms [Jn 14:2]). Inner wholeness is marked by the true shalom of God, which replaces pain and tears with healing and compassion (Rev 21:4). Feelings of insecurity and alienation will be replaced with security and intimacy (Rev 21:3). Here is the ultimate fulfillment of Isaiah's prophecy regarding the suffering servant, that 'upon him was the chastisement that made us whole' (Is 53:5 RSV)." "Whole" in *Dictionary of Biblical Imagery*, eds. Leland Ryken et al. (Downers Grove, IL: InterVarsity, 2000), 944.

35. R. W. Yarbrough, "Atonement," in *New Dictionary of Biblical Theology*. A redeemed people from every tribe, nation, and tongue will dwell in the heavenly city because their names are written in the Lamb's book of life (Rev. 21:27). Only blood-bought sinners saved by the Lamb will dwell in the heavenly city (Rev. 5:9–10). The heavenly city will display a beautiful mosaic of redemption. Peoples from every tribe and tongue will bring their honor and glory into the city and offer praise to God and to the Lamb (Rev. 21:24–26).

36. Christopher J. H. Wright, *The Mission of God: Unlocking the Bible's Grand Narrative* (Downers Grove, IL: IVP Academic, 2006), 529–30.

37. D. A. Carson, *A Call to Spiritual Reformation: Priorities from Paul and His Prayers* (Grand Rapids, MI: Baker, 1992), 189.

38. The Heidelberg Catechism, Question and Answer 1. http://www.ccel.org/creeds/heidelberg-cat.html.

Concluding Prayer

1. *The Valley of Vision: A Collection of Puritan Prayers and Devotions,* ed. Arthur Bennett (Edinburgh: The Banner of Truth, 1975), 284–85.

Bibliography

Abel, Gene, J. V. Becker, M. Mittleman, J. Cunningham-Rathner, J. L. Rouleau, and W. D. Murphy. "Self-Reported Sex Crimes of Nonincarcerated Paraphiliacs." *Journal of Interpersonal Violence* 2, no. 1 (1987): 3–25.

Aland, B., K. Aland, J. Karavidopoulos, C. M. Martini, and B. M. Metzger, eds. *The Greek New Testament*, 4th rev. ed. Stuttgart: Deutsche Biblegesellschaft, 2001.

Allen, Jon. *Coping with Trauma: A Guide to Self-Understanding*. Washington, DC: American Psychiatric Press, 1995.

Allender, Dan B. "Forgive and Forget and Other Myths of Forgiveness." In *God and the Victim: Theological Reflections on Evil, Victimization, Justice, and Forgiveness*. Edited by Lisa Barnes Lampman. Grand Rapids, MI: Eerdmans, 1999.

_____. *When Trust Is Lost: Healing for Victims of Sexual Abuse*. Grand Rapids, MI: RBC Ministries, 1992.

Allender, Dan B., and Tremper Longman III. *The Cry of the Soul: How Our Emotions Reveal Our Deepest Questions About God*. Colorado Springs: NavPress, 1999.

American Medical Association. *Strategies for the Treatment and Prevention of Sexual Assault*. Chicago: American Medical Association, 1995.

Amir, Menachem. *Patterns in Forcible Rape*. Chicago: University of Chicago Press, 1971.

Arata, C. M. "Coping with Rape: The Roles of Prior Sexual Abuse and Attribution of Blame." *Journal of Interpersonal Violence* 14 (1999): 62–78.

Archard, David. *Sexual Consent*. Boulder: Westview, 1998.

Arendt, Hannah. *The Human Condition: A Study of the Central Dilemma Facing Modern Man*. Garden City: Doubleday, 1959.

Arnold, Magda B. *Emotion and Personality*, Vol. 1: *Psychological Aspects*. New York: Columbia University Press, 1960.

Atkeson, B. M., K. S. Calhoun, P. A. Resick, and E. M. Ellis. "Victims of Rape: Repeated Assessment of Depressive Symptoms." *Journal of Consulting and Clinical Psychology* 50 (1982): 96–102.

Baker, A. W., and S. P. Duncan. "Child Sexual Abuse: A Study of Prevalence in Great Britain." *Child Abuse & Neglect: The International Journal* 9 (1985): 457.

Bal, Mieke. *Death and Dissymmetry: The Politics of Coherence in the Book of Judges.* Chicago Studies in the History of Judaism. Chicago: University of Chicago Press, 1988.

Baloian, B. *Anger in the Old Testament.* New York: Peter Lang, 1992.

Basile, K. C., and L. E. Saltzman. *Sexual Violence Surveillance: Uniform Definitions and Recommended Data Elements.* Atlanta: Centers for Disease Control and Prevention, National Center for Injury Prevention and Control, 2002.

Bass, Ellen, and Laura Davis. *Beginning to Heal: A First Book for Men and Women Who Were Sexually Abused as Children.* New York: HarperCollins, 2003.

_____. *The Courage to Heal: A Guide for Women Survivors of Child Sexual Abuse.* New York: Harper & Row, 1988.

Beale, G. K. *We Become What We Worship: A Biblical Theology of Idolatry.* Downers Grove, IL: InterVarsity, 2008.

Benedict, Helen. *Recovery: How to Survive Sexual Assault for Women, Men, Teenagers, Their Friends and Families.* New York: Columbia University Press, 1994.

Bennett, Arthur, ed. *The Valley of Vision: A Collection of Puritan Prayers and Devotions.* Edinburgh: Banner of Truth, 1975.

Bergen, R. K. *Wife Rape: Understanding the Response of Survivors and Service Providers.* Thousand Oaks, CA: Sage, 1996.

Beste, Jennifer Erin. *God and the Victim: Traumatic Intrusion on Grace and Freedom.* New York: Oxford University Press, 2007.

Bock, Darrell L. "Luke–Acts." In *New Dictionary of Biblical Theology.* Edited by T. Desmond Alexander and Brian S. Rosner. Downers Grove, IL: InterVarsity, 2001.

Bonhoeffer, Dietrich. *The Cost of Discipleship.* New York: Touchstone Books, 1995.

_____. "Who am I?" In *Letters and Papers From Prison,* 347–8. New York: Touchstone, 1997.

The Book of Common Prayer. New York: Oxford University Press, 1979.

Bridges, Jerry. *The Gospel for Real Life: Turn to the Liberating Power of the Cross . . . Every Day.* Colorado Springs: NavPress, 2002.

Briere, John N. *Child Abuse Trauma: Theory and Treatment of the Lasting Effects.* London: Sage, 1992.

Briere, John N., and D. M. Elliot. "Prevalence and Symptomatic Sequelae of Self-Reported Childhood Physical and Sexual Abuse in a General Population Sample of Men and Women." *Child Abuse & Neglect: The International Journal* 27 (2003): 1205–22.

Briere, John N., and M. Runtz. "University Males' Sexual Interest in Children: Predicting Potential Indices of 'Pedophilia' in a Nonforensic Sample." *Child Abuse & Neglect: The International Journal* 13 (1989): 65–75.

Briere, John N., R. Woo, B. McRae, J. Foltz, and R. Sitzman. "Lifetime Victimization History, Demographics, and Clinical Status in Female Psychiatric Emergency Room Patients." *Journal of Nervous and Mental Disease* 185 (1997): 95–101.

Brooks, Thomas. *Heaven on Earth*. The Complete Works of Thomas Brooks. Edited by Alexander B. Grosart, Vol. 6. Edinburgh: James Nichol, 1866.

Brown, Francis, Samuel Rolles Driver, and Charles Augustus Briggs. *Enhanced Brown-Driver-Briggs Hebrew and English Lexicon*. Electronic ed. Oak Harbor, WA: Logos Research Systems, 2000.

Brownmiller, Susan. *Against Our Will: Men, Women, and Rape*. New York: Ballantine, 1993.

Bruce, F. F. *The Epistle to the Hebrews*. New International Commentary of the New Testament. Grand Rapids, MI: Eerdmans, 1996.

Brueggemann, Walter. *Old Testament Theology: Essays on Structure, Theme, and Text*. Minneapolis: Fortress, 1992.

_____. *The Message of the Psalms: A Theological Commentary*. Minneapolis: Augsburg, 1984.

_____. *Theology of the Old Testament: Testimony, Dispute, Advocacy*. Minneapolis: Fortress, 1997.

Burgess, Ann Wolbert. "Rape Trauma Syndrome." In *Rape and Society: Readings on the Problem of Sexual Assault*. Edited by Patricia Searles and Ronald J. Berger, 239–45. Boulder: Westview, 1995.

Burgess, Ann Wolbert, and Lynda Lytle Holmstrom. "Rape Trauma Syndrome." In *Forcible Rape: The Crime, the Victim, and the Offender*. Edited by Duncan Chappell, 320–25. New York: Columbia University Press, 1977.

Burnam, M. A., J. A. Stein, J. M. Golding, J. M . Siegel, S. B. Sorenson, A. B. Forsythe, and C. A. Telles. "Sexual Assault and Mental Disorders in a Community Population." *Journal of Consulting and Clinical Psychology* 56 (1988): 843–50.

Burt, M. R. "Cultural Myths and Supports for Rape." *Journal of Personality and Social Psychology* 33 (1980): 217–30.

Cahill, Ann J. *Rethinking Rape*. Ithaca: Cornell University Press, 2001.

Calvin, John. *Commentary on the Book of Psalms, Vol. 1. Calvin's Commentaries*. Translated by James Anderson. Edinburgh: Calvin Translation Society, 1845.

_____. *Commentaries on the Epistle of Paul the Apostle to the Hebrews*. Translated by John Owen. Edinburgh: Calvin Translation Society, 1853.

_____. *Institutes of the Christian Religion*. Edited by J. T. McNeill. Translated by Ford Lewis Battles. 2 vols. Philadelphia: Westminster, 1960.

_____. "Preface to Olivetan's New Testament." In *Calvin: Commentaries*, ed. Joseph Haroutunian. Library of Christian Classics 23: 69–70. Louisville, KY: Westminster, 1958.

Carson, D. A. *A Call to Spiritual Reformation: Priorities from Paul and His Prayers*. Grand Rapids, MI: Baker, 2006.

Carson, D. A., R. T. France, J. A. Motyer, and Gordon J. Wenham. *New Bible Commentary: 21st Century Edition*. Downers Grove, IL: InterVarsity, 1994.

Cartledge, T. W. *1 & 2 Samuel*. Macon, GA: Smyth & Helwys, 2001.

Catalano, Shannon M. *Criminal Victimization, 2005*. Washington, DC: Bureau of Justice Statistics, 2006.

Catty, Joselyn. *Writing Rape, Writing Women in Early Modern England: Unbridled Speech*. New York: St. Martin's, 1999.

Cheong, Robert Kenneth. "Towards an Explicitly Theocentric Model of Forgiveness Based on God's Two-fold Commandment of Love." PhD diss., Southern Baptist Theological Seminary, 2005.

Chrysostom, John. "Homily on Ephesians I.I.8." In *Galatians, Ephesians, Philippians, Ancient Christian Commentary on Scripture* Vol. 8. Edited by Mark J. Edwards. Downers Grove, IL: InterVarsity, 1999.

Classen, C., O. Palesh, and R. Aggarwal. "Sexual Revictimization: A Review of the Empirical Literature." *Trauma, Violence, & Abuse* 6, no. 2 (2005): 103–4.

Cole, Graham A. *God the Peacemaker: How Atonement Brings Shalom*. New Studies in Biblical Theology. Downers Grove, IL: InterVarsity, 2009.

Courtois, C. *Healing the Incest Wound: Adult Survivors in Therapy*. New York: W. W. Norton, 1988.

_____. "Theory, Sequencing, and Strategy in Treating Adult Survivors." *Treating Victims of Child Sexual Abuse* 51 (1991): 47–60.

Coxell, A., M. B. King, G. C. Mezey, and D. Gordon. "Lifetime Prevalence, Characteristics, and Associated Problems of Non-Consensual Sex in Men: Cross Sectional Survey." *British Medical Journal* 318 (1999): 846–50.

Deliramich, A., and M. Gray. "Changes in Women's Sexual Behavior Following Sexual Assault." *Journal of Behavior Modification* 32, no. 5 (2008): 611–20.

Dempster, Stephen G. *Dominion and Dynasty: A Theology of the Hebrew Bible.* New Studies in Biblical Theology, vol. 1. Downers Grove, IL: InterVarsity, 2003.

_____. "Exodus and Biblical Theology: On Moving into the Neighborhood with a New Name." *Southern Baptist Journal of Theology* 12, no. 3 (2008): 12.

Desai, S., I. Arias, and M. P. Thompson. "Childhood Victimization and Subsequent Adult Revictimization Assessed in a Nationally-Representative Sample of Women and Men." *Violence and Victims* 17 (2002): 639–53.

DeSilva, David A. "Despising Shame: A Cultural-Anthropological Investigation of the Epistle to the Hebrews." *Journal of Biblical Literature* 113, no. 3 (1994): 439–61.

Dorais, M. *Don't Tell: The Sexual Abuse of Boys.* Montreal: McGill-Queens University Press, 2002.

Douglas, Mary. *Purity and Danger: An Analysis of the Concepts of Pollution and Taboo.* London: Routledge & Kegan Paul, 1966. Reprint, London: Routledge, 1984.

Driscoll, Frances. *The Rape Poems.* Port Angeles, WA: Pleasure Boat Studio, 1997.

Driscoll, Mark, and Gerry Breshears. *Death by Love: Letters from the Cross.* Wheaton, IL: Crossway, 2008.

_____. *Doctrine: What Christians Should Believe.* Wheaton, IL: Crossway, 2010.

Dube, S. R., R. F. Anda, C. L. Whitfield, D. W. Brown, V. J. Felitti, M. Dong, and W. H. Giles. "Long-term Consequences of Childhood Sexual Abuse by Gender of Victim." *American Journal of Preventive Medicine* 28 (2005): 430–38.

Dumbrell, William J. *Search for Order: Biblical Eschatology in Focus.* Eugene, OR: Wipf and Stock, 2001.

Edwards, Jonathan. "God's Excellencies." In *The Works of Jonathan Edwards.* Vol. 10, *Sermons and Discourses 1720–1723.* Edited by Wilson H. Kimnach. New Haven, CT: Yale University Press, 1992.

Elliot, Diana M., Doris S. Mok, and John Briere. "Adult Sexual Assault: Prevalence, Symptomatology, and Sex Differences in General Population." *Journal of Traumatic Stress* 17, no. 3 (2004): 203–11.

Elliott, Matthew A. *Faithful Feelings: Rethinking Emotion in the New Testament.* Grand Rapids, MI: Kregel, 2006.

Enns, Peter. "Exodus, Book of." In *New Dictionary of Biblical Theology*. Edited by T. Desmond Alexander and Brian S. Rosner. Electronic ed. Downers Grove, IL: InterVarsity, 2001.

Faravelli, C., A. Glugni, S. Salvatori, and V. Ricca. "Psychopathology after Rape." *American Journal of Psychiatry* 61, no. 8 (2004): 1483–85.

Federal Bureau of Investigation. *Crime in the United States 2000*. Washington, DC: Government Printing Office, 2001.

Federal Bureau of Investigation. *Uniform Crime Report*. Washington, DC: Government Printing Office, 1973.

Finkelhor, D. "Epidemiological Factors in the Clinical Identification of Child Sexual Abuse." *Child Abuse & Neglect: The International Journal* 17 (1993): 67–70.

_____. *Sexually Victimized Children*. New York: Free Press, 1979.

_____. "What's Wrong with Sex Between Adults and Children?" *American Journal of Orthopsychiatry* 49, no. 4 (1979): 692–97.

Finkelhor, D., G. Hotaling, I. A. Lewis, and C. Smith. "Sexual Abuse in a National Survey of Adult Men and Women: Prevalence, Characteristics, and Risk Factors." *Child Abuse & Neglect: The International Journal* 14 (1990): 19–28.

Finkelhor, D., and K. Yllo. *License to Rape: Sexual Abuse of Wives*. New York: Holt, Rinehart, and Winston, 1985.

Fisher, B. S., F. T. Cullen, and M. G. Turner. *The Sexual Victimization of College Women*. Washington, DC: U.S. Department of Justice, National Institute of Justice, 2000.

Fortune, Marie. *Sexual Violence: The Unmentionable Sin*. New York: Pilgrim, 1984.

Fossum, Merle A., Marilyn J. Mason. *Facing Shame: Families in Recovery*. New York: W. W. Norton Company, 1989.

Frank, E. and B. D. Stewart. "Depressive Symptoms in Rape Victims: A Revisit." *Journal of Affective Disorders* 7 (1984): 77–82.

Frank, E., S. M. Turner, and B. Duffy. "Depressive Symptoms in Rape Victims." *Journal of Affective Disorders* 1 (1979): 269–277.

Frazier, Patricia A. "A Comparative Study of Male and Female Rape Victims Seen at Hospital-Based Rape Crisis Programs." *Journal of Interpersonal Violence* 8 (1993): 65–79.

_____. "Perceived Control and Distress Following Sexual Assault: A Longitudinal Test of a New Model." *Journal of Personality and Social Psychology* 84, no. 6 (2003): 1257–69.

_____. "The Role of Attribution and Perceived Control in Recovery from Rape." *Journal of Personal and Interpersonal Loss* 5 (2000): 203–25.

_____. "Victim Attribution and Post-Rape Trauma." *Journal of Personality and Social Psychology* 59 (1990): 298–304.

Frazier, Patricia A., and L. Schauben. "Causal Attributions and Recovery from Rape and Other Stressful Life Events." *Journal of Social and Clinical Psychology* 13 (1994): 1–14.

Frazier, Patricia, A. Heather Mortenson, and Jason Steward. "Coping Strategies as Mediators of the Relations Among Perceived Control and Distress in Sexual Assault Survivors." *Journal of Counseling Psychology* 52 (2005): 267–78.

Freedman, S., and R. Enright. "Forgiveness as an Intervention Goal with Incest Survivors." *Journal of Consultation and Clinical Psychology* 64, no. 5 (1996): 983–92.

Freud, Sigmund. *Civilization and Its Discontents*. Translated by Joan Riviere. London: Hogarth, 1963.

_____. *A Short Account of Psychoanalysis*. Standard Edition, vol. 19. Edited and translated by James Strachey. London: Hogarth, 1953–74.

Goldingay, John. *Old Testament Theology*. vol. 1, *Israel's Gospel*. Downers Grove, IL: InterVarsity, 2003.

Gonsiorek, John C., Walter Bera, and Don LeTourneau. *Male Sexual Abuse: A Trilogy of Intervention Strategies*. Newbury Park, CA: Sage, 1994.

Gray, Mark. "Amnon: A Chip Off the Old Block? Rhetorical Strategy in 2 Samuel 13:7–15: The Rape of Tamar and the Humiliation of the Poor." *Journal for the Study of the Old Testament* 77 (1998): 39–54.

Graziano, R. "Treating Women Incest Survivors: A Bridge Between 'Cumulative Trauma' and 'Post-Traumatic Stress.'" *Social Work in Health Care* 17, no. 1 (1992): 69–85.

Greenberg, Moshe. "Some Postlulates of Biblical Criminal Law." In *Yehezkel Kaufmann Jubilee Volume: Studies in Bible and Jewish Religion Dedicated to Yehezkel Kaufmann on the Occasion of his Seventieth Birthday*. Edited by Menahem Haran. Jerusalem: Magnes, 1960.

Grenz, Stanley. *Theology for the Community of God*. Grand Rapids, MI: Eerdmans, 2000.

Groves, Alan J. "Atonement in Isaiah 53." In *The Glory of the Atonement: Biblical, Theological, and Practical Perspectives*. Edited by C. E. Hill and F. A. James III. Downers Grove, IL: InterVarsity, 2004.

Hall, R. *Ask Any Woman: A London Enquiry into Rape and Sexual Assault.* London: Falling Wall, 1985.

Hanson, K. C. "How Honorable! How Shameful! A Cultural Analysis of Matthew's Makarisms and Reproaches." *Semeia* 68 (1996): 81–112.

Hanson, R. F., D. G. Kilpatrick, S. A. Falsetti, H. S. Resnick, and T. Weaver. "Violent Crime and Mental Health." In *Traumatic Stress: From Theory to Practice.* Edited by J. R. Freedy and S. E. Hobfoll, 129–61. New York: Plenum, 1995.

Harney, Patricia A., and Charlene L. Muehlenhard. "Rape." In *Sexual Coercion: A Sourcebook on Its Nature, Causes and Prevention.* Edited by Elizabeth Grauerholz and Mary A. Koralewski. Lexington, KY: Lexington Books, 1991.

Hart, Timothy C. "Violent Victimization of College Students." U.S. Department of Justice: Office of Justice Programs, Bureau of Justice Statistics Special Report, 2003.

The Heidelberg Catechism. http://www.ccel.org/creeds/heidelberg-cat.html.

Heitritter, Lynn, and Jeanette Vought. *Helping Victims of Sexual Abuse: A Sensitive Biblical Guide for Counselors, Victims, and Families.* Minneapolis: Bethany House, 2006.

Helm, Herbert W. Jr., Jonathan R. Cook, and John M. Berecz. "The Implications of Conjunctive and Disjunctive Forgiveness for Sexual Abuse." *Pastoral Psychology* 54 (2005): 23–34.

Hengel, Martin. *Crucifixion in the Ancient World and the Folly of the Message of the Cross.* Translated by John Bowden. Philadelphia: Augsburg Fortress, 1977.

Herman, Judith Lewis. "Complex PTSD: A Syndrome in Survivors of Prolonged and Repeated Trauma." In *Psychotraumatology: Key Papers and Core Concepts in Post-traumatic Stress.* Edited by George S. Everyl Jr. and Jeffrey M. Lating, 94–95. New York: Plenum, 1995.

Hodge, Charles. *Systematic Theology.* Vol. 3. Peabody, MA: Hendrickson, 1999.

Holeman, V. "The Relationship Between Forgiveness of a Perpetrator and Current Marital Adjustment for Female Survivors of Childhood Sexual Abuse." PhD diss., Kent State University, 1994.

Holeman, V., and R. Myers. "Effects of Forgiveness of Perpetrators on Marital Adjustment for Survivors of Sexual Abuse." *The Family Journal* 6, no. 3 (1998): 182–8.

Holmer, Paul. *Making Christian Sense.* Louisville, KY: Westminster, 1984.

Holmes, G. R., L. Offen, and G. Waller. "See No Evil, Hear No Evil, Speak No Evil: Why Do Relatively Few Male Victims of Childhood Sexual Abuse

Receive Help for Abuse-Related Issues in Adulthood?" *Clinical Psychology Review* 17 (1997): 69–88.

Holmes, W. C., and G. B. Slap. "Sexual Abuse of Boys: Definition, Prevalence, Correlates, Sequelae, and Management." *Journal of the American Medical Association* 280 (1998): 1855–62.

Hoyenga, K. B., and K. T. Hoyenga, *The Question of Sex Differences: Psychological, Cultural and Biological Issues*. Boston: Little, Brown, 1979.

The Hymnal 1982. Harrisburg, PA: Church Publishing, 1985.

Jeffery, Steve, Michael Ovey, and Andrew Sach. *Pierced for Our Transgressions: Rediscovering the Glory of Penal Substitution*. Wheaton, IL: Crossway, 2007.

Johnson, Eric L. *Foundations of Soul Care: A Christian Psychology Proposal*. Downers Grove, IL: IVP Academic, 2007.

Johnson, H., and V. Pottie Bunge. "Prevalence and Consequences of Spousal Assault in Canada." *Canadian Journal of Criminology* 43, no. 1 (2001): 27–45.

Kaufman, A., P. Divasto, R. Jackson, D. Voorhees, and J. Christy, "Male Rape Victims: Noninstitutionalized Assault." *American Journal of Psychiatry* 137 (1980): 221–23.

Keller, Timothy. *Counterfeit Gods: The Empty Promises of Money, Sex, and Power*. New York: Dutton, 2009.

————. "The Gospel in All Its Forms." *Christianity Today*, May 2008.

Kelly, Liz. *Surviving Sexual Violence*. Minneapolis, MN: University of Minnesota Press, 1988.

Kierkegaard, Søren. *A Kierkegaard Anthology*. Edited by Robert Bretall. Princeton, NJ: Princeton University Press, 1973.

Kilpatrick, D. G., and A. Seymour. "Rape in America: A Report to the Nation." National Victims Center, Arlington, VA, and Crime Victims Research and Treatment Center, Charleston, SC, 1992.

Kilpatrick, D. G., B. E. Saunders, A. Amick-McMullan, C. L. Best, L. J. Veronen, and H. S. Resnick. "Victim and Crime Factors Associated with the Development of Crime-Related Post-Traumatic Stress Disorder." *Behavior Therapy* 20 (1989): 199–214.

Kilpatrick, D. G., B. E. Saunders, L. J. Veronen, C. L. Best, and J. M. Von. "Criminal Victimization: Lifetime Prevalence, Reporting to Police, and Psychological Impact." *Crime and Delinquency* 33 (1987): 479–89.

Kilpatrick, D. G., and L. J. Veronen. "Treatment of Fear and Anxiety in Victims of Rape." Washington, DC: National Institute of Mental Health, 1984.

Kilpatrick, D. G., L. J. Veronen, and P. A. Resick. "The Aftermath of Rape: Recent Empirical Findings." *American Journal of Orthopsychiatry* 49 (1979): 658–69.

Kilpatrick, D. G., P. A. Resick, and L. J. Veronen. "Longitudinal Effects of a Rape Experience." *Journal of Social Issues* 37 (1981): 105–22.

Kimerling, R., A. Rellini, V. Kelly, L. P. Judson, and L. Learman. "Gender Differences in Victim and Crime Characteristics of Sexual Assault." *Journal of Interpersonal Violence* 17 (2002): 526–32.

Klump, Meredith. "Posttraumatic Stress Disorder and Sexual Assault in Women." *Journal of College Student Psychotherapy* 21, no. 2 (2006).

Koss, M. "Rape: Scope, Impact, Interventions and Public Policy Responses." *American Psychologist* 48 (1993): 1062–69.

Koss, M., A. Figueredo, and R. Prince. "Cognitive Mediation of Rape's Mental, Physical, and Social Health Impact: Test of Four Models in Cross-Sectional Data." *Journal of Consulting and Clinical Psychology* 70 (2002): 926–41.

Koss, M., and Mary Harvey. *The Rape Victim: Clinical and Community Interventions*. Newbury Park, CA: Sage Library of Social Research, 1991.

Koss, M., C. A. Gidycz, and N. Wisniewski. "The Scope of Rape: Incidence and Prevalence of Sexual Aggression and Victimization in a National Sample of Higher Education Students." *Journal of Consulting and Clinical Psychology* 55 (1987): 162–70.

Koss, M., and T. E. Dinero. "Discriminant Analysis of Risk Factors for Sexual Victimization among a National Sample of College Women." *Journal of Consulting and Clinical Psychology* 57 (1989): 242–50.

Köstenberger, Andreas J., and Peter T. O'Brien. *Salvation to the Ends of the Earth: A Biblical Theology of Mission*. Downers Grove, IL: InterVarsity, 2001.

Kraus, C. Norman. *Jesus Christ Our Lord: Christology from a Disciple's Perspective*. Scottsdale, AZ: Herald, 1990.

Lane, William L. *Hebrews 9–13*. Word Biblical Commentary, vol. 47B. Nashville, TN: Word, 1991.

Lew, M. *Victims No Longer: Men Recovering from Incest and Other Sexual Child Abuse*. New York: HarperCollins, 1990.

Lindquist, Scott. *The Date Rape Prevention Book: The Essential Guide for Girls and Women*. Naperville, IL: Sourcebooks, 2000.

Lipka, Hilary. *Sexual Transgressions in the Hebrew Bible*. Sheffield, England: Sheffield Phoenix Press, 2006.

Lisak, D., J. Hopper, and P. Song. "Factors in the Cycle of Violence: Gender Rigidity and Emotional Constriction." *Journal of Traumatic Stress* 9 (1999): 721–43.

Luther, Martin. *Commentary on St. Paul's Epistle to the Galatians*, Translated by Theodore Conrad Graebner. Grand Rapids, MI: Zondervan, 1939.

_____. *Day by Day We Magnify Thee: Daily Readings*. Minneapolis, MN: Fortress, 1982.

_____. *The Heidelberg Disputation*. http://www.academici.com/blog.aspx?bid=3373.

_____. *Luther's Werke*. Weimar, 1883.

_____. *Luther's Works*, Vol. 31, *Career of the Reformer*. Edited by Harold J. Grimm and Helmut T. Lehmann. Minneapolis, MN: Fortress Press, 1957.

Lyons, W. *Emotion*. Cambridge: Cambridge University Press, 1980.

Machen, J. Gresham. "What the Bible Teaches About Jesus." In *Selected Shorter Writings*. Edited by D. G. Hart. Phillipsburg, NJ: Presbyterian and Reformed, 2004.

Mackey, T., S. M. Sereika, A. Weissfeld, S. S. Hacker, J. F. Zender, and S. L. Heard. "Factors Associated with Long-term Depressive Symptons of Sexual Assault Victims." *Archives of Psychiatric Nursing* 6 (1992): 10–25.

Mahoney, P., and L. Williams, "Sexual Assault in Marriage: Prevalence, Consequences and Treatment for Wife Rape." In *Partner Violence: A Comprehensive Review of 20 years of Research*. Edited by J. Jasinski and L. M. Williams. Thousand Oaks, CA: Sage, 1998.

Maker, A. H., M. Kemmelmeier, and C. Peterson. "Child Sexual Abuse, Peer Sexual Abuse, and Sexual Assault in Adulthood: A Multi-risk Model of Revictimization." *Journal of Traumatic Stress* 14 (2001): 351–68.

Malina, Bruce J. *The New Testament World: Insights from Cultural Anthropology*. Louisville: Westminster, 2001.

Marcel, Gabriel. *Homo Viator: Introduction to the Metaphysics of Hope*. Chicago: Regnery, 1951.

McCarter, P. K. *II Samuel*. Anchor Bible Commentary 16. New York: Doubleday, 1984.

McFarlane, Alexander, and Bessel van der Kolk. "Trauma and Its Challenge to Society." In *Traumatic Stress*. Edited by Bessel van der Kolk, Alexander McFarlane, and Lars Weisaeth. New York: Guilford, 1996.

Meyer, B., and S. Taylor. "Adjustments to Rape." *Journal of Personality and Social Psychology* 50 (1986): 1226–34.

Meyers, M. F. "Men Sexually Assaulted as Adults and Sexually Abused as Boys." *Archives of Sexual Behavior* 18 (1989): 203–15.

Morris, Leon. *The Atonement: Its Meaning and Significance.* Downers Grove, IL: InterVarsity, 1983.

Morrison, Toni. *The Bluest Eye.* New York: Pocket Books, 1970.

Murray, John. *The Atonement.* Philadelphia: P&R, 1962.

_____. *Redemption Accomplished and Applied.* Grand Rapids, MI: Eerdmans, 1984.

National Center for Victims of Crime and Crime Victims Research and Treatment Center. *Rape in America: A Report to the Nation.* Arlington, VA: National Center for Victims of Crime, 1992.

Norris, F. H., "Epidemiology of Trauma: Frequency and Impact of Different Potentially Traumatic Events on Different Demographic Groups." *Journal of Consulting and Clinical Psychology* 60 (1992): 409–18.

Owen, John. *Communion with God.* Edited by R. K. Law. Carlisle, PA: Banner of Truth, 1991.

Packer, J. I. *Knowing God.* Downers Grove, IL: InterVarsity, 1973.

Packer, J. I., and Mark Dever. *In My Place Condemned He Stood: Celebrating the Glory of the Atonement.* Wheaton, IL: Crossway, 2007.

Parrot, Andrea. "Incest." In *Human Sexuality: An Encyclopedia.* Edited by V. L. Bullough and B. Bullough. New York: Garland, 1994.

Peterson, David. *Where Wrath and Mercy Meet: Proclaiming the Atonement Today.* Carlisle, UK: Paternoster, 2001.

Plantinga, Cornelius Jr., *Not the Way It's Supposed to Be: A Breviary of Sin.* Grand Rapids, MI: Eerdmans, 1995.

Powlison, David. "Anger Part 1: Understanding Anger." *The Journal of Biblical Counseling* 14, no. 1 (1995).

_____. *Suffering and the Sovereignty of God.* Edited by John Piper and Justin Taylor. Wheaton, IL: Crossway, 2006.

Pratt, Richard L. Jr., *Designed for Dignity: What God Has Made It Possible for You to Be.* Phillipsburg, PA: P&R, 1993.

Proudfoot, W. "Religious Experience, Emotion, and Belief." *Harvard Theological Review* 70 (1977): 348.

Reid, D. G. "Violence." In *New Dictionary of Biblical Theology.* Edited by T. Desmond Alexander and Brian S. Rosner. Electronic ed. Downers Grove, IL: InterVarsity, 2001.

Rennison, Callie Marie. *Criminal Victimization in the United States, 1999: Statistical Tables*. Washington, DC: U.S. Department of Justice, Office of Justice Programs, 2001.

_____. *National Crime Victimization Survey: Criminal Victimization 2001*. Washington, DC: U.S. Department of Justice, Office of Justice Programs, 2002.

Renvoize, Jean. *Innocence Destroyed: A Study of Child Sexual Abuse*. New York: Routledge, 1993.

Resick, P. A., "The Psychological Impact of Rape." *Journal of Interpersonal Violence* 8 (1993): 223–55.

_____. "Reactions of Female and Male Victims of Rape or Robbery." Washington, DC: National Institute of Mental Health, 1988.

Resnick, H. S., D. G. Kilpatrick, B. S. Dansky, B. E. Saunders, and C. L. Best. "Prevalence of Civilian Trauma and Posttraumatic Stress Disorder in a Representative National Sample of Women." *Journal of Consulting and Clinical Psychology*, 61, no. 6 (1993): 984–91.

Rothbaum, B. O., E. B. Foa, D. S. Riggs, T. Murdock, and W. Walsh. "A Prospective Examination of Post-Traumatic Stress Disorder in Rape Victims." *Journal of Traumatic Stress* 5, no. 3 (1992): 455–75.

_____. "The Incidence and Prevalence of Intrafamilial and Extrafamilial Sexual Abuse of Female Children." *Child Abuse & Neglect: The International Journal* 7 (1983): 133–46.

Russell, D. E. H. *Rape in Marriage*. Indianapolis, IN: Indiana University Press, 1990.

Ryken, Leland, Jim Wilhoit, Tremper Longman, Colin Duriez, Douglas Penney, and Daniel G. Reid, eds. *Dictionary of Biblical Imagery*. Downers Grove, IL: IVP Academic, 1998.

Sailhamer, John H. *The Life of Christ*. Grand Rapids, MI: Zondervan, 1995.

_____. *The Meaning of the Pentateuch: Revelation, Composition, and Interpretation*. Downers Grove, IL: InterVarsity, 2009.

Saliers, Don E. *Soul in Paraphrase: Prayer and Religious Affections*. Nitro, WV: OSL Publications, 1991.

Sanday, Peggy Reeves. "The Socio-Cultural Context of Rape: A Cross-Cultural Study," *Journal of Social Issues* 37 (1981): 5–27.

Sarkar, N. N., and Rina Sarkar. "Sexual Assault on Woman: Its Impact on Her Life and Living in Society." *Sexual and Relationship Therapy* 20 (2005): 407–19.

Sontag, Susan. *The Body in Pain: The Making and Unmaking of the World*. New York: Oxford University Press, 1987.

_____. *Regarding the Pain of Others*. New York: Farrar, Straus and Giroux, 2002.

Schaeffer, Francis A., and Udo Middelmann. *Pollution and the Death of Man*. Wheaton, IL: Crossway, 1992.

Sherman, Robert. *King, Priest, and Prophet: A Trinitarian Theology of Atonement*. New York: T&T Clark, 2004.

Shriver, Donald Jr., *An Ethics for Enemies: Forgiveness in Politics*. New York: Oxford University Press, 1995.

Smedes, Lewis B. *Forgive and Forget: Healing the Hurts We Don't Deserve*. San Francisco: Harper & Row, 1984.

_____. *Shame and Grace*. San Francisco: HarperCollins, 1993.

Snyder, Howard N. *Sexual Assault of Young Children as Reported to Law Enforcement: Victim, Incident, and Offender Characteristics*. Washington, DC: U.S. Department of Justice, Bureau of Justice Statistics, 2000.

Sorenson, S. B., J. A. Stein, J. M. Siegel, J. M. Golding, and M. A. Burnam, "The Prevalence of Adult Sexual Assault: The Los Angeles Epidemiologic Catchment Area Project." *American Journal of Epidemiology* 126 (1987): 1154–64.

Sproul, R. C. *Faith Alone: The Evangelical Doctrine of Justification*. Grand Rapids, MI: Baker Books, 1999.

_____. *The Holiness of God*. Wheaton, IL: Tyndale, 1985.

Steketee, G., and E. B. Foa. "Rape Victims: Post-Traumatic Stress Responses and Their Treatment: A Review of the Literature." *Journal of Anxiety Disorders* 1 (1987): 69–86.

Stiebert, Johanna. *The Construction of Shame in the Hebrew Bible: The Prophetic Contributions*. Sheffield: Sheffield Academic, 2002.

Storms, Sam. *One Thing: Developing a Passion for the Beauty of God*. Ross-shire, Scotland: Christian Focus, 2004.

Suchocki, Marjorie. *The Fall to Violence: Original Sin in Relational Theology*. New York: Continuum, 1994.

Stott, John R. W. *The Cross of Christ*. Downers Grove, IL: InterVarsity, 1986.

Styron, William. *Darkness Visible: A Memoir of Madness*. New York: Vintage, 1990.

Tangney, June Price, and Ronda L. Dearing. *Shame and Guilt*. New York: Guilford, 2002.

Taylor, L., and N. Gaskin-Laniyan. "Sexual Assault in Abusive Relationships." *National Institute of Justice Journal* 256 (2007): 1–3.

Tjaden, P., and N. Thoennes. "Extent, Nature, and Consequences of Intimate Partner Violence: Findings from the National Violence Against Women Survey." Washington, DC: U.S. Department of Justice, 2000.

_____. "Prevalence, Incidence, and Consequences of Violence Against Women: Findings from the National Violence Against Women Survey." Washington, DC: U.S. Department of Justice, 1998.

Trible, Phyllis. *Texts of Terror: Literary-Feminist Readings of Biblical Narratives.* Minneapolis, MN: Augsburg Fortress, 1984.

Tripp, Paul David. *A Quest for More: Living for Something Bigger Than You.* Greensboro, NC: New Growth, 2008.

Turretin, Francis. *Institutes of Elenctic Theology.* Edited by James T. Dennison, Jr. Translated by George Musgrave Giger. 3 vols. Phillipsburg, NJ: P&R, 1992.

Ullman, Sarah E. "Social Reactions, Coping Strategies, and Self-Blame Attributions in Adjustment to Sexual Assault." *Psychology of Women Quarterly* 20 (1996): 505–26.

United States Department of Justice. Bureau of Justice Statistics. *National Crime Victimization Survey, 2004.* http://www.icpsr.umich.edu/NACJD/NCVS/.

_____. *National Crime Victimization Survey, 2007.* http://www.icpsr.umich.edu/NACJD/NCVS/.

van der Kolk, Bessel, and Alexander McFarlane. "Black Hole of Trauma." In *Traumatic Stress: The Effects of Overwhelming Experience on Mind, Body, and Society.* Edited by Bessel van der Kolk, Alexander McFarlane, and Lars Weisaeth. New York: Guilford, 1996.

Van Dijk-Hemmes, Fokkelien. "Tamar and the Limits of Patriarchy: Between Rape and Seduction (2 Samuel 13 and Genesis 38)." In *Anti-Covenant: Counter-Reading Women's Lives in the Hebrew Bible.* Bible and Literature 22. Edited by Mieke Bal. Sheffield, England: Almond, 1989.

Volf, Miroslav. *End of Memory: Remembering Rightly in a Violent World.* Grand Rapids, MI: Eerdmans, 2006.

_____. *Exclusion and Embrace: A Theological Exploration of Identity, Otherness, and Reconciliation.* Nashville, TN: Abingdon, 1996.

_____. *Free of Charge: Giving and Forgiving in a Culture Stripped of Grace.* Grand Rapids, MI: Zondervan, 2006.

Voltaire, *Toleration and Other Essays.* Translated by Joseph McCabe. New York: G. P. Putnam's Sons, 1912.

Vos, Geerhardus. *Grace and Glory: Sermons Preached in Chapel at Princeton Theological Seminary*. Grand Rapids, MI: The Reformed Press, 1922.

Waites, Elizabeth. *Trauma and Survival: Post-traumatic and Dissociative Disorders in Women*. New York: Norton, 1993.

Wanke, G. "āpār dust." In vol. 2 of *Theological Lexicon of the Old Testament*. Edited by Mark E. Biddle. Translated by Ernst Jenni and Claus Westermann. 3 vols. Peabody, MA: Hendrickson, 2001.

Warfield, B. B. "The Emotional Life of Our Lord." In *The Person and Work of Christ*. Philadelphia, PA: Presbyterian & Reformed, 1950.

Watson, Thomas. *The Lord's Prayer*. 1692. Reprint, Carlisle, PA: Banner of Truth, 1999.

Watts, Rikki E. "Exodus." In *New Dictionary of Biblical Theology*. Edited by T. Desmond Alexander and Brian S. Rosner. Downers Grove, IL: InterVarsity, 2001.

Weil, Simone. *Waiting for God*. New York: Putnam, 1951.

Welch, Ed. *When People Are Big and God Is Small: Overcoming Peer Pressure, Codependency, and the Fear of Man*. Phillipsburg, PA: P&R, 1997.

Wenham, G. J. *Leviticus*, The International Commentary on the Old Testament. Grand Rapids, MI: Eerdmans, 1979.

Wertheimer, Alan. *Consent to Sexual Relations*. Cambridge Studies in Philosophy and Law. Cambridge: Cambridge University Press, 2003.

White, Aaronette. "I Am Because We Are: Combined Race and Gender Political Consciousness among African American Women and Men Anti-Rape Activists." *Women's Studies International Forum* 24, no. 1 (2001): 12–13.

_____. "Talking Feminist, Talking Black: Micromobilization Process in a Collective Protest Against Rape." *Gender & Society* 13, no. 1 (1999): 97.

Whitsett, Doni. "The Psychobiology of Trauma and Child Maltreatment." *Cultic Studies Review* 5, no. 3 (2006): 367.

Widom, C. S., and S. Morris. "Accuracy of Adult Recollections of Childhood Victimization: Part 2. Childhood Sexual Abuse." *Psychological Assessment* 9 (1997): 34–46.

Wilkerson, Mike. *Redemption: Freed by Jesus from the Idols We Worship and the Wounds We Carry*. Wheaton, IL: Crossway, 2011.

Williamson, G. I. *Westminster Confession of Faith for Study Classes*. Philadelphia, PA: Presbyterian and Reformed, 1964.

Williamson, Paul R. *Sealed with an Oath: Covenant in God's Unfolding Purpose.* New Studies in Biblical Theology 23. Downers Grove, IL: InterVarsity, 2007.

Wilson, H. "Forgiveness and Survivors of Sexual Abuse: Relationships among Forgiveness of the Perpetrator, Spiritual Well-being, Depression and Anxiety." PhD diss., Boston University, 1994.

Wood, Joanne V., W. Q. Elaine Perunovic, and John W. Less. "Positive Self-Statements: Power for Some, Peril for Others." *Psychological Science* 20, no. 7 (2009): 860, 861, 865.

Wright, Christopher. *The Mission of God: Unlocking the Bible's Grand Narrative.* Downers Grove, IL: InterVarsity, 2006.

Wright, N. T. *Colossians & Philemon.* Tyndale New Testament Commentary. Downers Grove, IL: InterVarsity, 1986.

_____. *Following Jesus: Biblical Reflections on Discipleship.* Grand Rapids, MI: Eerdmans, 1994.

Wright, Stephen I. "Luke." In *Theological Interpretation of the New Testament.* Edited by Kevin J. Vanhoozer. Grand Rapids, MI: Baker, 2008.

Yancey, Phillip. *What's So Amazing About Grace?* Grand Rapids, MI: Zondervan, 1997.

Yarbrough, R. W. "Atonement." In *New Dictionary of Biblical Theology.* Edited by T. Desmond Alexander and Brian S. Rosner. Electronic ed. Downers Grove, IL: InterVarsity, 2001.

Young, E. J. *Genesis 3.* Edinburgh: Banner of Truth, 1966.

Zahl, Paul F. M. *Grace in Practice: A Theology of Everyday Life.* Grand Rapids, MI: Eerdmans, 2007.

_____. *Who Will Deliver Us? The Present Power of the Death of Christ.* Eugene, OR: Wipf & Stock, 1983.

Zanna, M. P. "Message Receptivity: A New Look at the Old Problem of Open-Versus Closed-Mindedness." In *Advertising Exposure, Memory and Choice.* Edited by A. Mitchell. Hillsdale, NJ: Erlbaum, 1993.

General Index

Scripture Index

John

Romans

RE:LIT

Resurgence Literature (Re:Lit) is a ministry of the Resurgence. At www.theResurgence.com you will find free theological resources in blog, audio, video, and print forms, along with information on forthcoming conferences, to help Christians contend for and contextualize Jesus' gospel. At www.ReLit.org you will also find the full lineup of Resurgence books for sale. The elders of Mars Hill Church have generously agreed to support Resurgence and the Acts 29 Church Planting Network in an effort to serve the entire church.

FOR MORE RESOURCES

Re:Lit – www.relit.org
Resurgence – www.theResurgence.com
Re:Train – www.retrain.org
Mars Hill Church – www.marshillchurch.org
Acts 29 – www.acts29network.org